HAL's Legacy:
2001*'s Computer as Dream and Reality*

HAL's Legacy

2001's Computer as Dream and Reality

edited by David G. Stork

The MIT Press
Cambridge, Massachusetts
London, England

Third printing, 2000

©1997 Massachusetts Institute of Technology

Library of Congress Cataloging-in-Publication Data

HAL's legacy : 2001's computer as dream and reality / edited by David
    G. Stork.
        p.   cm.
    Includes index.
    ISBN 0-262-19378-7 (hc : alk. paper)
    1. Computer science. 2. Supercomputers. I. Stork, David G.
QA76.H265   1997
791.43'72—dc20
                                                            96-31375
                                                               CIP

To Stanley Kubrick
Ars sine scientia nihil est

Contents

Foreword   Arthur C. Clarke   *xi*
Preface   *xvii*

1   The Best-Informed Dream: HAL and the Vision of *2001*   *1*
David G. Stork

2   Scientist on the Set: An Interview with Marvin Minsky   *15*
David G. Stork

3   Could We Build HAL? Supercomputer Design   *33*
David J. Kuck

4   "Foolproof and incapable of error?" Reliable Computing and Fault Tolerance   *53*
Ravishankar K. Iyer

5   "An Enjoyable Game": How HAL Plays Chess   *75*
Murray S. Campbell

6   "The Talking Computer": Text to Speech Synthesis   *101*
Joseph P. Olive

7 When Will HAL Understand What We Are Saying? Computer Speech
   Recognition and Understanding   *131*
   Raymond Kurzweil

8 "I'm sorry, Dave, I'm afraid I can't do that": How Could HAL
   Use Language?   *171*
   Roger C. Schank

9 From *2001* to 2001: Common Sense and the Mind of HAL   *193*
   Douglas B. Lenat

10 Eyes for Computers: How HAL Could "See"   *211*
    Azriel Rosenfeld

11 "I could see your lips move": HAL and Speechreading   *237*
    David G. Stork

12 Living in Space: Working with the Machines of the Future   *263*
    Donald A. Norman

13 Does HAL Cry Digital Tears? Emotions and Computers   *279*
    Rosalind W. Picard

14 "That's something I could not allow to happen":
    HAL and Planning   *305*
    David E. Wilkins

15 Computers, Science, and Extraterrestrials: An Interview with
    Stephen Wolfram   *333*
    David G. Stork

16   When HAL Kills, Who's to Blame? Computer Ethics   *351*
         Daniel C. Dennett

Contributors   *367*
Index   *377*

Arthur C. Clarke in the Set of the Pod Bay

Foreword: The Birth of HAL

Arthur C. Clarke

"Is it true, Dr. Chandra, that you chose the name Hal to be one step ahead of IBM?"

"Utter nonsense! Half of us come from IBM and we've been trying to stamp out that story for years. I thought that by now every intelligent person knew that H-A-L is derived from Heuristic ALgorithmic."

Afterwards, Max swore that he could distinctly hear the capital letters.
—2010: Odyssey Two

Sometimes you just can't win. I deliberately inserted that passage into *Odyssey Two* because for decades I too had been "trying to stamp out that story." I don't know when or how it originated, but believe me it's pure coincidence, even though the odds against it are 26^3 to 1. (Much less, of course, if you eliminate ridiculous—or vulgar—combinations.)

I was embarrassed by the whole affair, and I felt that IBM, which was very helpful to Stanley Kubrick during the making of *2001*, would be annoyed. (Bell Telephone and PanAm—remember them?—also provided useful services. How difficult it is to foresee the future! At least Hilton and Howard Johnson are still with us, though they are not yet in space.)

Well, recently I gave a satellite address to an IBM conference in Europe and was pleasantly surprised to discover that all had been forgiven. In fact, because Big Blue now seems quite proud of the link and no longer fears guilt by association, I've happily abandoned my attempt to set the record straight.

Of course, I'm pleased that the distinguished contributors of this book are also trying, so to speak, to put the record straight—even though the hindsight of specialists is bound to be more accurate than the foresight of a writer and filmmaker—especially in a field as rapidly changing as computer science. A great deal has happened since Stanley and I worked so hard to learn all we could about that nascent field (and about space travel too, for that matter).

Although I've never considered *2001* as a strict prediction—but as more of a vision, a way thinks could work—I have long kept track, informally, of how our vision compares with computer science reality. Some things we got right—even righter than we ever had a reason to suspect. Others, well, who could have known?

In analyzing these issues, the contributors to *HAL's Legacy* have done us all a great service. They've given us so much more than a scorecard for the film and novel. These creators of the real technology and science have shown the reasons for the way things developed—and may continue to develop—to 2001 and beyond. Their clear analysis of the details of *2001*—a single chess move, say, or the click of an (analog!) camera, the use of the single word *take*—illuminates both science and science fantasy. They also present informed and exciting speculations about the future of computing and artificial intelligence. I have learned a lot from this book and have been especially happy to know how its contributors were affected by *2001*.

Still, there are many things about HAL no one else could explain. For instance, why was he 'born' at Urbana, Illinois? Though I have long forgotten most of the reasons for decisions we made a third of a century ago, I remember this one clearly.

My applied mathematics tutor at King's College, Cambridge, when I took my degree in 1947–1948 was the distinguished cosmologist George McVittie. He taught me the elements of perturbation theory, which I have used in several of my stories—as I acknowledged in *Reach for Tomorrow*. During the 1950s George moved to the United States, where he took up a post at the University of Illinois, Urbana.

I was happy to pay this fitting tribute to him, for I am now sure he must have been involved in establishing the Supercomputer Center at Urbana. A few months ago I came across a photograph of the now-famous Bletchley Park team that was responsible for breaking the ENIGMA cypher during World War II. There in the middle was, needless to say, Alan Turing; and standing shyly at the back was George. I had had no idea that he was involved, for of course he never mentioned his association with one of the war's greatest secrets. (How ironic that Alan Turing, who perhaps contributed more than any other individual to the Allied victory, would never have been allowed into Bletchley under normal security regulations.) Bletchley Park's COLOSSUS, which I suppose had something like the capability of a 1995 laptop computer, is widely regarded as one of the ancestors of today's programmable computers. Without it, the war might well have been lost—or at least greatly prolonged.

Another Bletchley story, perhaps apocryphal, is an account of Winston Churchill's inspection of the staff there. He is supposed to have remarked to the superintendent, "When I told you to leave no stone unturned, I didn't expect you to take me so literally." Those Bletchley boffins sure were a weird crew!

Then there is the issue of the date of HAL's birth. When writing the novel, I dimly recall choosing 1997 because it seemed close enough to the launch time for *Discovery*. But why January 12? No particular reason, though I later realized that it was a Sunday. The engineers were working hard on the weekend!

In 1972, four years after the release of *2001*, I put together my reminiscences of the production, together with thousands of words of deathless prose not used in the final novel, in *The Lost Worlds of 2001*. In chapter 11, "The Birth of Hal," I reveal that the ship's computer was originally named Socrates (or, alternatively, Athena) and was conceived of as a fully mobile robot. Here's a snatch of dialogue I had completely forgotten but which undoubtedly—though perhaps unconsciously—presaged things to come. Although I have always assumed that lipreading was Stanley's idea—and have also said I thought it the only thing in the movie that was technically improbable!—this passage suggests I should share some of the blame.

"Bruno," asked the robot, "What is life?"

Dr. Bruno Foster, director of the Division of Mobile Adaptive Machines, carefully removed his pipe in the interests of better communication. Socrates still misunderstood about 2 percent of spoken words; with that pipe, the figure went up to five.

"Sub-program three three zero," he said carefully. "What is the purpose of the universe? Don't bother your pretty little head with such problems. End three three zero."

Socrates was silent, thinking this over. Sometime later in the day, if he understood his orders, he would repeat the message to whichever of the lab staff had initiated that sequence.

It was a joke, of course. By trying out such tricks, one often discovered unexpected possibilities, and unforeseen limitations, in Autonomous Mobile Explorer 5—usually known as Socrates or, alternatively, "That damn pile of junk." But to Foster, it was also something more than a joke, and his staff knew it.

One day, he was sure, there would be robots that would ask such questions—spontaneously, without prompting. And a little later, there would be robots that could answer them.

Then there is the issue of HAL's death. In the early 1960s at Bell Laboratories I had heard a recording of an Illiac computer singing "Bicycle Built for Two." I thought it would be good for the death scene—especially the slowing down of the words at the end. Imagine my surprise, then, when I recently came upon a 1918 poem, "In the Theater," about brain surgeon Lambert Rogers operating to remove a brain tumor. Near the end of the poem the patient on the operating table speaks to the surgeon:

Then, suddenly, the cracked record in the brain,
a ventriloquist voice that cried, "You sod,
leave my soul alone, leave my soul alone,"—
the patient's dummy lips moving to that refrain,
the patient's eyes too wide. And, shocked,
Lambert Rogers drawing out the probe
with nurses, students, sister, petrified.

"Leave my soul alone, leave my soul alone,"
that voice so arctic and that cry so odd
had nowhere else to go—till the antique

gramophone wound down and the words began
to blur and slow, ". . . leave . . . my . . . soul . . . alone . . ."
to cease at last when something other died.
And silence matched the silence under snow.
—Dannie Abse

I will always remember my collaboration with Stanley Kubrick as some of the most intellectually stimulating (and demanding!) work of my career. Anecdotes such as those of Dr. Minsky's recounts in chapter 2 bring back fond memories of the set. Speaking of the set, I do not know how many actors Stanley interviewed before he settled on Douglas Rain as the voice of HAL; but I am almost certain that one of them was Martin Balsam, who comes to a memorably sticky end in *Psycho*. Apparently Martin made some recordings but decided the role wasn't for him. So here is another piece of unknown Kubricana—like the custard-pie fight in the war room of *Dr. Strangelove* that never made it into the final version. (Did you ever wonder what those tables of goodies were doing at the back of the room?) I still hear Douglas Rain's silky voice every time I tell my computer to do something stupid and it says reproachfully, "I'm sorry, Dave, I can't do that."

Further Readings

Dannie Abse. *Collected Poems 1948–76.* London: Hutchinson, 1977.

Jerome Agel, ed. *The Making of Kubrick's 2001.* New York: Signet, 1970. Responses to the film, as well as some discussion of the filming.

Piers Bizony. *2001: Filming the Future. London, UK:* Aurum Press, 1994. This beautiful large-format book is the product of many years of devoted research. It gives the entire history of the film and is full of original art work, engineering drawings, and stills taken during production, most of which have never appeared before.

Arthur C. Clarke. *2001: A Space Odyssey.* London: Hutchinson/Star, 1968. A novel based on the original screenplay by Stanley Kubrick and Arthur C. Clarke.

Arthur C. Clarke. *The Lost Worlds of 2001*. New York: New American Library, 1972. Clarke's view of the writing of the script, the later novel, and alternative chapters, plots, and so on.

Arthur C. Clarke, *2010: Odyssey Two*. New York: Ballantine Books, 1982. The sequel to *2001*, explains several issues in the first novel and the film.

Andrew Hodges. *Alan Turing: The Enigma*. New York: Simon and Schuster, 1983. The definitive biography of one of the deepest thinkers at the dawn of the modern computer age.

Neil McAleer. *Odyssey: The Authorized Biography of Arthur C. Clarke*. London: Victor Gollancz, 1992.

Operating Manual for the HAL 9000 Computer: Revised Edition. Oakland, Calif.: Miskatonic University Press, 2010. This edition, essential for all surviving users of this versatile machine, advises the fitting of small explosive charges at key points in the mainframe.

Preface

I am a HAL Nine Thousand computer, Production Number 3. I became operational at the HAL Plant in Urbana, Illinois, on January 12, 1997.
—HAL, 2001: A Space Odyssey (the novel)

At a dinner party some time ago, an acquaintance, a nonscientist, asked me in a casual way about my duties as chief scientist at a research lab. I said that one of my great joys was overseeing a wide range of projects, to varying extents, and I mentioned a few of them: pattern recognition, machine learning, neural networks, computer-chip design, supercomputer design, image compression, expert systems, handwriting recognition, document analysis, uses of global networks such as the World Wide Web, novel human-machine interfaces, and so on. Then I turned to one of the areas of my particular expertise: lipreading by computer.

"Oh," she said, "Like HAL." Ah, a kindred soul, I thought. We spent quite some time discussing the state of the art and the challenges of computer lipreading, its possible applications, and so on. Later our discussion turned to other topics suggested by the movie—language understanding, chess, computer vision, artificial intelligence. It was clear that she was interested in the current state of the art and that many years before the film had both caught her imagination and helped her identify crucial issues in today's computer science. One of the questions she asked was, "How realistic was HAL?"

This book is for people like her. And because no one is an expert in all the topics covered in the film, even scientists are sure to learn from the accounts of other areas. The book is much more than an answer to her question, though. It has four major goals, which it addresses in varying proportions in the sixteen chapters.

Analysis

It is a testament to Clarke and Kubrick's achievement that *2001* still holds up to close scrutiny in the late 1990s. Under the expert eyes of the contributors, the most innocuous aspects of scenes—a line of computer code on a screen, a chess move, the use of a word, the form of a button—reveal a great deal. Even though I've seen the film several dozen times, I have learned an immense amount from the contributors. *HAL's Legacy* seeks to do for *2001* what good art history does for a major painting; namely, make the viewer see it in a new light—a tall order, to be sure!

Teaching

The film illustrates key ideas in several disciplines of computer science, and thus provides a springboard for discussions of the field in greater depth, including our own research. Descriptions of the world computer chess champion Deep Blue system, the commercially successful VOICE recognition system, the massive CYC artificial-intelligence project, the award-winning Mathematica software system, and much more are here discussed by their creators at a level accessible to the general reader.

Prognostication

It is natural, too, to look to the future. Several contributors make informed and fascinating predictions based on developments in the field. What are the most promising approaches toward artificial intelligence? Will we ever be able to "reverse engineer" a human brain and represent it in a computer?

Reflection

2001 transcends the label of "science fiction movie" and captures many of the central metaphors of *our* time, telling us much about society and its aspirations. The film has even been praised by the pope! Many people have been deeply affected by the film, among them several contributors who reflect here about its influence on their own careers and on computer science in general.

Clearly, *HAL's Legacy* differs from books on the making of the film or its cinematography. It differs, too, from books that analyze the science shown in movies or on television—science that is incidental and just "goes along for the ride." To an extent unprecedented and never duplicated in a feature film, the makers of *2001* were as careful as possible to get things right; when they did make errors, they often did so in illuminating ways.

Now seems like the perfect time for *HAL's Legacy*. Birthdays are an important theme in the film (there are at least five of them), and in the novel, HAL "becomes operational . . . on January 12, 1997." Kubrick changed the year to 1992 for the film version—perhaps to give HAL a longer lifetime and so make his death more poignant. On the 1992 date, I—along with colleagues, faculty, and assorted Silicon Valley friends—held a birthday party for HAL. I was interviewed by several papers, and an Associated Press photo of me cutting the HAL cake (shaped like his console, complete with red LED under a clear plastic hemisphere) appeared worldwide. I was pleasantly surprised to learn that much of the general public was interested in HAL too.

It has been particularly rewarding for me to work with this group of contributors—all of whom were chosen because of their preeminence in their respective subfields. I have known a few of them personally for many years; Azriel Rosenfeld was on my dissertation committee. Others I met serving on panel discussions. I'll never forget the time I came dressed in a suit while fellow panelist Marvin Minsky showed up in a Pac Man T-shirt. Yet others I knew primarily through their books—Dan Dennett and Don Norman, for example—and still others are inventors of products I use regularly (e.g., Steve Wolfram's Mathematica). At our meetings and dinners in Stanford, Urbana, and Cambridge, and through frequent written messages, we passed many ideas back and forth. Although I had strong ideas about what I wanted them to write, they all had the good sense to ignore me when appropriate. At times I felt like someone trying to herd cats.

Even at a distance, there was a great sense of camaraderie. As we approached one of the important publishing deadlines, one contributor, who was still late with a chapter, replied to my frantic entreaties thus: "Dave, I honestly think you ought to sit down calmly, take a stress pill and think things over." A later message read, "I still have every confidence in the success of my chapter," which at first brought bemusement but then a diffuse sense of dread.

It has been a privilege to correspond with Arthur C. Clarke, whose work inspired us all. Throughout the preparation of this book he has been gracious, enthusiastic, and helpful.

Although I did my writing and editing at home, often late into the night and on weekends, I would like to thank my colleagues at the Ricoh California Research Center for their support of our ongoing research, which influenced this book in numerous ways: Greg Wolff, K. V. Prasad, Michael Angelo (yes, that's his real name), Morten Pedersen (visiting from the Technical University of Denmark), Stanford graduate students Vicky Lu, Chuck Lam, and (especially) Marcus Hennecke (by the time this book is released, *Dr.* Hennecke!). Thanks also go to Director Peter Hart for making CRC such a great place to work.

This book was improved indirectly by a large number of people. One colleague pointed out a used bookstore selling an out-of-print book about the filming of *2001*; an acquaintance asked a "naive" question that ultimately led to a new section in a chapter; a student told me about a *2001* World Wide Web site; an intrepid cab driver took me through the blizzard of '96 to interview Marvin Minsky. Piers Bizony, whose book on the filming of *2001* both inspired and informed me, made several transatlantic phone calls and helped me track down photographs. I also had a somewhat eerie telephone conversation with Douglas Rain, the Canadian actor who played the voice of HAL. Thanks go also to the efficient staff at Turner Broadcasting for their assistance providing stills from the film.

An extra-special thanks goes to my editor at the MIT Press, Bob Prior. He was the only person in the publishing industry who "got" the idea of *HAL's Legacy* instantly, as proven by his enthusiastic response to my proposal. Michael Rutter, also at the Press, helped obtain illustrations and kept track of numerous production details. Sandra Minkkinen helped to orchestrate the editing and production process for the entire project, and copy editor Roberta Clark improved the text immeasurably.

Deep appreciation goes to my immediate family—Nancy, Alex, and Olivia—for putting up with my many late nights and weekend hours working on the book. I am happy to say that groggy Saturday mornings after marathon editing sessions are now a thing of the past, and we can spend more time doing what we all love so much: hiking Mount Tamalpais and the Marin headlands and kayaking on Squibnocket Pond.

David G. Stork
Stanford, California
January 12, 1996

1 *"The Best-Informed Dream": HAL and the Vision of 2001*

David G. Stork

With most science fiction films, the more science you understand the *less* you admire the film or respect its makers. An evil interstellar spaceship careens across the screen. The hero's ship fires off a laser blast, demolishing the enemy ship—the audience cheers at the explosion. But why is the laser beam visible? There is nothing in space to scatter the light back to the viewer. And what slowed the beam a billionfold to render its advance toward the enemy ship perceptible? Why, after the moment of the explosion, does the debris remain centered in the screen instead of continuing forward as dictated by the laws of inertia? What could possibly drag and slow down the expanding debris (and cause the smoke to billow) in the vacuum of outer space? Note too the graceful, falling curve of the debris. Have the cinematographers forgotten that there is no gravity—no "downward"—in outer space? Of course, the scene is accompanied by the obligatory deafening boom. But isn't outer space eternally silent? And even if there were some magical way to hear the explosion, doesn't light travel faster than sound? Shouldn't we *see* the explosion long before we *hear* it, just as we do with lighting and thunder? Finally, isn't all this moot? Shouldn't the enemy ship be invisible anyway, as there are no nearby stars to provide illumination?

But with other, less numerous films, the more science you know the more you appreciate a film and esteem its makers. *2001* is, of course, the premier example of this phenomenon. Director Stanley Kubrick and author Arthur

C. Clarke consulted scientists in universities and industry and at NASA in their effort to portray correctly the technology of future space travel. They tried to be plausible as well as visionary. Every detail—from the design of the space ship, the timing of the mission, and the technical lingo to the typography on the computer screens and the space stewardesses' hats (bubble-shaped and padded to cushion bumps in the zero gravity of space travel)—was carefully considered in light of the then-current technology and informed predictions. The film, which has been used in the training of NASA astronauts, doesn't look dated even though thirty years have passed since its release.

We acknowledge, of course, that science fantasy is a literary or cinematic genre and need not get the science right to succeed as art. Indeed, *2001* succeeds on the strength and boldness of its vision, the profundity of its central thesis, and the clarity and unsurpassed mastery of its cinematic technique. Nevertheless, the incorporation of science and technology—*real* science and technology—is a vital part of its success, a part that has not, until now, received adequate consideration.

It is widely believed that architects design their best buildings when they are confronted by obstacles and challenges. Think of Frank Lloyd Wright's Fallingwater house, nestled among rock outcrops and perched over a stream. So too, faithfulness to scientific constraints led Kubrick and Clarke to create especially brilliant cinematic solutions. Would a lesser director have obeyed the laws of physics and portrayed Frank's murder or Dave's reentry through the emergency airlock in *silence*?

Virtually all the film's rare departures from scientific veracity were deliberate compromises by Kubrick and Clarke. For instance, even though *Discovery*'s speed is extremely high by terrestrial standards, the ship would not appear to move relative to the stars. The filmmakers were well aware of this. But when test sequences showing the stars motionless in the background made the ship look too static, they compromised and introduced a slow drift of the stars. (This solution was immensely challenging technically and required meticulous microalignment of many separate sequences.) Similarly, although in reality half of *Discovery* would have been invisible to any cosmic viewer—because it would receive no light from the sun—Clarke and Kubrick, realizing that such a half-visible ship would distract the audience, reluctantly illuminated all of it. In short, the filmmakers knew and cared about getting the science right and made as few artistic exceptions to accuracy as possible. Their care extended, too, to HAL, the central and surely the most memorable character in the film.

But before we turn to HAL, we might ask: Why analyze the science in the film at all? Why not just consider the film as art, with its own conventions and logic? We believe that, just as an art history book can deepen our understanding of a painting or sculpture, scientific analyses can lead to a richer aesthetic experience of the film. We seek to see the film from an additional, fresh perspective—not to diminish its art, but to appreciate it more fully. Such a scientific analysis also provides those of us who are not working scientists an opportunity to learn more about the research going on in real laboratories and about the recent history of science—computer science in particular.

Consider, for example, how such a perspective augments a traditional cinematic view in relation to the issue of software. In Clarke's novel (adapted from the screenplay), HAL's birthday is January 12, 1997, whereas in Kubrick's passage in the screenplay it is 1992. Why the difference? A traditional analysis (centered on character development, plot devices, and so forth) might suggest that Kubrick wanted to make HAL's life somewhat longer in order to make his death more poignant. But from our—and Clarke's—technological perspective, the 1992 date is implausible; there is simply no need for such a long history. Who would use a nine-year-old computer on the most technologically sophisticated and challenging adventure in the history of mankind? In fact, HAL's software could be downloaded onto a 1997-vintage computer in a few days (and wouldn't require inserting millions of floppy disks). Consequently, there is no scientific reason for the early birthday.

Taking our scientific and technological perspective a step farther, we can then ask: What else does this lack of appreciation of software imply, and how was it manifested in the film? Kubrick and Clarke—and indeed all but a few computer visionaries in the 1960s—failed to understand the important and unique nature of software: that it is general purpose, infinitely malleable, and can be divorced from hardware. This lack of understanding helps explain the excessive number of control buttons we see in the film, especially in the pods. Currently, jetliners and fighter jets are equipped with numerous computer screens that display different types of information and replace mechanical buttons. One good computer screen with windows and software buttons would have sufficed for *Discovery*. But *2001* was made before the Macintosh computer interface was developed, so we can't blame Kubrick and Clarke for overlooking this important trend, nor for the click of the (analog) shutter of a bulky camera where software (and smaller, digital cameras) would be used today. And, as Stephen Wolfram points out, the snippets of computer code visible on HAL's screens are reminiscent of BASIC or Fortran, popular computer languages at the time the film was made. Presumably, the software written for HAL's hardware is much less intuitive (i.e., easy for humans to understand) than languages developed since then.

In short, our technical analysis of the software issues suggested by the film draws together such details as HAL's birthday, the click of a camera, and the plethora of buttons, as well as snippets of code on the screens. It's hard to imagine how a traditional cinematic or literary analysis could shed such light or deepen our understanding of the film in this way.

In fact, *2001* is suffused—explicitly and implicitly—with the motif of birthdays: everything from the "dawn of humanity" and the explicit date when HAL "became operational," to the birthday of Heywood Floyd's daughter "Squirt" (played by Kubrick's daughter Vivian), to Frank's birthday (complete with his parents singing "Happy Birthday" via a radio transmission delayed by the immense distances of inter-planetary space), to the final scene—the birth of a star child. All this, of course, occurs at the birth of the millennium.

As the chapters in this book illustrate, the film ranges widely over issues that are still salient in computer science (and in space travel), and presents a rich array of "predictions"—though Clarke prefers to consider them "visions." It is a testament to the thoroughness of its makers that the film remains as vital and moving today as when it came out. It is appropriate that we analyze these points now, at yet another birthday, the time the novel says HAL "became operational": January 12, 1997.

The overarching technical issue associated with HAL—and the one that captures the imagination, is his artificial intelligence (AI). *2001* is, in essence, a meditation on the evolution of intelligence, from the monolith-inspired development of tools, through HAL's artificial intelligence, up to the ultimate (and deliberately mysterious) stage of the star child.

How well does Kubrick and Clarke's vision stand up to the reality of 1997? Let's state the obvious: HAL doesn't exist, and there is no chance that some miraculous change in funding or insight will yield AI at the level portrayed in HAL by the year 2001. We have learned that artificial intelligence—a notably hazy matter we don't even have a good definition for—is one of the most profoundly difficult problems in science—on a par with going to the moon, identifying the fundamental constituents of matter, and unlocking the puzzle of life. But we've gone to the moon, and we seem to be on the way to understanding these other mysteries. *Why* don't we have AI?

Marvin Minsky (who, incidentally, nearly lost his life consulting on *2001*!) argues (in chapter 2) that the field made such good progress in its early days that researchers became overconfident and moved on prematurely to more immediate or practical problems—for example, chess and speech recognition. They left undone the central work of understanding the general computational principles—learning, reasoning and creativity—that underlie intelligence. Without these, he believes, we will end up with a growing collection of dumb experts and will never achieve AI.

Stephen Wolfram (in chapter 15) agrees that we have overlooked deep principles but thinks the missing pieces lie in the domain of complex systems—a field he helped launch—where simple elements can interact to produce unexpectedly complex behavior. Just as the simple laws of physics applied to simple water molecules can give rise to the wonderfully complex vortex flow of a stream around a rock, so the relatively simple rules governing nerve cells (neurons) may lead to a complex cognitive system. His insight, though, is that we shouldn't be thinking so much in terms of mathematics (i.e., equations) as, instead, algorithms (i.e., computer programs).

Ray Kurzweil (chapter 7), on the other hand, says that we already know how to achieve AI—just reverse engineer a brain! In a few decades, he suggests, we may be able to scan an entire human brain, down to the level of nerve cells and their interconnections. We need then merely (!) encode all that information into a computer to make a virtual brain every bit as intelligent as a human brain that is its model.

However, for Doug Lenat (chapter 9), there is no silver bullet for achieving AI. We first need to encode an enormous amount of common-sense knowledge into a computer through a laborious process of hand entering information gleaned from a wide range of sources—such as encyclopedias. With such a "primed knowledge pump," a computer might be able to learn more by reading books and interacting with its environment, scientists and other experts, and, perhaps, other developing computers. That, at least, is the theory. Daniel Dennett (in chapter 16) stresses the need for a computer to explore the world, and learn from its interactions.

The contributors to this anthology share a general consensus that nothing in principle prevents us from creating artificial intelligence—not quantum gravity, not some secret mystical *élan vital*. Other than that, there are numerous disagreements. Naturally, this is healthy for the field—let a thousand flowers bloom! I confess that my own background and sentiments are close to Dennett's and Lenat's, although I might stress the role of learning somewhat differently than they do. It will be hard indeed to go from low levels and up through the enormous range of levels to create the exquisitely organized systems needed for language or scene analysis. In my own area of expertise, pattern recognition (admittedly a small part of the AI puzzle, though an essential one), we seem to understand the central principles. It is *applying* them that has proven extremely difficult. Even if Kurzweil is right in believing that we can someday reverse engineer a brain, such an effort would tell us little about *how* the brain learns or represents information.

The fact that we have not achieved AI (for whatever reason) should not, however, blind us to the fact that in some domains we have met and even surpassed the vision of a HAL. As David Kuck (chapter 3) points out, recent advances in computer design and the spectacular and continuous rate of improvement in hardware summarized by Moore's law tell us that we could soon build a computer the size and power of HAL. Ravishankar Iyer, reviewing the progress in computer reliability, shows how we could make the hardware of a massive computer like HAL reliable, even for a prolonged space mission. Alas, the techniques for insuring reliable hardware are more effective than those for software, and this is surely an imposing, but not insurmountable, barrier. In principle, there seems to be nothing to prevent us from making a large computer that is fault-tolerant. Does this sound too much like the hubris of HAL and his designers? As Frank points out in that context, making a computer with no errors "sounds a little like famous last words."

Still, in limited-application domains, we *have* made steady improvements. We have computer chess systems that beat all but a few dozen human grandmasters, and they are improving every year. It seems all but certain that the world's best chess player will soon be a computer—perhaps even by the year 2001. In chapter 5, Murray Campbell, a member of IBM's Deep Blue team that challenged Garry Kasparov in February of 1996, analyzes *2001*'s chess scene in fascinating detail. Campbell also reflects on the changing public perception of chess machines, as illustrated in the film.

We have made several important strides toward automated speech recognition, especially in the initial stages of transcribing raw sound into phonemes. Kurzweil summarizes that progress and applies his own commercial VOICE speech-recognition system to the *2001* soundtrack. He finds that the system's simple phonological transcription is good, and can be particularly accurate when restricted to just two talkers (e.g., Frank and Dave in the quiet spaceship). General speech recognition, however, relies very heavily on semantics, common sense, context and world knowledge. (For example, how do we give a computer the ability to distinguish among such homonyms as *their, they're,* and *there*?) We are still far from solving problems like this one.

Similarly, in my own research (chapter 11), I have developed speechreading (lipreading) systems that use both sight and sound. These systems outperform purely acoustical speech recognizers in noisy rooms. Alas, no current system even remotely approaches HAL's proficiency at speechreading in silence. In fact, the lipreading scene in the pod is the only one Clarke thought was technologically implausible for the year 2001. Automatic speech recognition and speechreading will always be limited by the problems of representing semantics, common sense, and world knowledge—profoundly difficult issues that will occupy science for many decades to come.

As humans, we take our faculties of vision for granted, but making computers see has proven to be extremely difficult. In chapter 10, Azriel Rosenfeld discusses some of the successes of research in "early" vision, such as edge and motion detection, face tracking, and the recognition of emotions (which he illustrates with images from *2001*). Full vision, however, would include the ability to analyze scenes. Imagine, for example, a computer that could look at an arbitrary scene—anything from a sunset over a fishing village to Grand Central Station at rush hour—and produce a verbal description. This is a problem of overwhelming difficulty, relying as it does on finding solutions to both vision and language and then integrating them. I suspect that scene analysis will be one of the last cognitive tasks to be performed well by computers.

Other capabilities have proven remarkably difficult to develop, including one that Clarke wasn't sure we could solve by 2001: making a computer produce natural-sounding speech. In chapter 6, Joe Olive reviews the development of computer speech generation, such as the systems needed to convert text to speech for the blind. Although these experimental systems work adequately for short utterances or single words, with sentences (let alone entire speeches) they cannot convey the human subtleties of stress and intonation. A convincing artificial speaking system would require the system to understand what it is saying—again, an extremely hard and unsolved problem.

Reading Roger Schank's discussion of language in chapter 8 is like seeing the Wizard of Oz behind the curtain. With a few simple tricks, we could duplicate some of HAL's linguistic performance. For instance, it would be a fairly straightforward task to record a large number of canned stories and have HAL play them back when he hears appropriate "trigger" questions. Such a program might even persuade a casual or unsuspecting person that HAL understood language. Indeed, a noted computer program (ELIZA) around the time of *2001*'s release, sought to mimic a Rogerian therapist; in limited dialogues it convinced naive users that they were conversing with a real person. Such demonstrations tell us more about the novelty of computer discourse of the time and the gullibility of users than they do about true machine intelligence. ELIZA and its descendants are a far, far cry from true language understanding and general intelligence.

In the film, HAL makes several plans: to test whether the AE35 unit was in fact faulty, to navigate the ship, to search for extraterrestrial life around Jupiter, and to kill the crew. Such planning, Dave Wilkins points out in chapter 14, requires the identification of subgoals, anticipating obstacles, retracing steps, and so on. His review of the progress in planning by computer demonstrates the difficulty of solving even apparently simple problems in a rarefied and idealized world of stacking blocks. The bottom line is that planning is *hard*! HAL was not particularly good at it, and neither are current computer systems.

As the characters in the film admit, it is hard to tell whether HAL's emotions are programmed in to make him easy to talk to, or whether they are genuine. Rosalind Picard (chapter 13) discusses HAL's emotions—his pride, anger, fear, paranoia, concern—as well as his ability to recognize emotion in crew members—and how current research approaches similar problems. If emotions are essential for computer cognition, as she and Minsky and Norman argue, how will we deal with such "affective" computers? Would you trust an affective computer with your spreadsheets?

Don Norman (in chapter 12) underscores the importance of emotion, and points to a notion of machine (and human) intelligence much broader than the kind of logical intellect that preoccupies the field. He looks at what it might be like to live in space and work with computers for extended periods. His discussion stresses the need to take into consideration the "softer" aspects of cognition, those related to emotions, making mistakes, and so forth.

It's interesting that Kubrick and Clarke seem to want us to have stronger feelings toward HAL than we do toward the crew. HAL is the only one in the film to show emotions: "I'm afraid. I'm afraid. I'm losing my mind. I can feel it. I can feel it." In contrast, the dull, robotlike astronauts sleepwalk through boring meetings and chat about ham sandwiches. (Three other characters are known solely through the trace of their biological functions during hibernation.) When the BBC announcer, Mr. Amer, greets the crew, they mumble indistinctly in response. HAL, however, answers with clarity, animation, and interest: "Everything is going extremely well." By the middle of the movie, we have grown accustomed to HAL and accept the fact that he has more personality than the crew. While we may be shocked and surprised at the death of Frank, HAL's plaintive "I'm afraid . . . I'm afraid" evokes our sympathy.

In fact, the audience's sympathy (or anger or both) toward HAL makes more poignant a number of ethical questions. Does HAL *murder* Frank and the three hibernating crewmen? If so, who (or what) should be punished? Is it immoral to disconnect HAL (without a trial!)? Daniel Dennett argues that higher-order intentionality and responsibility are necessary conditions for moral responsibility—and hence blame—and that HAL exhibits such intentionality. After all, he tells Dave "I want to help you" (though, of course he says this to try to stop Dave from dismantling him).

A broad question touched on throughout this book is whether we should try to make computers intelligent by mimicking a human brain or, instead, exploit their particular strengths—such as rapid search and large memories. So far, different domains have tried different approaches. Researchers in computer chess, for instance, began by trying to reproduce the methods of human grandmasters—in particular recognizing key configurations of pieces on the board—but found that this approach quickly led to such difficulties as determining and representing the key properties of the arrangements. Massive and rapid searches of possible sequences of moves have proven more successful. This approach is used for Deep Blue, which has rapid search capacities that are distinctly unlike those of human grandmasters (although grandmaster Garry Kasparov has commented that Deep Blue plays like an intelligent human). Likewise, the best computer speechreading systems operate not at all like humans. Both of these applications are limited and—as valuable and interesting as they may be—do not lead us toward true AI.

Kurzweil's brain-scan approach is the most extreme of the duplicate-a-human-brain approaches. Certain cognitive abilities—in particular, language and our species-specific common sense—are distinctive to human beings. There are strong arguments for trying to copy these capacities in computers. While this would not require duplicating a brain to the level of nerve cells, it would, presumably, involve identifying the specific methods we use to carry out myriad tasks.

Another theme suggested by *2001* is society's perception of computers, contemporaneous and future. Were public fears about computers in the 1960s borne out? The fact that Frank takes his loss to HAL at chess without the slightest surprise reflects an attitude that is radically different from the public's perception in that decade when the thought of a computer becoming the world chess champion evoked anger and hostility.

As we approach 2001, we might ask why we have not matched the dream of making a HAL. The reasons are instructive. In broad overview, we have met, and surpassed, the vision of HAL in those domains—speech, hardware, planning, chess—that can be narrowly defined and easily specified. But in domains such as language understanding and common sense, which are basically limitless in their possibilities and hard to specify, we fall far short. Perhaps too we need to ask whether, as a culture, we are willing to support the undertaking of producing artificial intelligence.

The vision that produced HAL was clearly that "bigger is better." In fact, one of the major trends that the filmmakers did not foresee was that there was "room at the bottom"; that is, that computers would become smaller and smaller and evolve into doorknobs and pocket pagers. There are no personal computers or personal digital assistants in *2001*; Frank and Dave take notes with pen on paper tablets on clipboards. The role of networks is not explored, although it is unclear how they would have been incorporated into the story even if the creators had been fantastically prescient enough to predict them.

Yet another, and final theme to consider is the influence of science fantasy on budding scientists. In an earlier era, Buck Rogers films—as crude as they were—fired the imaginations of future employees of NASA and aerospace corporations. Implicit, and occasionally explicit, throughout this book is the fact that nearly all the contributors were deeply influenced by *2001* when it was released in 1968. I was myself introduced to the notion that a computer might someday be able to lipread by that famous scene in the pod, and I have spent years trying to devise computer lipreading systems. In that sense, many scientists are themselves a part of HAL's legacy.

When *2001* was released, one perceptive film reviewer called it "the best informed dream" of the future. In the following chapters, we look at that dream to see just how well-informed and how prescient it was and to gain a deeper understanding and appreciation of this truly remarkable film.

2   *Scientist on the Set: An Interview with Marvin Minsky*

David G. Stork

David G. Stork: You—along with John McCarthy, Claude Shannon, Nathaniel Rochester, and others—are credited with founding the field of artificial intelligence (AI) at the famous Dartmouth conference in 1956. A decade later, in the mid-sixties, when Clarke and Kubrick began work on *2001*, where was the field of AI? What were you trying to do?

Marvin Minsky: Well, we were trying to make intelligent machines. There were lots of good students working on interesting and important problems. In 1964 Tom Evans's program ANALOGY had excellent results on automated analogies—you know, figure A is to figure B as figure C is to what . . .

Jim Slagel wrote a program that could get an *A* on an MIT calculus exam. This is a tricky domain because, unlike simple arithmetic, to solve a calculus problem—and in particular to perform integration—you have to be smart about which integration technique should be used: integration by partial fractions, integration by parts, and so on. Around 1967 Dan Bobrow wrote a program to do algebra problems based on symbols rather than numbers.

It was somewhat later, 1974, that Eugene Charniak wrote a program to try to do word problems in algebra—of the sort, "Mary bought two pounds of flour at fifty cents a pound, and bought three days later a pound of sugar at two dollars. How much did she spend altogether?" He found this was extremely difficult, and basically his program didn't work.

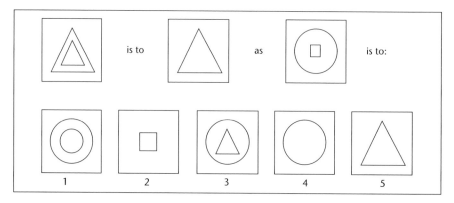

Figure 2.1
A Sample Problem of the General Sort Solved by Evans's ANALOGY Program

Stork: Was this because of insufficiently sophisticated language understanding, or instead lack of common sense or world knowledge?

Minsky: World knowledge. For instance, in the flour problem, how would the computer know that Mary didn't buy three *days*? In fact, somewhat later, around 1970, Terry Winograd addressed a simple Blocks World environment made up of simple objects and actions—"put the big block next to the smallest block," and so on—and showed that one could have a fairly seamless transition from syntax to semantics. So language, as difficult as a domain as it is, was not the obstacle to Charniak's program.

Stork: In the late sixties did you really think that toy world domains such as Blocks World captured all the essential aspects of intelligence?

Minsky: I did then, and I *still* do! In fact, I think it was the move away from such problems that is the main reason for lack of progress in AI. The problem is that in working on specific problems (such as chess, character recognition, and so on), there is no depth.

  I think a key to AI is the need for several representations of the knowledge, such that when the system is stuck (using one representation) it can jump to use another. When David Marr at MIT moved into computer vision, he generated a lot of excitement, but he hit up against the problem of knowledge representation; he had no good representations for knowledge in his vision systems. Bit by bit, people recognized the severity of the knowledge-representation problem, but only Doug Lenat took it seriously enough to base a research program on it. What I find astonishing is that Lenat—who is working on this now, in the nineties—is still considered a pioneer. Doug renounced trying to make intelligence in a particular domain, and I think this is a huge advance. I think Lenat is headed in the right direction, but someone needs to include a knowledge base about learning.

If the group at SRI hadn't built Shakey, the first autonomous robot, we would have had more progress. Shakey should never have been built. There was a failure to recognize the deep problems in AI; for instance, those captured in Blocks World. The people building physical robots learned nothing.

Stork: Oh, but doesn't the physical world force you to confront problems you might otherwise try to sneak around or overlook—for instance, friction?

Minsky: If it was an aspect of the problem that you overlooked in a simulation, then you would have overlooked it in a physical robot too. There was great effort expended building real walking machines, but we learned much more from pure simulations. For the real systems, you never knew if it worked or if it didn't work because a cloud went over the window and changed the lighting. When Mark Rayburn realized that, and went into simulations of walking machines, then we started making progress. By the way, it was his simulations that helped out in *Jurassic Park*—without them, there would have been only a few dinosaurs. Based on his techniques, Industrial Light and Magic could make whole herds of dinosaurs race across the screen.

Stork: Could you give a very broad overview of the techniques in AI?

Minsky: There are three basic approaches to AI: Case-based, rule-based, and connectionist reasoning.

The basic idea in case-based, or CBR, is that the program has stored problems and solutions. Then, when a new problem comes up, the program tries to find a similar problem in its database by finding analogous aspects between the problems. The problem is that it is very difficult to know which aspects from one problem should match which ones in any candidate problem in the other, especially if some of the features are absent.

In rule-based, or expert systems, the programmer enters a large number of rules. The problem here is that you cannot anticipate every possible input. It is extremely tricky to be sure you have rules that will cover everything. Thus these systems often break down when some problems are presented; they are very "brittle."

Connectionists use learning rules in big networks of simple components—loosely inspired by nerves in a brain. Connectionists take pride in not understanding how a network solves a problem.

Stork: Is that really so bad? After all, the understanding is at a higher, more abstract level of the learning rule and general notions of network architectures.

Minsky: Yes, it *is* so bad. If you just have a single problem to solve, then fine, go ahead and use a neural network. But if you want to do science and understand how to choose architectures, or how to go to a new problem, you have to understand what different architectures can and cannot do. Connectionist research on this problem leaves much to be desired.

Stork: What were you doing in the mid-sixties?

Minsky: I was interested in heterarchical systems for AI—ones that consisted of many interacting parts—applied to the same environment as Winograd. We wanted to solve robot problems and needed some vision, action, reasoning, planning, and so forth. We even used some structural learning, such as was being explored by Patrick Winston.

After about 1970, Winograd and his students tried to add more stuff. A major problem with AI research then was that Ph.D. dissertations were huge programs, and only the writer knew how they worked. Winograd thought you needed a second database, on how the design was done, so that all the theses could be unified. But we didn't have a good tool for knowledge representation. So Winograd and colleagues developed KRL—knowledge representation language—but this didn't work out, and the project fizzled. It turned out that it took as much time to cast a dissertation into KRL as it took to write the dissertation program in the first place! Thus this line of research was declared a failure, as summed up by Winograd's statement to the effect that you can't write big, smart programs.

Stork: But before that, again back to the mid-sixties, wouldn't you agree that the field was quite optimistic? After all, in a *Life* magazine article, you were quoted as saying "In from three to eight years we will have a machine with the general intelligence of an average human being. I mean a machine that will be able to read Shakespeare, grease a car, play office politics, tell a joke, have a fight. At that point the machine will begin to educate itself with fantastic speed. In a few months it will be at genius level and a few months after that its powers will be incalculable."

Minsky: Oh, that *Life* quote was made up. You can tell it's a joke. Herbert Simon said in 1958 that a program would be chess champion in ten years, and, as we know, the IBM group has done extremely well, but even now [Deep Blue] is not the undisputed champion.

As for optimism, it depends on what you mean. I believed in realism, as summarized by John McCarthy's comment to the effect that if we worked really hard, we'd have an intelligent system in from four to four hundred years.

Stork: What was your relationship to the filming of *2001*?

Minsky: Stanley Kubrick knew we had good graphics around MIT and came to my lab to find out how to do it. We had some really good stuff. I was very impressed with Kubrick; he knew all the graphics work I had ever heard of, and probably more.

Stork: Did he use any of your images or image techniques directly?

Minsky: No. At that time, all our images were 512 by 512 pixels—far too coarse for film audiences, and, more importantly, far too coarse for what we all knew would be available by the year 2001. Our images were on a twenty-inch raster-scan TV screen, before good color rendition. Kubrick was quite secretive, however, and I never really knew just what he would or wouldn't be using from MIT.

Stork: What kinds of images did you show Kubrick?

Minsky: We were showing him spectacular, out-of-this-world fractal images—you know, where a simple function was iterated again and again. For instance, one could start with a simple line segment, and then at one end, splice on two shorter line segments at some angle. At the end of each of *those* you add two more, and so on and so on. Pretty soon you have a simple tree. You can make some spectacular fireworks this way too.

The problem was that none of these were images that a HAL would be showing to the crew, so Kubrick never used any of our images.

Stork: Were you looking at such fractals just for fun? What was the research?

Minsky: In 1963 I had made some sketches for a "recursive structure" based on my fractal and bifurcating work. It looked so humanoid. We never built such a robot, but we used it in simulation.

Stork: What was it like on the set in England?

Minsky: The moon set at Shepperton, south of the Thames near London, was *very* impressive—*very* realistic. I remember clearly the excavation set with its lights and the monolith.

The staff at the MGM Borehamwood studios built the pods so well—I was very jealous. When I later saw the scene where the pod was used to open the emergency door to *Discovery,* I was particularly impressed. I thought that they must have built very sophisticated gearing and motor mechanisms just for that scene. Then I learned just how naive I was. In fact, the scene was filmed with stop action with a stagehand *inside Discovery* turning the handle. The pod arm just followed along! I was a bit disappointed.

I remember seeing the monster in *Little Shop of Horrors* and being suitably impressed there too. Later I met Bran Ferren at Disney, who was responsible for it. He said yes it was difficult—not the engineering, but giving complicated instructions to forty people simultaneously pulling levers and ropes to control the monster!

Stork: What else about working with them?

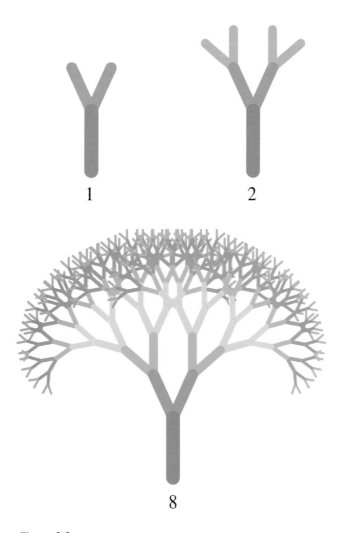

Figure 2.2
Fractal Image Generation
One simple rule is successively applied: Add two shorter and thinner segments to each line segment. Repeat.

David G. Stork

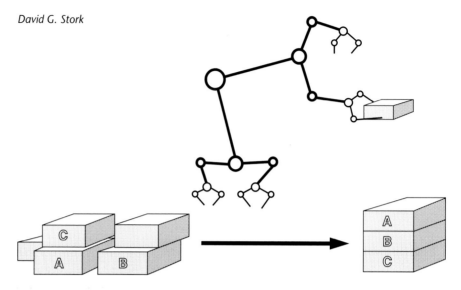

Figure 2.3
Minsky's Recursive Structure Robot Design

Minsky: I remember showing Kubrick superballs, before they had been sold in England. You know, those fantastic rubber balls that bounced so high. He loved them, and bounced them all over the halls.

As you know, Kubrick's initial alien artifact was a clear tetrahedron. But when he showed it to people, they all said, "what's that?" After all, it isn't a pyramid, or cube. Stanley was so upset that he dropped the tetrahedrons, though in the Stargate section of the film they appear briefly.

Stork: But wasn't this about the time of Buckminster Fuller, geodesic domes, the cult of the carbon bond, and so on?

Minsky: To an extent. Nevertheless, in the general public, a tetrahedron was somewhat foreign. Thus, instead, of course, Kubrick decided on the famous black monolith.

Stork: So, you said before that you didn't know what the final film would be like.

Minsky: Right. I remember sitting with Carl Sagan at the Boston opening of *2001* and thinking that it was the most awesome film I'd ever seen.

Stork: Why?

Minsky: Everything! I especially liked the putting down of the humans. All that boring dialogue and the dumb staff meetings, meetings to "beef up morale"! And after the momentous statement that the monolith must have been deliberately buried, one of the moon astronauts says "Well, how about a little coffee?" I always thought that it was Kubrick's idea that the universe was too majestic for short-sighted people. Of course, HAL stole the show.

Stork: In virtually all of Clarke's writing he comes across as an optimist, whereas all of Kubrick's films show a dark pessimism. Did you sense this interplay in *2001*?

Minsky: Certainly, though I never tried to identify which scene was due to which author. Clearly, though, the last scene is due to Clarke, based on his story "Childhood's End." Nevertheless, I think both are quite mystical, in a way. Kubrick's vision seemed to be that humans are doomed, whereas Clarke's is that humans are moving on to a better stage of evolution.

Stork: Did you see the screenplay beforehand?

Minsky: No. I had no detailed idea, really, what the film would be about.

Stork: In fact, most of the actors, and even some of the principals didn't know what the film was about, specifically. Douglas Rain, the Canadian actor who was the voice of HAL, did all his recording in a weekend, not really knowing how it fit in. Keir Dullea—playing David in the pod during the Stargate scene—was told to "look amazed" and had no idea what the final film would show.

Minsky: I heard that the same thing occurred in a scene in *Alien,* where the creature pops out of the chest of a crewman. The other actors didn't know what was to happen; the director wanted to get true surprise.

I was on the ferris wheel set in Borehamwood, England, just before it was done. It was a technical marvel, made at some unheard-of expense. The basic idea was that the ferris wheel (along with the camera attached to it) would rotate. The actor would always be at the bottom, running like a mouse in a treadmill. In the final footage, the viewer naturally assumes that the camera is still and it is the actor who runs around the circular room. Very clever.

For the scenes in which the camera follows the actor as he runs "around the walls," filming was trickier. Here the camera *also* stayed near the bottom of the treadmill, supported by a thin metal plate that slipped through the black cracks between the floorboards, all the way around the circumference. It was quite a set, and difficult and unpleasant for the actors—they could only stay in the set for about eight minutes.

Well, the set had lots of difficulties. For one thing, the stage crew occasionally left tools or lightbulbs on the set. Then, when it started rotating, the bulbs would fall free and pop on the ground.

Once when I was standing at the base, they started rotating the set and a big, heavy wrench fell down from the 12 o'clock position of the set, and got buried in the ground a few feet from me. I could have been *killed*! Kubrick was livid and quite shaken and fired a stagehand on the spot.

Once, later, Kubrick called me to talk about AI, and our conversation drifted to the issue of nuclear weapons and nuclear war. He thought all the disarmament and nuclear nonproliferation treaties were beside the point. Countries as a whole were too reasonable to ever start a nuclear war. The real danger was in an accident, or some madman getting ahold of a weapon. Why didn't the politicians realize *that*, Kubrick wanted to know. So I tried to console him and said that he had done more than anyone to alert the world to that possibility through his film, *Dr. Strangelove.*

Kubrick was silent for quite some time, and then said, "Oh, I forgot about that."

Stork: Did you work with Clarke too?

Minsky: He lived for a couple of weeks in the top floor of my house in Massachusetts, and we talked about a lot of science fiction—but stories other than *2001,* such as his book *Against the Fall of Night,* about a city run by machines. The city is great. The computer knows where all its atoms are and cleans up the city every night; I thought it was very clever.

I asked Clarke about language, and although he was optimistic about artificial intelligence, he thought that natural intonation in computers was harder. He wanted to know how long it would take computers to speak with

Figure 2.4
The Ferris Wheel Set of the Main Cabin of *Discovery*
The actors walked and remained at the bottom while the camera and the set rotated around them. In the film, the audience sees the set as fixed and the actors walking around the walls.

proper, natural intonation. Gort, the superintelligent machine in *The Day the Earth Stood Still,* couldn't speak well.

Stork: But might that not be cinema's way of letting the viewer know *this is a robot?*

Minsky: Yes! It is a convention, just like the way cinematographers slow down the motion to let you know that the action is really fast! Every kid can pretend to be a superfast athlete, like a karate master, by moving really slow! I suppose we owe all this to Eadweard Muybridge who took the stop-action shots of a horse running in order to show that all four feet were off the ground at the same time.

We can credit Clarke with inventing the "fifty-year horizon": that it was really out of the question to predict what the world would look like in fifty years. He had this wonderful quote, something to the effect of "any sufficiently advanced technology is indistinguishable from magic."

Stork: Yes, and the film only described about a fifty-year jump into the future. Kubrick went to extraordinary lengths to develop remarkable special effects, all to make the film look realistic—not the wizardry of exploding Death Stars, and so forth—in part, I suppose, to make the audience believe in the plausibility of the basic premise, that an alien civilization had visited the earth and moon.

Minsky: Yes, and whereas some films, and *Star Trek* in particular, insert technobabble, Kubrick and Clarke were very careful to stick as closely as they could to science.

I was once on the set of *Star Trek*—the TV version, not the film—and spoke to Gene Roddenberry, its creator. I said that with the tremendous, large, and loyal following the show had, wouldn't it be a great opportunity to insert even just a little "real" science?

Gene thought for a moment and then said, "no—too dangerous."

Stork: It is clear that some of the problems have been solved, chess for instance. However, we can presume that there is no Deep Blue on board *Discovery*—that's too much hardware just for the crew's amusement. But we have no program that has general intelligence that can play chess reasonably.

Minsky: But we *could* have! Only a small community has concentrated on general intelligence. No one has tried to make a thinking machine and *then* teach it chess—or the very sophisticated oriental board game Go. So Clarke made the same mistake that Herbert Simon made in the sixties, that AI was progressing so well and would continue to progress that we should start by concentrating on particular problems, such as Go or chess. But that's the wrong idea. The bottom line is that we really haven't progressed too far toward a truly intelligent machine. We have collections of dumb specialists in small domains; the true majesty of general intelligence still awaits our attack.

To give you one idea of some of the dumb things that have diverted the field, you need only consider situated action theory. This is an incredibly stupid idea that somehow swept the world of AI. The basic notion in situated action theory is that you don't use internal representations of knowledge. (But I feel they're crucial for any intelligent system.) Each moment the system—typically a robot—acts as if it had just been born and bases its decisions almost solely on information taken from the world—not on structure or knowledge inside. For instance, if you ask a simple robot to find a soda can, it gets all its information from the world via optical scanners and moves around. But it can get stuck cycling around the can, if things go wrong. It is true that 95 percent or even 98 percent of the time it can make progress, but for other times you're stuck. Situated action theory never gives the system any clues such as how to switch to a new representation.

When the first such systems failed, the AI community missed the important implication: that situated action theory was doomed to fail. I and my colleagues realized this in 1970, but most of the rest of the community was too preoccupied with building *real* robots to realize this point.

Stork: Would you like to help dispel the story about HAL having anything to do with IBM?

Minsky: Oh, that if you advance each letter in HAL by one letter you get IBM? Everyone denied that there was any connection. In fact, HAL comes from Heuristically programmed ALgorithmic computer. Heuristics are, of course, rules of thumb, tricks or techniques that might work on a problem, or often work, but aren't guaranteed. Algorithmic implies inviolate rules, such as *If A then B, and A, therefore B*. HAL was supposed to have the best of both worlds.

It is worth remembering that Nathaniel Rochester at IBM referred to the IBM 701 computer as "smart," and it nearly got him fired. Up to about 1985, IBM had a rule against employees stating that a machine could be smart, or had artificial intelligence. The highest officials at IBM thought it was a religious offense—that only God could create intelligence. Of course, they also wanted to reassure their potential customers that IBM products would only do what they were programmed to do!

Stork: It has been said that science fiction seeks to "metaphorize" the present in future terms. If so, what would *2001* say about the public's view of computers in the mid-sixties?

Minsky: Well, the person on the street at the time the film was made both loved computers and was scared of them. It's worth mentioning that there are no benevolent superintelligent computers in film—except, I suppose, in *The Day the Earth Stood Still*.

Stork: Do you think that is the nature of high intelligence?

Minsky: No, I think that's the nature of Hollywood.

Stork: Did Kubrick and Clarke fail to see important trends in computation, for instance the PC revolution? After all, Dave and Frank take notes in *Discovery* using pen on paper on a clipboard!

Minsky: I basically agree with Alan Kay, who said something to the effect that "the best way to predict the future is to invent it." Of course, Clarke came up with the idea of communications satellites in 1945 and promoted them in a short story, "I Remember Babylon." It's hard to do a better prediction than that!

But, as for PCs, for the most part no one in the film needed them; HAL took care of almost everything. It is true that the trend has been toward smaller and smaller computers. We're working on *wearable* computers, and I think the first ones will be connected to screens in your eyeglasses so you can see the virtual images anywhere, anytime.

Stork: What are you working on now?

Minsky: I'm writing a book, *The Emotion Machine,* a sort of sequel to my *The Society of Mind.*

Stork: Does this have much to do with the kind of "affective computing" that Roz Picard is pursuing?

Minsky: Not too much. Roz is working on detection of emotion from images of the face, tone of voice, and so on, as well as giving the computer some sort of emotion in its output. I'm more interested in reasoning about emotion.

I think it is a deep problem how we construct goals, and especially how we change our approach to a problem, to know when one method of attack isn't working and that we have to try a different approach. Emotion influences this.

Stork: Of course, HAL detects and shows more emotion than any other character in *2001.* Do you think Kubrick was prescient about the need for emotion?

Minsky: As I stress in my book, I don't think you can make AI without subgoals, and emotion is crucial for setting and changing subgoals. Kubrick probably put the emotion in to make good cinema, but it also happens to be very good science. For instance, HAL explains that the Jupiter mission is too important to be jeopardized by humans. It is through emotion that he sets the goals and subgoals, ultimately killing the humans—except, of course, Dave.

Stork: But if you want computers to be reliable, you probably don't want to put in emotion. After all, imagine the air traffic computers having emotions. You wouldn't want to take away humans and leave life-and-death decisions to emotional computers, would you?

Minsky: But it's the humans that cause us to crash! The planes are really so far apart that the chance for them to crash is small. There are so many chances for human errors!

Stork: Was your science influenced by science fiction?

Minsky: Oh, absolutely. I read about equal parts of Jules Verne and H. G. Wells—Verne for space and Wells for nonspace. But, of course, according to Einstein, time and space are really the same thing!

Specifically, I got interested in tele-operators from reading Heinlein's books. And if we had all read the books by Brunner more carefully, we would have had screens in our eyeglasses twenty years ago.

Stork: Now for the converse: How was your science *fiction*—specifically your book *The Turing Option*—influenced by your science?

Minsky: Well, I thought that science fiction was a good venue for exploring the implications of AI. It helps you to be clearer about the implications of your work. In *The Turing Option*, I was particularly interested in the value of information, such as corporate secrets. It was also a lot of fun to write!

Stork: Do you read current science fiction—William Gibson, for example?

Minsky: I'm not interested in novels about how to break machines. I started, but couldn't read *Neuromancer,* and didn't see any new ideas in it. The cyberpunk authors are primarily interested in atmosphere rather than ideas, and that doesn't satisfy me.

Stork: So, you seem dismayed by many of the directions in AI? What would you advocate for the field to bring us closer to building a HAL?

Minsky: We have got to get back to the deepest questions of AI and *general* intelligence and quit wasting time on little projects that don't contribute to the main goal. We can get back to them later.

Stork: Supposing the field follows your suggestion, how long until we can make a HAL?

Minsky: I'm still a realist: If we work really hard—and smart—we can have something like a HAL in between four and four hundred years. I suppose if we're lucky, then, we can make it by 2001!

Further Readings

Harry Harrison and Marvin Minsky. *The Turing Option*. New York: Warner Books, 1992. A science fiction novel about computers, artificial intelligence, and espionage.

Marvin Minsky. *The Society of Mind*. New York: Simon and Schuster, 1985. Both a model of the human mind and a blueprint for artificial intelligence as a society of specialized agents, each solving problems in a limited domain.

Marvin Minsky. *The Emotion Machine*. (In preparation.) A sequel to *The Society of Mind* exploring the role of emotions and desires for guiding and arbitrating among large numbers of specialized, but dumb, agents.

3   *Could We Build HAL? Supercomputer Design*

David J. Kuck

For most of the trip in *Discovery 1*, HAL seems to be everywhere and yet nowhere, ubiquitous and yet hidden. On the one hand, we see his red eye on every wall, corridor, and panel of the ship, and even in the pods. His display screens appear prominently on numerous consoles; the speakers carrying his voice can only be avoided in the privacy of a pod. On the other hand, we don't really *see* HAL at all. Only when Dave floats into the grandeur of HAL's "brain room" does his full size strike us: he is as big as a house! Surely constructing a machine of that magnitude is a tremendous—and tremendously expensive—engineering feat.

Could we build a computer like HAL today? For any given technology what determines how powerful a computer we can produce? What might be the general design—the computer architecture—of a HAL suited to tasks as diverse as controlling a spaceship and discussing personal psychology with the crew? What types of hardware components would we use? How would the hardware support the complex software required to carry out the many humanlike functions of which HAL is capable?

Those of us who have spent our professional lives designing and building high-performance computers are constantly aware that we live in a Golden Age in which computer hardware continually becomes more powerful and less expensive. This trend has gone on for half a century, since the invention of the modern computer and the transistor in the 1940s. Many distinct types of computer architecture have been built and used in various applications.

This has made some people optimistic that the components and system architecture for building a massive supercomputer like HAL are, or soon will be, within our grasp.

Examining the specific predictions of both the book and film versions of *2001* with the 20/20 vision of hindsight allows us to observe now that some of them were far too optimistic and others were not optimistic enough. In fact, over the past fifty years, progress in computer engineering and computer science has been breathtaking in some aspects and disappointing in others. While some computer systems have become workhorses and milestone systems against which all successor systems are judged, others have shown great promise but delivered too little to attract a wide following. In this chapter, we examine the realities of the past thirty years, in terms of the 1960s Clarke-Kubrick vision that predicted HAL would be developed by 1997.

2001, the novel, outlines a three-stage sequence of breakthroughs that led, in the 1980s, to techniques for the automatic generation of artificial neural networks. In the third stage, as Clarke describes it, "artificial brains could be grown by a process strikingly analogous to the development of a human brain." However, even in 2001, developing such systems was very expensive, "and only a few units of the HAL 9000 series had yet been built."

The two prior breakthroughs described in the novel were, first, the invention in the 1940s of "such clumsy, high-speed morons as ENIAC and its successors," which were based on vacuum tubes. "Then in the 1960s, solid-state microelectronics had been perfected," making it "clear that artificial intelligences at least as powerful as Man's need be no larger than office desks."

The novel explains that the precise details of the process of growing these brains "would never be known, and even if they were, they would be millions of times too complex for human understanding." The neural networks were "generated automatically—self replicated—in accordance with any arbitrary learning program."

The ENIAC breakthrough of the 1940s was indeed correctly stated by Clarke, with the benefit of twenty years of hindsight. The second event too was accurately identified as a breakthrough, with the qualification that saying solid-state microelectronics were "perfected" in the 1960s was overly optimistic. At that time, it would have been difficult to predict that the speed and size of microelectronic devices would continue to evolve dramatically for the next thirty years. Indeed, not until the 1980s did microprocessors and memory chips become commodity items.

The third breakthrough, attributed by Clarke to the 1980s, was far off the mark. The notion of artificial neural nets is as old as computers themselves; and indeed there was renewed interest in them in the 1980s. The idea is that a large collection of relatively simple network elements, perhaps with some overall separation of functions, could be presented with long training sequences from which the network would learn a given function. The individual elements would change slightly in response to each step of the training process; in the end, the neural net would be able to solve the problem for which it was trained. Over the years, researchers have attempted to base the elements of artificial neural nets, roughly, on the neurons and synapses of the human brain.

While 1980s research has led to working neural net systems and real products ranging from speech-recognition systems to mutual fund stock-picking software, the results have not constituted a major breakthrough. Most of the systems developed are actually software *simulations* of neural networks that run on normal computers, and most of them solve problems by traditional computational methods. In certain cases, the neural nets are competitive with (or even better than) traditional computational methods.

The real computing breakthrough of the 1980s, however, turned out to be the commodity development of computers. These microprocessor-based systems, whose capabilities far exceed ENIAC's, have uses ranging from personal workstations and home computers with easy-to-use "do what I mean" software to microprocessors embedded in automobiles and airplanes to replace or enhance electrical and mechanical components. This breakthrough was accompanied by development of a ubiquity of application software available for solving real problems or, in some cases, simply for entertaining people.

As a consequence of the development of commodity microprocessors, and because solid-state device speeds have been pushed almost as far as seems possible for the types of microelectronic devices in common use, parallelism in computing also underwent a major advance in the 1980s. This happened in high-performance scientific and engineering computing as well as in commercial computing. Parallel computer applications now include weather forecasting, geophysical oil exploration, radar and sonar signal processing, and simulations of air flow around airplanes and under auto hoods and of cars crashing into solid walls. On the commercial side, insurance-company databases, bank processing, and junk mail engines now all rely on parallel computers.

Although the architecture of HAL is not described in the novel, we can make informed guesses about what it might have been like. To be as large and powerful as he is described, HAL would have to be a parallel system. Parallel computers are collections of components much like those found in familiar PCs, but they are interconnected in ways that allow fast communication and, therefore, cooperation in solving a single problem. Whereas the human brain and artificial neural nets are both massive parallel systems built from neurons, parallel computers are composed of microprocessors, memory units, and a complex interconnection network, which are, in turn, built from silicon transistors.

Technical Predictions

One concrete number given in the novel describes the memory unit Bowman pulls out as a "marvelously complex three-dimensional network, which could lie comfortably in a man's hand yet contained millions of elements." In hindsight, we see that the available bases for prediction in the 1960s were already fairly close to what *2001* offers as a thirty-year prediction. ILLIAC 4, the first large-scale parallel supercomputer, was being designed as the book was being written; when completed in the early 1970s, it had the first solid-state computer memory. Each of the sixty-four processors' memories had 2K (K=1,024) 64-bit words—employing some fraction of a million transistors—

on a board small enough for a person to carry with both hands. So each processor had 16K bytes of memory, and the whole supercomputer had 1MB (1 megabyte is about a million 8-bit words). This was large for the time but inadequate for any laptop today! The very conservative nature of Clarke's prediction is underscored by today's commodity memory technology; even a modern 8-MB PC memory contains several hundred million transistors.

So how *does* one make a rational prediction about computer and micro-electronics technology? Two basic hardware characteristics, which vary over time, allow us to predict future system size and capability. One is the *feature size* in semiconductor chips: How small can wires and transistors become? The answer determines how far electrons must travel on each processing step. The other factor is the *clock speed* of computer circuits: How frequently does information move to the next step in a computer's operation. A third determinant—how fast electrons move when the clock allows them to—is determined by a physical invariant, the speed of light.

The other components of computer system performance—system architecture and software—are much harder to describe and to predict than hardware is, because they are human syntheses and thus much less constrained by physical laws. The rest of this chapter outlines various aspects of how these technologies have advanced over the past thirty years. It also describes difficulties in the evolution of higher-performance systems that use architecture and software alone. We begin, however, with the purely hardware aspects of performance.

Microelectronic Feature Sizes

In the past decade, feature size has passed through the 1-micron (a millionth of a meter) level and will approach 0.1 micron for commodity parts by 2001. Moore's law (named after a 1964 observation by Gordon E. Moore of Intel) holds that *"The number of elements in advanced integrated circuits doubles every year."* This law is widely and loosely quoted, sometimes with the time period being stretched to eighteen months or more; it reflects the tremendous progress made since the first planar transistor was produced in 1959.

The microelectronic integration of many of these flat transistors on one chip made the microprocessor possible. By a series of steps that are reminiscent of lithography, millions of electronic components are built up on postage-stamp-sized semiconductor chips. It is clear, however, that Moore's law is an observation about technological progress that will not continue forever.

There are two obvious contributors to the increases described by Moore's law: the reduction of feature sizes within the chip and the growth of the chip size itself; the latter is now about one-inch square, but most of the progress has come from smaller feature sizes. The fundamental limitations on feature size are determined by the wavelength of light used in the lithography process of manufacturing semiconductor chips. Continued progress at historical rates seems assured beyond the next decade and is relatively straightforward. Even with a drop-off in Moore's law to doubling every two years, memory-size increases of ten times in seven years seem plausible for many decades to come.

Memory speeds have not kept pace with processor speeds, however. In the past few decades, memory speeds (once comparable to processor speeds) have lagged behind. Traditional computers performed typical operations in about one memory access period. Although current microprocessors can perform one operation per clock period, memory accesses require about fifty clocks; this imbalance makes complex, fast-access cache-memory systems (used to "hide" copies of reusable information in one-chip memory) very important components of modern microprocessors.

The prognosis of much larger memories at about constant speeds matches well with the development of parallel systems. Each processor added to a system adds a memory unit as well; and if the processor/memory speed ratio is constant, cache systems will evolve to yield well-balanced, high-performance microprocessor-memory components. This leads to the prediction that memory size will grow linearly with processor count and hence with peak system performance.

Any hint that there may be excess memory capacity in the future, however, can be immediately dismissed by realizing another fundamental limitation of computing, the Law of Large Memory: "*Software abhors vacant memory and immediately fills any vacancies.*"

Clock Speed

Every step inside a computer is driven by an electronic clock whose ticks move the system's state forward. In the time between clock ticks, data bits move between adjacent pairs of registers, much as students move between classrooms when the bell rings, each following a different path, generally with a different path length.

The clock period can be made as fast as desired within a broad range; but to be practical, data must move forward a substantial distance in each clock tick. When a system is designed the clock is adjusted to accommodate the longest delay in the hardware of the computer. These delays are determined by physical laws; the speed of signal on a wire is less than the speed of light in free space, about one foot per nanosecond (one nanosecond [ns] is one billionth of a second). Since each operation is performed in one or more clock periods, speeding up the clock speeds up all of the computer's operations. But the laws of physics eventually set insurmountable limits to practical clock-speed increases.

Early computers had clock speeds in the millisecond range; by the 1960s they had passed though the microsecond level; and we are now approaching the nanosecond level—an increase of roughly a factor of a million in fifty years. Together with perhaps a factor of 10 achieved by other architectural advances, uniprocessors have increased their speed by a factor of about 10 every seven years, averaged over the fifty-year history.

Computer-clock periods are stated either in units of time or as frequencies measured in units of one per time. Because the square-wave, computer-clock frequency is analogous to the frequency of sinusoidal natural sound and electromagnetic waves, it is given in terms of units of hertz, megahertz (MHz), and so on.

About the time *2001* was written in the 1960s, the CDC 6600 had a 100-ns clock period; in the early 1970s, ILLIAC 4 had a 40-ns clock. By 1976, the Cray 1 had a 12.5-ns clock period, and, fifteen years later, the Cray 2 attained a 4-ns clock. Thus, in recent years, the fastest system clocks have speeded up by a factor of less than 1.7 per seven years—because the physical limits are being hit. Similarly, the Intel x86-line clock period improved from 210 ns in the 8086 of 1978 to 15.2 ns in the Pentium of 1993, a factor of about 14 over fifteen years, or about 3.7 every seven years—thus demonstrating the same slowing trend as supercomputers. The fastest commercially available clock speed today is 2 ns, in the Hitachi S-3800 vector supercomputer.

Computer System Performance

The fastest microprocessor today is the Digital Equipment Corporation's (DEC) Alpha processor. DEC's 1992 announcement of the Alpha and its 5-ns clock period promised that the Alpha line would achieve performance growth of a factor of 1000 over its twenty-five-year lifetime. The company projected a gain of ten times from clock-speed improvements (it announced 300 MHz in 1994), an additional ten times from uniprocessor architectural gains, and ten times from parallel processing. Because it maintains the traditional system speed gain of about ten times every seven years, this projection is in accord with the prediction that maximum clock speeds will reach about 1 ns in the next decade; but then it posits a gain of only about two times per seven years over the next twenty-five years (a bit more than the Cray attained in the 1980s); the remaining 100-factor increase comes from architecture and software. Thus DEC is projecting that the cube root of future performance gains will come from clock speed, whereas almost *all* of the historical gains came from the clock. Most of the rest of the increase in their projection comes from parallelism, because uniprocessor speed gains are now substantially tied to executing more than one operation in parallel within each microprocessor.

The Intel-system performance record of the past fifteen years, which is based on a typical metric (MIPS, millions of instructions executed per second), shows a total gain factor of 336. Thus, architecture and software have provided a significant improvement in performance. Depending on the exact period chosen, Intel microprocessors have recently been attaining about the square root of their performance gains through clock-speed advances. Today Intel is beginning to ship parallel processor boards to help overcome the inevitable clock-speed squeeze.

In summary, while historically system performance improvements were in direct linear proportion to the clock speed, in the past decade this has dropped to a square-root effect and, in the next two decades, appears likely to drop to a cube-root effect. In fact, data in a Business Week (1993) article that was generally very optimistic predicts a mere 800-MHz clock rate (1.25 ns cycle time) for microprocessors in 2011.

In fact, if automobile speed had improved by the same factor as computer speed has in the past fifty years, cars that travelled at highway speed limits in the 1940s would now be traveling at a different speed limit—the speed of light! The cube root of historic computer-speed gains, however, would have carried 1940s cars only to modern airplane speeds. Thus, unless parallel processing can be efficiently exploited, twenty-first-century computer progress will look more like the progress of twentieth-century transportation than like the spectacular progress of twentieth-century computing.

The crucial point here is that the relatively easy historical computer-speed gains from clock-speed advances are now being replaced by gains from software and architecture. These latter gains, unfortunately, have not occurred across-the-board. In fact, they are so variable that modern general-purpose supercomputers often show variations of 10 to 100 times in computational rates on different types of jobs (Corcoran 1991). Of course, it is always possible to design special-purpose hardware that runs very fast. This is done in digital signal processors (e.g., as used in modems and communications equipment); graphics processors; multimedia processors (e.g., Chromatic and Microunity); chess machines (e.g., IBM's Deep Blue which contains 256 chess processors plus 32 standard microprocessors); and, potentially, even in HAL-like systems. To succeed in the real world marketplace, though, this approach must be general purpose enough to sustain a sufficient production volume and lifetime.

It is important to realize that the clock-speed squeeze discussed above does not depend on whether the eventual limit on the clock period for current technology is 1 ns or even 0.1 ns, but rather on the fact some physical limit is being hit. Technology breakthroughs are always possible; to succeed they must provide low-cost engineering solutions to commodity computer circuit-speed problems, not merely laboratory possibilities.

Are such breakthroughs likely in the near future? Over the past fifteen years, development of the gallium arsenide high-speed computer circuit has been a big disappointment; Cray Computer Corporation used it in its failed attempt to produce the Cray 3. Superconducting devices have long been proposed as computer building blocks. More recently, optical computers that switch light, not electricity, have gained attention; and from time to time various quantum mechanical effects have been proposed as physics principles for innovative devices. Even biological and DNA computers are currently under study for certain applications in the distant future.

For any new technology to succeed in the near future, however, it must be competitive with the CMOS and BiCMOS devices (relatively simple to build and fast and effective transistors) that have become the fabric of computers. Since there are no plausible alternatives on the five-to-ten-year horizon, clock-speed considerations alone would lead one to the inevitable conclusion that parallel architecture and software are in the short run the only escapes from the speed trap imposed by nature on general-purpose computer hardware.

Supercomputer System History Since 2001

In the mid-1960s, when Clarke and Kubrick designed HAL, the Control Data Corporation's CDC 6600 was the world's dominant supercomputer. It had parallelism within its single central processor. The first large-scale parallel system, ILLIAC 4, with its sixty-four high-speed processors, was just being developed. In the thirty years since then, parallelism has blossomed in response to the clock-speed squeeze.

Today, parallel systems are categorized as shared-memory parallel (SMP) systems or distributed-memory parallel (DMP) systems. All the processors in an SMP system can access any word in the system memory directly. DMP systems are a connected set of microprocessors, each with its own memory, that communicate with each others' memories by sending and receiving messages. SMP systems are widely offered as departmental servers and are now appearing on desktops, whereas DMP systems can be either networks of workstations or special-purpose supercomputers; the latter can be massively parallel-processor (MPP) systems of more than a thousand processors.

The supercomputers of Control Data evolved from the CDC 6600 of the 1960s through the 7600 and Cyber 205 systems. The 6600 was designed by James Thornton and Seymour Cray. Thornton also designed the CDC STAR 100 line, which evolved into the Cyber 205 in the 1970s. Cray left CDC in the early 1970s to start Cray Research, Inc., and left that company in the 1980s to found Cray Computer Corporation.

The traditional Cray Research line of supercomputers evolved in various ways during the past two decades but has kept a solid customer base by maintaining a common instruction set, improving its architecture, and providing a hardware performance monitor plus software to allow for some degree of performance tuning and portability between model changes. The massively parallel, distributed-memory systems of the past decade have rarely followed this model. Cray Research attempted to gain a market share in both worlds by introducing its Cray T3D and T3E MPP systems, which are sold as attachments to Cray's traditional SMP systems. The idea is that the SMP system would handle parts of a computation, but suitable parts would be handed off to an attached MPP system for superfast execution. Despite these efforts, Cray's revenues have dropped sharply in the 1990s, because of competition from other supercomputer vendors as well as rapid advances in uniprocessor cost/performance ratios.

In 1983, Thinking Machines Corporation (TMC) began business in an aura of artificial intelligence applications. It featured LISP (a language of artificial intelligence researchers) as a programming language and named its MPP system the Connection Machine—some thought to link it with the connectionist models of the mind. Its first system, the CM-1, used up to 64,000 single-bit processors and had a single-instruction multiple-data (SIMD) architecture. After market exposure, the CM-1 and successor CM-2 systems provided Fortran programming and were mostly used for traditional scientific and engineering computations. However, the performance successes users achieved with these SIMD systems had to be seriously reconsidered when TMC produced a successor CM-5 system in 1992; the new system used a different instruction set and a multiple-instruction, multiple-data (MIMD) architecture. Although the company claimed upward compatibility for CM-2 codes to the CM-5 system, achieving high performance required users to rethink many aspects of codes for the totally new architecture, which contributed to customer defection and TMC's downfall.

The Intel Supercomputer Systems Division in Oregon dates from 1984. It has produced five generations of MPPs, beginning with the iPSC/1, an array of Intel 80286 microprocessors, through the Paragon system, which has as many as 1,024 clusters consisting of two Intel i860 microprocessors with shared memory for computation. Intel's current system, Teraflops, is based on the Intel Pentium-Pro microprocessor and contains up to nine thousand microprocessors in four-processor SMP clusters. Thus, Intel has changed both instruction sets and interconnection architectures, although it has retained MIMD control and a global DMP software model over the years.

Despite these and a number of other efforts, practical parallel processing is not yet available for general computing. Nevertheless, parallel desktop SMP systems are now arriving at the level of workstations from Sun Microsystems and PCs based on the Pentium-Pro. Parallel systems are therefore becoming commodity items, and their practical application will be driven by the need for speed, their low cost, and new software developments.

However, supercomputers have fallen on hard times, and many of the startup companies of the 1980s have failed. Cray Research suffered revenue losses and in 1996 was bought by Silicon Graphics; the latter company, which was established in the 1980s, focuses on workstations and SMP servers whose graphics capabilities were demonstrated in the films *Jurassic Park* and

Toy Story. Intel's Supercomputer Systems Division had difficulty selling machines in the general marketplace and abandoned its Paragon line in 1996, and Thinking Machines closed down its hardware business in 1995.

So where could HAL be built in 1997? Arthur Clarke placed the HAL plant in Urbana, Illinois, the home of the University of Illinois. This was plausible, because beginning in the early 1950s, the Digital Computer Lab and Computer Science Department produced four ILLIACs and the Cedar system. I directed the Center for Supercomputing R&D (CSRD), which finished Cedar, an SMP system, in the early 1990s. Cedar pioneered several ideas aimed at scalable parallel performance that would have been useful in building HAL.

A key architectural problem is how to interconnect parallel processors and memories. A Cedar innovation to this problem was the Omega network, whose shuffle-exchange interconnection pattern moves data in the style of a perfect playing-card shuffle. IBM's SP line of parallel systems in the 1990s has adopted this interconnection network, because it can be scaled up to large numbers of processors. Another key architectural problem is how to build scalable parallel systems in which performance remains good over a wide range of processor counts. Cedar was a hierarchical SMP system built from clusters of smaller SMP systems; several of the MPP systems listed above used DMP-interconnected SMP clusters. CSRD also pioneered in parallelizing Fortran and LISP compilers to ease the programming efforts for parallel systems. These ideas are now widely used on all systems; in fact, Kuck and Associates Inc., a University of Illinois spinoff, produces high-performance compiler technology for all the major computer companies. CSRD also developed highly tunable parallel algorithm libraries, including the widely used BLAS3, Basic Linear Algebra kernels, which could have been used to maximize HAL's performance in speech, vision, and various control functions.

But in 1997 the only American parallel-computer manufacturers that could build HAL are IBM (basing him on its new SP3 line, perhaps); Cray/Silicon Graphics; or, perhaps Convex/HP (Convex was a 1990s startup Hewlett Packard rescued in the 1990s); or Intel (as a Teraflops companion). The Japanese Big 3—Fujitsu, NEC, and Hitachi—have all continued work in supercomputing, including parallel computing, but they have not been leaders in parallelism. In the 1980s the Japanese government sponsored a major effort called the Fifth Generation Project, which attempted to develop many aspects of computing for artificial intelligence, but it led to little practical technology. Nor have European efforts at parallel computing produced any viable, ongoing businesses.

A central problem of parallel processing is the difficulty of programming the systems effectively. Imagine the difficulties of describing in advance how to prepare and cook a multicourse meal on a four- or eight-burner range so that each course comes out properly cooked at just the right moment for serving. Current software on most architectures suffers from the fact that, as a last resort, users have to bear a substantial programming burden that should be borne by well-designed architectures and software. However, motivated by the clock-speed squeeze, many software developers are moving their applications onto these machines, and software tools to meet the demands are improving.

High-Performance Computing versus Machine Intelligence

Computer scientists and artificial intelligence (AI) specialists have failed to fulfill many aspects of the Clarke-Kubrick vision. They have not created computer systems that can mimic the behavior of the human brain; nor have they been able to build systems that can learn to imitate many human skills. However, in the past thirty years, systems have been created that far exceed human capabilities in many more areas than were anticipated in the mid-1960s.

Denigrating whatever computers can do has traditionally been easy. Computers are really morons—the book states—with large memories and fast arithmetic/logical abilities that humans program to carry out one trivial step at a time. Consider, however, what computers can do today using the complex application software systems that have been developed. And consider how far these capabilities are from what any scientist, engineer, or businessman can do without computers. There is, of course, a thin line of distinction between what is computed and what the user does with computed results, but I refer here to the fact that computed results, in whatever form, often change or influence people's technical and business decisions. The Boeing 777, for example, was totally computer-simulated before it was constructed.

The Turing test of machine intelligence is satisfied if an uninformed observer cannot distinguish a computer from a human via typed communication alone. This ignores the issue of defining a *human,* in that Garry Kasparov is not simply *a human chess player* and that nobel laureates are not merely *human technical specialists.* Our Alien Turing test, on the other hand, is something that *Discovery 1* astronauts, or those traveling to other galaxies, might be able to use.

Suppose that astronauts encounter aliens who have encyclopedic memories of facts and images, plus superfast recall and logical-processing abilities, as well as sensors that allowed them to look inside human bodies to spot abnormalities, or look under the earth's surface to distinguish valuable oil pools from water and rock. Such aliens could also perceive the future by foreseeing, approximately, when a mechanical part will fail or, roughly, what tomorrow's weather will be. Given a detailed description of a computer system or the structure of a building, the aliens would be able to simulate the behavior of complex systems over time and decide, for example, how much stress from external voltages, or from an earthquake, the systems could absorb before failing. Surely, the analytical and problem-solving abilities of these alien minds over a range of complex topics would not be confused with human minds.

The Alien Turing test of machine intelligence would be satisfied if an uninformed observer could not distinguish a computer from an alien with respect to their respective abilities to solve the problems on a given list. If we administered the test to these aliens and to today's high-performance computers, the computer systems we have evolved would pass it easily. The Alien Turing test mentioned above is merely to suggest that in the 1960s computers were only beginning to solve complex problems for ordinary people, and a prediction that they would be as useful as they are in so many areas would have been very farsighted indeed. Of course, the AI predictions of *2001* were reasonable for science fiction, as such thoughts are always exciting—appealing to some people and threatening to others.

The Turing test asks: Can computers ever become as good as human minds are, at doing what the human mind has evolved to do best? The Alien Turing test can also be termed the Anti-Turing test, as it really poses the inverse problem: Can a human or alien ever become as good as the most powerful computers are at what *they* have evolved to do best? Although the human mind will continue to evolve and accumulated knowledge will allow abstract thought to rise to new heights, the best human minds and the most powerful computers do not appear to be on converging paths.

However, it is tempting to compare the gross physical characteristics of supercomputers and human brains. Obviously, the human brain is very compact in size relative to any of today's supercomputers. What about the number of elements or devices contained in each? Because the brain's methods of representing and storing information and functioning are not well understood, direct comparisons with the number of computer components can only be suggestive of relative complexity. With this in mind, we note that the brain appears to have between one and ten trillion neurons, plus many more interconnecting synapses that are very important to its functioning.

On the other hand, modern microprocessors have up to ten million elementary switches for logical/arithmetic operations, thus a 10,000-processor MPP (e.g., the Intel Teraflops) would have 100 billion switches. This is, at most, 10 percent of the neuron estimate. The main memory (RAM) of a 10,000-processor computer with 80 MB per processor would contain one trillion bits (0–1 information); the disk or CD ROM storage would be much larger. Following Moore's Law, even at a decreased growth rate, future computers are likely, in terms of physical capacity, to match the human brain. This, of course, implies nothing about how such a machine might function, relative to a human brain.

It is important to realize that AI could succeed without a manmade architecture that matches or is an analog of the brain. So, even if we do not understand the details of how the brain works, programming a high-performance general-purpose computer, designing a special-purpose artificial neural network computer, or synthesizing some distributed hybrid collection of these, might do a major part of the job that HAL did. It is clear that the human brain operates in parallel in order to carry out its many functions simultaneously. So present-day parallel computers may be headed in a direction that will someday support systems with more intelligence than any machine has demonstrated to date. In this discussion I have referred to the *evolution* of computers in order to underscore the sometimes slow and sometimes rapid changes in computer system architecture that have occurred over the past fifty years. In the future, a sufficient number of independent developments in AI and computer architecture may allow us to build much more powerful reasoning systems.

We can summarize our discussion by observing that very little is currently known about how to relate the functioning of brains to the functioning of computers. However, another significant computing breakthrough of the past thirty years is clear: the Anti-Turing test can be defined through a list that includes many problems important to everyone, not to just a few specialized scientists and engineers. An integral part of this breakthrough is the fact that people who are not computer specialists can now use computers directly for solving many difficult problems in science, engineering, and business.

Conclusion

In the thirty years since the film was made, computing has progressed dramatically, in terms of hardware technology, system architecture, application software, and cost to end users. Because of their massive ability to crunch numbers and symbols and recent progress in simulating time-varying processes ranging from games to engineering systems and scientific questions, computers are now ubiquitous in the real world. However, fifty years after computers were invented attempts to use them in most applications are still at the development stage. These intense efforts will continue into the next century—and beyond.

The application that jumped to the forefront of the minds of computer scientists and laymen as soon as modern computers were invented was artificial intelligence, under various definitions. This idea motivated the Clarke-Kubrick vision of HAL in *2001*. Under any general definition, however, AI has so far been a failure. In retrospect, however, it doesn't seem significant that AI has failed to live up to its early promises. We don't need the kind of AI that could pass the Turing test, because we already have millions of good human minds—produced, as *2001* points out, by unskilled labor.

However, other parts of the Clarke-Kubrick vision of HAL have become very useful and important, and some of these applications are discussed in this volume. For example, speech recognition, handwriting recognition, computer vision, and even computer chess and other advanced games of skill are in wide use today. Moreover, it is now easy to predict that future computers will routinely solve much more difficult problems than those we imagine today. Many aspects of computational engineering design are rapidly evolving; weather forecasting is still weak, even with the most powerful computers; and people in many areas of science and technology still use computers in rudimentary ways. Their importance, however, is certain to grow far beyond today's most complex and successful applications.

Additionally, computers are now being deployed in distributed processing. For example, one or more computers at each bank site are linked together to produce a bank's network. The same idea is used in complex mechanical systems (e.g., in automobiles, airplanes, or space systems). In an airplane, microprocessors can help control the engines, landing gear, navigation system, and so on; then these subsystems are networked to help operate the entire airplane. Indeed, HAL would have been a distributed system containing powerful parallel systems for various parts of the cognitive functions as well as for the various control functions. In fact, the human brain has a great number of similarly independent sections for controlling and processing vision, hearing, speech, and various types of cognitive activities; and each of these sections is a highly parallel collection of neurons. There are, thus, strong analogies between the history and progress of computing in the past thirty years and what we would need to build HAL.

Because of a clock-speed squeeze in the semiconductor-based technology that has been used for the last fifty years, parallelism now seems to be a necessity for future computer architectures. As parallel computing continues to develop, unpredictable breakthroughs will occur. As more and more formidable results allow us to tick off the items on the Anti-Turing test, perhaps someday even the Turing test will be satisfiable—in the sense that a computer or collection of computers will be able to emulate or challenge the minds of many of the world's most powerful humans. We have already seen this happen with chess, and it seems clear that it is likely for certain other activities. However, it is not obvious, especially with the loss of emphasis on manned space travel, that a HAL-like system will ever be sufficiently interesting to induce governments or corporations to fund its development.

Acknowledgments

My thanks to Oxford University Press for permission to use extensive material from my 1996 work, which is reprinted and modified here.

Further Readings

Anon. "In Supercomputing, Superconfusion." *Business Week* 3311 (March 22, 1993): 89–90. An analysis of the complex financial underpinnings of the supercomputer industry.

Elizabeth Corcoran. "Calculating reality." *Scientific American* 264, 1 (January 1991): 100–109. Discussion of the use of supercomputers to simulate complicated physical processes.

P. P. Gelsinger, P. A. Gargini, G. H. Parker, and A. Y. C. Yu. "Microprocessors circa 2000." *IEEE Spectrum* (October 1989): 43–47. Careful predictions about the performance characteristics of future microprocessors.

David J. Kuck. *High-Performance Computing: Challenges for Future Systems*. New York: Oxford University Press, 1996. A fairly detailed and technical book on future problems and opportunities in the supercomputer industry.

Robert N. Noyce. "Microelectronics." *Scientific American* 237, 3 (September 1977): 63–69. Discusses Moore's law, and developments in the fundamental technologies of computer chips.

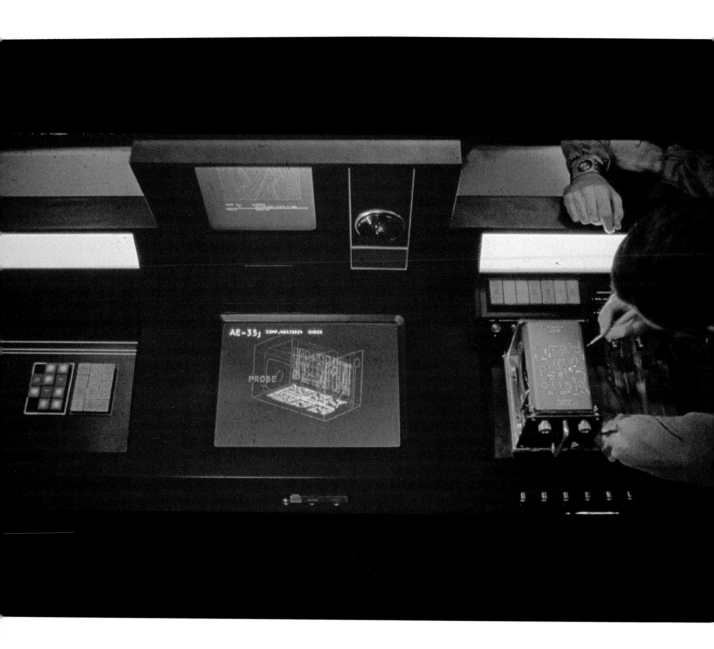

4   *"Foolproof and incapable of error?" Reliable Computing and Fault Tolerance*

Ravishankar K. Iyer

According to HAL, "No 9000 computer has ever made a mistake or distorted information. We are all, by any practical definition of the words, foolproof and incapable of error." Yet, during a "chat" with Frank about the oddness of the mission, HAL appears to malfunction. He suddenly announces, "I've picked up a fault in the AE35 unit. It's going to go 100 percent failure within seventy-two hours." When Frank retrieves the unit and runs diagnostics on it, he is baffled: "I'm damned if I can find anything wrong with it." Almost simultaneously the crew receives a report from HAL's twin 9000 on earth, which gives a different reading. "It's puzzling. I don't think I've ever seen anything quite like this before," HAL admits, but refuses to consider the explanation that he has himself malfunctioned in some way. Instead, he calmly suggests that they "put the unit back in operation and let it fail."

When asked to account for the discrepancy between the two identical computers, HAL is unperturbed and attributes it to human error. "This sort of thing has cropped up before, and it has always been due to human error. The 9000 series has a perfect operational record," he insists, without offering any idea of what human error might have caused the problem. HAL is totally satisfied. Even when Frank persists in asking whether there's ever been even insignificant computer errors, HAL dismisses the possibility airily: "None whatsoever, Frank. Quite honestly, I wouldn't worry myself about that."

The audience, however, never learns directly whether the unit actually is broken, because Frank is killed before he finishes replacing it. Yet, it becomes increasingly clear that something *is* very wrong with HAL. His behavior kills Frank and the hibernating crew members and threatens Dave. The eerily soundless deaths of the hibernating scientists as the computer screen flashes its messages are particularly alarming.

COMPUTER MALFUNCTION

LIFE SUPPORT FUNCTIONS TERMINATED

HAL's justification for killing Frank and Dave—that they are trying to disconnect him and thus threaten a mission they do not completely understand—only indirectly applies to the other crew members. HAL has clearly run amok.

The Puzzle of HAL's Failure

A crucial element of any reliable system is its ability to detect and recover from its own internal errors. The notions of *fault tolerance* (i.e., operating despite minor faults) and *error recovery* are thus central to the development of dependable computing. No computer system will ever be immune to the possibility of malfunction. Even HAL's creators included a COMPUTER MALFUNCTION message in his program. However perfect HAL may have been in the past, he is—by his own admission—in an unprecedented situation and, we suspect, dealing with an unforeseen amount of stress—that is, difficulty in resolving competing goals. Only later in the film, when Dave is trying to reenter the ship, do we learn the source of that stress.

Doubt about HAL's reliability is raised when Frank can detect no problem with the AE35 unit and Houston sends a different reading from the twin 9000. This situation—in which different but equally authoritative sources give conflicting information—is what is known as the Byzantine generals' problem. It is a notoriously difficult problem.

But *why* does HAL break down? We begin to sense the problem in HAL's conversation with Frank about the oddness of the mission. It is perhaps this "oddness," and the unusual system demands of keeping all the vital information about the mission from the crew, that causes HAL's error-detection and diagnostic programs to fail and renders the system error-prone in a particularly pernicious way.

Although HAL's confidence in his reliability makes it easy for him to attribute the discrepancy to human error, Frank and Dave feel that the error is HAL's. Given what we now know about computer error, the entire scenario—from HAL's seemingly routine "I've picked up a fault in the AE35 unit," to his refusal to let Dave back into the ship—is best understood as a case of an error in a complex system that cannot successfully diagnose its own malfunction. This lack of self-diagnostic capability enables the error to propagate and manifest itself in increasingly distorted and disastrous ways. HAL's certainty that he is right is a clear symptom of this type of breakdown. In this chapter, we take a close look at the history, state of the art, and future of methods of detecting and recovering from errors in complex systems.

Fault Tolerance in Historical Perspective

A strong impetus for fault tolerance first arose in the early 1960s in the space program, which needed systems that could survive without maintenance for extended periods of time. In the 1970s and 1980s, manned space flights provided a further boost to research in fault tolerance, and reliability techniques advanced rapidly. Other applications were in long-distance space probes, defense and telecommunication systems, and, more recently, in a wide range of commercial products and environments. The numerous international and regional symposia and workshops on the topic, and a steady stream of journal articles and graduate theses, attest to the vigor and vitality of the issue of fault tolerance.

Invention of the integrated circuit brought a significant improvement in chip reliability—but also a vast increase in system complexity and a comparable growth in the application domain. As hardware reliability improved, research and development branched off in several directions. One focused on developing applications for situations in which even rare failures would be catastrophic; in the late seventies, control of fly-by-wire aircraft was such an application and helped spur important architectural advances in fault-tolerant computers. Another line of research considered the impact of transient and intermittent errors, as opposed to permanent failures, and led to increased interest in on-line hardware/software recovery and its effect on system reliability and availability.

In the 1980s, with the increase in the use of commercial computer applications, a strong economic motive emerged. The costly interruption of services affected the public at large—in banking, airlines, and commercial markets. This business use may have been the major factor in bringing practical fault tolerance to the marketplace. Several established and new companies developed fault-tolerant computers for both internal use and the commercial market. The development of fault-tolerant computers for electronic switching systems (e.g., the ESS series) and of highly available systems for transaction processing (e.g., Tandem Guardian systems) are two well-known examples.

The explosion in software applications created the need to both evaluate and test the reliability of software systems. Researchers developed new techniques for predicting software reliability and for designing systems to tolerate software defects. Several of these techniques found their way into the design of systems for ultrareliable applications such as aerospace computing. Software dependability continues, however, to be of major concern for both system designers and users. In addition, the vastly enhanced application domain has made it necessary to broaden the definition of *fault;* software and hardware specifications and implementations, as well as operator interventions, are now recognized as increasingly important sources of system failure. In the 1960s, when Clarke created HAL, system reliability was something akin to an article of faith. Only humans made mistakes.

Distributed processing introduced undependable and low-bandwidth communications, new sources of faults and impediments to fault diagnosis. A new kind of error—fault-induced inconsistency among redundant computations—appeared and stimulated a vast body of research, including study of the Byzantine generals' problem.

The rapid increase in system complexity, on one hand, and the concern for events that occur only rarely, on the other, have made it difficult to verify fault-tolerant design, manufactured prototypes, and operational systems. Testing, the usual way of demonstrating that a component or system meets its requirements, is inadequate for either complex systems or fault-tolerant designs for extremely high-dependability applications. Researchers are addressing this issue by a combination of advances in stochastic models and experimental/statistical techniques, and by using such formal methods as automatic proving techniques for composing correct systems from proven components and abstractions for describing faults and fault behavior. The problem of verifying designs for response to rare events also arose in systems with severe security requirements. Recent work on automating fault injection and on measuring fault behavior is aimed at making these methods easier and more effective to use with such systems. Although progress in mechanizing fault-tolerant design and measuring fault behavior has been impressive, we do not yet know how to verify highly critical systems such as HAL.

The measurement and modeling of system dependability have also advanced in significant ways. Measurement shows that we need to model software and hardware jointly in order to account for workload variations and imperfect fault coverage; we also need to distinguish models of fault-tolerant systems from traditional reliability models. Finally, the problems of degradable performance and real-time constraints have led some researchers to develop combined models of performance and reliability.

Where Is Fault Tolerance Today?

The study of fault-tolerant computing has paralleled the development of modern computers. One of the earliest contributors was John von Neumann, designer of the first stored-program machine. His work at the Institute for Advanced Studies addressed the problem of synthesizing reliable computers from unreliable components and he developed the techniques of redundancy and replication that are commonly used in computers today. Their development was fueled by the failures of components based on vacuum-tube logic. (The early days of tube and discrete-transistor machines were very fruitful ones for the development of fault tolerance engineering. A notable "bug" in the ILLIAC turned out to be a real-life moth and halted the machine for a considerable period of time!)

For purposes of discussion, we can divide techniques for achieving reliability in ground and space-borne systems roughly into two categories. The first, that of *fault-avoidance methods,* focuses on prevention—trying to avoid the possibility of a fault. This strategy relies on conservative design techniques, use of high-reliability components, and extensive testing of components and the system. However, even the most conservative design rules, careful choice of components, and testing cannot keep failures from creeping in during the operational life of a system. Hence we need techniques that let the system tolerate the occurrence of failures while continuing to operate, with full or limited capacity. The category of methods to do this is termed *fault tolerance.*

Fault tolerance is achieved by providing redundancy in hardware, software, information, or calculations (time redundancy) in a way that either masks or corrects the effects of a fault. Hardware redundancy entails using additional components (gates, memories, or communication links) to provide the extra information needed to mask the effect of a fault. Software redundancy is analogous; it provides for backup software modules that may be able to negate the effect of a software fault. Time redundancy, usually provided by software, involves reexecuting the failed instructions or calculations, using different techniques.

Fault tolerance relies on accurate fault *detection,* which is generally achieved by error-detecting codes. Once a fault is detected, so-called static or dynamic means provide fault tolerance. *Static redundancy* includes such error-correcting codes as hamming codes or triple modular redundancy; *dynamic redundancy* methods reconfigure the system to maintain critical functions, use spare components, or employ graceful degradation. *Graceful degradation* is when a small or relatively minor error leads to a small drop in performance—a mild corruption of some data, say, or a reduction in overall speed. The latter is achieved by duplicating critical components that are thought most likely to develop a fault.

Reliability and availability are different ways of designating a system's vulnerability to faults. *Reliability,* although it has an exact mathematical definition, is often stated as the mean time to failure (MTTF) for a given system. *Availability,* the ability of a system to withstand faults, describes how rapidly a system recovers from a fault. The notion of severity also plays a role in assessing the vulnerability of a system to faults. In a complex distributed system on which, like HAL, a major human undertaking depends, severe failures are those that endanger the undertaking or human life. Other, minor failures may affect specific, noncritical components. An evaluation of a system's reliability and availability measures usually clearly states the type of failures considered.

Where are the failures most likely to occur? Even though we have made major advances in developing highly reliable hardware components, from a software perspective the situation remains far from satisfactory. Today, we believe, the majority of failures occur in software and communications and are usually transient in nature.

In the following sections we deal first with the broad subject of hardware fault tolerance by discussing such important characteristics of hardware fault-tolerance techniques as hardware redundancy, information redundancy, and time redundancy, as well as the development of self-checking circuits. Next, we consider, the question of software fault tolerance. With software failures fast becoming the dominant failure mode of complex computer systems, this has become an important area of research. Several Apollo and Challenger missions had to be aborted because of software faults; and recently sections of the AT&T network were virtually paralyzed by a software bug.

Next, we address the question of testing and of designs for testability. Because availability of defect-free parts is basic to designing fault-tolerant systems, efficient testing strategies for determining the presence of defects and faults in components are critical. Finally, we examine the issue of evaluation, which is decisive from the perspectives of both designer and user. We look at the methods and tools used to determine the dependability of the overall system and to make comparative evaluations, outlining both analytical and measurement-based methods.

Hardware Fault Tolerance

Redundancy—whether of components, information, or calculations in time—is the cornerstone of hardware fault tolerance.

Hardware Redundancy

There are three basic forms of hardware redundancy: passive, active, and hybrid. *Passive hardware redundancy* relies on "voting" mechanisms to mask the occurrence of faults by using the concept of majority voting. Such systems do not require a fault-detection mechanism or system reconfiguration. In the most common form of passive redundancy, triple modular redundancy (TMR), there are three copies of the hardware necessary to perform the required operation and a voter to determine the output of the system. The primary difficulty with this method is the voter; if it fails, the entire system fails. This problem is often avoided by using three voters and providing for three independent outputs. (Figure 4.1 shows the two forms of TMR.) Voting can be performed by either a hardware voter—which works very quickly but requires a lot of extra hardware logic—or a software voter—which also uses some existing processors to perform normal computations but is generally slow. Another version of the TMR approach, N-modular redundancy (NMR), uses *n* copies of a module instead of three. The NASA space shuttle onboard computer system uses four computers and performs operations on the basis of a majority vote.

Active hardware redundancy, on the other hand, attempts to achieve fault tolerance by fault detection, fault location, and fault recovery. The most common form of fault detection employs duplication and comparison; it has two identical copies of hardware performing the same computations in parallel and comparing the results (as shown in figure 4.2). One commercial product, from Stratus Computers, uses a pair-and-spare approach in which

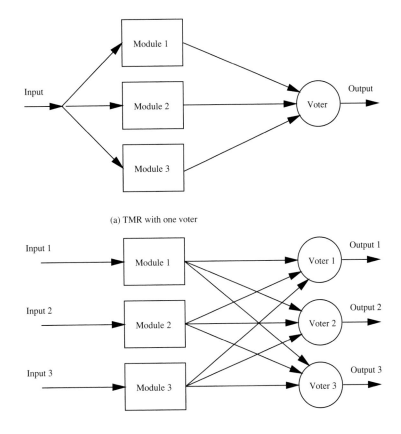

(a) TMR with one voter

(b) TMR with three voters

Figure 4.1
Triplication and Voting

two duplexed components are used for self-checking and fault tolerance. It contains two processor boards, each of which has two microprocessors in a duplicate-and-compare mode. (Recall the twin, ground-based HAL 9000 used for fault checking.)

Another form of fault detection includes off-line fault diagnosis: applying a set of test input patterns to various components of the system and comparing the outputs to the expected outputs for each component. Other forms of fault detection include periodically interleaving normal computations with diagnostic tests, or using self-checking hardware (which we describe below).

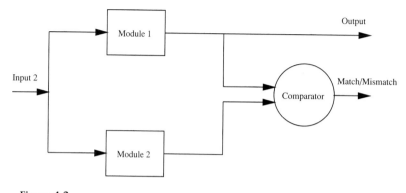

Figure 4.2
Duplication and Comparison

A second form of active hardware redundancy, called *standby sparing,* has one operational module and one or more standby, or spare modules. Various fault-detection schemes determine when a module has become faulty, while fault location finds the faulty module. The reconfiguration operation in standby sparing can be viewed conceptually as a switch whose output is selected from one of the modules that provide inputs to the switch. Standby sparing can bring a system back into full operation after a fault occurs but causes a momentary disruption in performance while reconfiguration is being performed.

Information Redundancy

Information redundancy systems supply additional information that makes fault detection, fault masking, and fault tolerance possible. Examples of information redundancy are error-detecting and error-correcting codes (ECC). *Parity codes* are used routinely in computers to check for errors in busses (local communication channels), memory, and registers. Cyclic redundancy checks detect errors in communication channels, tapes, and disks; M-out-of-N codes find errors in control store memories; and arithmetic codes identify errors in arithmetic units like adders and multipliers. These checks locate errors by decoding circuits that identify any word that is not legally permitted in the code. Error correction is performed by more extensive decoding

$$\mathbf{H}_1 = \begin{array}{c} \begin{array}{cccccc} d_0 & d_1 & d_2 & c_0 & c_1 & c_2 \end{array} \\ \left[\begin{array}{cccccc} 1 & 0 & 1 & 1 & 0 & 0 \\ 0 & 1 & 1 & 0 & 1 & 0 \\ 1 & 1 & 0 & 0 & 0 & 1 \end{array} \right] \end{array}$$

$$c_0 = d_0 \oplus d_2$$
$$c_1 = d_1 \oplus d_2$$
$$c_2 = d_0 \oplus d_1$$

$$\mathbf{H}_2 = \begin{array}{c} \begin{array}{cccccc} d_0 & d_1 & d_2 & c_0 & c_1 & c_2 \end{array} \\ \left[\begin{array}{cccccc} 1 & 0 & 1 & 1 & 0 & 0 \\ 1 & 1 & 0 & 0 & 1 & 0 \\ 1 & 1 & 1 & 0 & 0 & 1 \end{array} \right] \end{array}$$

$$c_0 = d_0 \oplus d_2$$
$$c_1 = d_0 \oplus d_1$$
$$c_2 = d_0 \oplus d_1 \oplus d_2$$

Figure 4.3
Parity Check Matrices for Two Simple Codes (d: databits, c: checkbits)

that associates a noncode-space word with the original code word transformed by the errors.

One such error-detecting code is the parity code, which, given an n-bit word, attaches an extra bit to convert it to an even or odd parity word. Any single-bit error in the parity-coded word is detected by a simple decoding circuit that uses a set of XOR (exclusive-OR) gates. Parity check codes characterized by the parity-check matrix H are the most common type. For example, consider a length-6 code, $n = 6$, with three information bits, k = 3, and three check bits, r = 3. The two H-matrices in Figure 4.3 provide the same error-correcting property. Because all the columns are distinct, the code can correct all single-bit errors. However, the parity check circuit for H_1, which is less complex than H_2, requires three 2-input XORs to compute the checks, whereas H_2 requires two 2-input XORs and one 3-input XOR; the encoder/decoder for the H_2 code will therefore be slower and more complex than that for the H_1.

In high-speed memories, single-bit error-correcting and double-bit error-detecting (SEC-DED) codes are most frequently used; because most semiconductor RAM chips are organized for one bit of data output at a time, the failure of one chip manifests itself as one-bit error.

Self-checking logic designs—like the logic board and subsystems in HAL—employ error-detecting codes and some extra hardware to detect faulty logic circuits that could be single points of failures in a system. Each self-checking circuit has encoded inputs and outputs and are widely used in the Electronic Switching Systems 3A processors and in aircraft and space-vehicle systems.

Time Redundancy

The basic concept behind time redundancy is that repeating computations two or more times and comparing the results will uncover discrepancies. If an error is detected, performing the computations again will determine whether the disagreement remains or disappears. Such approaches, although useful for detecting errors resulting from temporary faults, cannot protect against errors resulting from permanent, systemic faults. One form of time redundancy that can handle permanent faults modifies the way the computations are performed the second time.

Software Fault Tolerance

Software plays a crucial role in a computer system's ability to tolerate design and manufacturing faults and failures that result from wear. Most software errors are due to problems in design or implementation, while faults in hardware are more likely products of design, manufacturing, wear and tear, or environmental upsets. In this section, we present an overview of the ways software design and implementation techniques can be used to detect and tolerate both software design errors and hardware faults.

Developing highly reliable software not only requires software fault-tolerance techniques but also the rigorous applications of fault-avoidance approaches. These approaches include the correct use of formal specification languages, structured programming, formal proof of correctness, and extensive testing at all levels of implementation. Software fault tolerance addresses the issues of detecting any design and implementation errors that remain in the software after testing and enabling a system to recover from them. (The same techniques can also be useful in recovery from environmentally induced hardware faults.)

The fundamental approach to detecting software design errors is the exploitation of diversity in implementation and design. This may take the form of diverse acceptance tests on the results of a computation, executable assertions, alternative software modules, or full diversity—through designing and implementing multiple versions of the complete software by different teams of software engineers. Diversity can be captured by encoding knowledge of the expected behavior at various levels of the software and then comparing what is expected against what is observed. Such encoding can be at the level of the process outputs, intermediate results, system behavior, or expected algorithm behavior. Two primary approaches to software fault tolerance—recovery blocks and *N*-version software—provide a complete framework for capturing diversity in both design and implementation and supply formal mechanisms for error detection, containment, and recovery.

Recovery Blocks

Recovery blocks implement diversity in the form of acceptance tests and alternative software modules. Software is partitioned hierarchically into self-contained modules called recovery blocks. Each block validates its own operation and either returns correct results or notifies the system of an error. As illustrated in Figure 4.4, each recovery block is composed of an acceptance test, the primary alternative software module, and the secondary software modules. The acceptance test is used to determine the correctness of a software module's results (error detection) and the alternative modules provide recovery from a detected error. Diversity can be captured in both the acceptance test and the secondary alternative software modules.

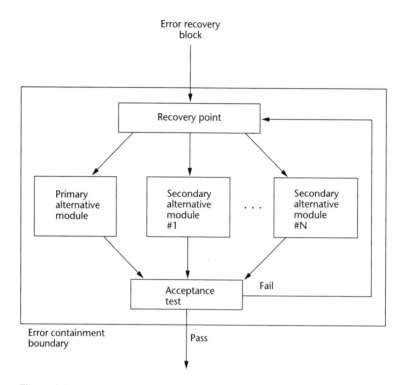

Figure 4.4
The Recovery-Block Approach to Software Fault Tolerance

N-*Version Programming*

The N-*version programming* approach to fault-tolerant software differs from recovery blocks in that it employs design diversity at the software-system level by designing and implementing multiple (*N*) versions of the software by different teams of programmers. Instead of employing a single acceptance test, *N*-version programming utilizes voters to reach a consensus of two or more outputs among the *N*-member versions. This approach necessarily relies on design diversity to detect programming errors in the *N* versions of the software.

Both approaches to fault tolerance can be implemented with distributed or parallel architectures in parallel with the primary module. Full design diversity can also be implemented by making a formal specification the basis of each recovery block and having diverse programming teams develop alternative modules and diverse acceptance tests.

Error-Detection Techniques

Although recovery blocks and *N*-version programming are the best-known approaches to providing complete frameworks for software fault tolerance of programming errors, a wide variety of other techniques are also employed. *Acceptance tests* and *executable assertions* often used to detect anomalies due to either programming errors or hardware failures are two examples of these techniques. Tests such as timers for detecting time-out conditions are also common.

Once an error has been detected, reexecution through *checkpointing and rollback* is an important technique of system recovery. In this method, the system simply rolls back to a known safe state and reexecutes the program. To be successful, the system state has to be saved, or "checkpointed," periodically to produce an error-free state from which to reexecute. Checkpointing schemes can be broadly classified as full or incremental. The former saves the entire active state of a processor while the latter saves only the differences between the current and a previous state. Checkpointing can be implemented at either the system or the application level.

Research on classic checkpointing and rollback recovery has been extensive. In graph-theoretic methods, the programmer decomposes the program into a sequence of tasks and decides where to insert the checkpoints between the tasks. Assuming that the execution time, checkpoint time, and the recovery time of each of these tasks are known in advance, the programmer can use algorithms to choose checkpoint locations so that the maximum checkpoint time, expected checkpoint time, or expected run time is attained.

In a parallel multiprocessor, or a network system such as HAL probably was, recovery through checkpointing and the rollback of one process may require a rollback of another process and result in a rollback to the initial state of the system. To avoid such a total rollback, a system must carry out periodic checkpointing in a way that maintains a consistent memory state.

In the multiprocessor cache-based checkpointing approach, there are two situations in which a process must be checkpointed. The first is when a cache block modified since the last checkpoint is to be written back to the shared memory, which happens when a cache block is replaced on cache miss. The second time is when another processor is to read a dirty block—that is, one that has been modified in a processor's cache since the time of the processor's last checkpoint. As checkpointing is initiated by the cache controller in hardware, it is transparent to system or application software. Checkpointing a process includes flushing the cache blocks modified since the last checkpointing session and saving the processor's internal registers.

In applications that use programmable computers, many fault-detection techniques can be implemented in software as extra lines of code to verify the consistency of a result (e.g., to check the magnitude of a signal). Capability checks are also performed to verify that a system possesses an expected capability: for example, to find out whether a processor can read or write to a given region of memory when a fault is present, or to verify that a processor can execute a specific instruction or set of instructions related to specific data.

Testing

Testing is the process of discovering faults, defects, or malfunctions in the system being examined. It is currently the most extensively used fault-avoidance technique and consists of presenting the system with a set of test vectors (inputs) and analyzing its responses for correctness. Designing a reliable computer system involves many levels of abstractions. Typically, from lowest to highest, they are: logic level, register level, instruction-set level, processor level, and system level. Testing closely coincides with these levels of abstraction and applies separate procedures to each level. The stimuli and responses defining a test experiment use information that is relevant to each level. Testing at logic level, for example, would employ binary vectors or vector sequences, while testing at higher levels would involve machine instructions, arithmetic numbers, textual data, messages, procedure, and application programs. *Testing*, therefore, is a very inclusive term for many different activities and environments. The theory and practice of testing are most well-defined and rigorous at the logic level. They become less precise as the level of abstraction rises. At the system level, testing is largely ad hoc and based on intuition and experience.

Testing begins when the semiconductor chip is being manufactured and continues at later stages of assembly and packaging of such components as printed circuit boards, at the hardware-system level, and—finally—the integrated system level, which includes the operating system and application software.

Testing continues after a system becomes operational and is deployed in the field. Field testing may be preventive or used during repair of an unoperational system. Testing for preventive maintenance is oriented toward finding defective chip or board faults that have not yet shown up during the system's normal operation. Such latent failures will eventually be exposed in system operation. In highly reliable systems, latent failures that are allowed to accumulate reduce the fault-tolerance capabilities of the system and require periodic testing to flush them out.

In a relatively simple computing system, testing for diagnosis and repair consists of narrowing down the location of a fault to a replaceable component—typically a board or a multichip module. The diagnosis of failures in a highly complex system like HAL, however, is still a major problem.

Evaluation

In the foregoing sections, we outlined a wide range of techniques useful for designing fault-tolerant systems. System designers also have to evaluate the relative efficiency of these techniques and decide what design trade-offs to make. Such analysis is an integral part of the design process and employs a wide range of mathematical techniques for modeling, analyzing, and measuring the dependability of fault-tolerant systems.

In the early design phase, before firm design decisions have been made, engineers can use mathematical models to conduct an extensive trade-off analysis. Once they have a detailed design and the overall architecture is in place, simulation is a powerful tool for assessing the fault tolerance and reliability of the design. Simulation is used to evaluate the behavior of a given system—from the chip level to the level of a system with a fault. By comparing the outputs from simulation of fault-free circuits with the faulty circuit, engineers can determine whether the test being applied detects the fault. A major issue still plaguing designers is how to understand the nature of the faults; that is, what model of fault behavior will allow us to evaluate a given system most accurately?

Once the system prototype exists, designers use extensive measurement-based monitoring schemes to evaluate the system's performance under a wide range of faults. Here again the problem is deciding what types of faults to inject, when in the system execution to inject them, and, finally, how to determine whether the system is fully tested. Taking measurements in the actual operational environment is also essential, to provide feedback on a system's ongoing health and viability.

Analytical models of computer system reliability, availability, and performability allow designers to make such trade-off decisions as choice of recovery scenarios, redundancy, and standby-sparing strategy. Researchers have developed a wide range of automated tools to help informed users evaluate complex structures.

The Future

Computer scientists' desire to attain, simultaneously, high performance and fault tolerance is clearly not just an intellectual exercise for the research literature. It is an important issue in the marketplace and will be more important in the future. Good solutions require that we achieve this goal in an integrated fashion, rather than by patching up problems one by one as they arise. A great deal of work will be necessary to deliver on this expanded definition of fault tolerance; for example, we still lack effective solutions for fault-tolerance in software and in human-software interfaces. We are, however, on the threshold of developing fault-tolerant design as an integral part of system design, a task we should pursue vigorously.

Fault-tolerance technology is rapidly diffusing into such fast-growing areas as database and telecommunications systems, which are being driven by applications in banking systems, medical systems, mobile computing, and the rapidly evolving Internet. Most future computing will probably be done, not on isolated mechanisms at finite locations, but as a highly diffused, dynamic activity in an all-pervasive information-processing web. This means that future fault-tolerant systems will need to be highly adaptive to changing environments.

Today, fault tolerance has a strongly mechanistic flavor. It assumes some kind of machine—hardware, design, code, operator function—that may break down before or during operation. It focuses on using redundancy to allow the machine to continue to generate acceptable results. However, new ways of thinking about fault tolerance are appearing that will require new abstractions. Though it may be a while before we know what the right questions are to ask about it, the issue of fault tolerance will surely continue to demonstrate its vitality and relevance in interesting, exciting, and unexpected ways. As such work progresses, we will become even more confident that an error such as HAL's can be avoided—or at least corrected automatically without loss of life.

Acknowledgments

This work was supported by the National Aeronautics and Space Administration under grant NAG-1-613, in cooperation with the Illinois Computer Laboratory for Aerospace Systems and Software (ICLASS), and by the Advanced Research Projects Agency under grant DABT63-94-C-0045. The findings, opinions, and recommendations expressed herein are those of the authors and do not necessarily reflect the position or policy of the United States Government and no official endorsement should be inferred. I am also deeply grateful to Frances Rigberg Baker, whose insights helped form the basis for the opening section, "The Puzzle of HAL's Failure," and who provided valuable editorial assistance with the chapter.

Further Readings

Barry W. Johnson. *Design and Analysis of Fault-Tolerant Digital Systems*. Reading, Mass.: Addison-Wesley, 1989. An introductory book for individuals with no exposure to fault tolerance computing. The reader is given a feel for what others have done in the past and the historical developments in fault tolerance.

P. A. Lee and T. Anderson. *Fault Tolerance: Principles and Practice,* 2nd. ed. New York: Springer-Verlag, 1990. A well-written book and easy to read. It is relevant to those interested in reliable computers as well as for practitioners. The early chapters go through the basic concepts and cover the most significant fault tolerant computers and their design merits.

Michael R. Lyu, editor. *Handbook of Software Reliability Engineering*. New York: McGraw-Hill, 1995. This recent handbook, with contributions from the leading experts in the field, describes current findings in developing reliable software systems. It is designed for a wide range of competency and interest levels.

Michael R. Lyu, editor. *Software Fault Tolerance*. Chichester, U.K.: John Wiley & Sons, 1995. This book, with contributions from the world's leading experts, contains state-of-the-art research in the design and validation of fault tolerant software. It is intended for a somewhat sophisticated reader.

Dhiraj K. Pradhan, editor. *Fault-Tolerant Computer System Design*. Upper Saddle River, N.J.: Prentice-Hall, 1996. This is a comprehensive volume on fault-tolerant computer design. Intended as a reference, with contributions by leaders in the field, it is aimed at the practicing engineer and knowledgeable reader.

G. Gordon Schulmeyer. *Zero Defect Software*. New York: McGraw-Hill, 1990. This book discusses the quality challenges that the software industry faces and the approaches necessary to achieve highly reliable software using real examples. The author argues that it is indeed possible to achieve zero software defects in field operation.

Martin Shooman. *Probabilistic Reliability: An Engineering Approach.* Malabar, Fla.: Robert E. Krieger, 1990. For the more mathematical reader, this book provides the fundamentals of reliability evaluation of complex systems. The material will appeal to an industrial reader with no formal training in the reliability field.

Daniel P. Siewiorek and Robert S. Swarz. *Reliable Computer Systems,* 2nd ed. Burlington, Mass.: Digital Press, 1992. This classic text serves as a comprehensive guide to the design evaluation and use of reliable computers. It includes the design of commercial as well as custom space-borne systems.

5 "An Enjoyable Game": How HAL Plays Chess

Murray S. Campbell

The chess scene in *2001* is just one example of the genius behind Clarke and Kubrick's screenplay. Although the game between HAL and astronaut Frank Poole is shown for only about thirty seconds, it conveys a great deal of information about HAL and the relationship between Frank and HAL. The fact that HAL can beat Frank at one of the world's oldest and most difficult games is clearly intended to establish HAL as an intelligent entity. But is this a correct conclusion? Does a machine need to be intelligent to play chess?

The question of whether HAL's chess ability demonstrates intelligence boils down to a question of *how* HAL plays chess. If, on the one hand, HAL plays chess in the "human style"—employing explicit reasoning about move choices and large amounts of chess knowledge—the computer can be said to demonstrate some aspects of intelligence. If, on the other hand, HAL plays chess in the computer style—that is, if HAL uses his computational power to carry out brute-force searches through millions or billions of possible alternatives, using relatively little knowledge or reasoning capabilities—then HAL's chess play is not a sign of intelligence.

This chapter attempts to resolve this question by examining in detail how HAL plays chess and by comparing HAL with Deep Blue, the world's current premier chess computer. I and my colleagues, Feng-hsiung Hsu and A. Joseph Hoane, Jr., developed Deep Blue at IBM's T. J. Watson Research Labs. It was the first machine in history to beat the human world champion, Garry

Kasparov, in a regulation chess game. The chapter also examines the strengths and weaknesses of computer-style chess by looking at some of the games between Kasparov and Deep Blue. Finally, we discover that HAL's first error occurred in the chess game with Frank.

Before we analyze how HAL plays chess, we need to put his game with Frank into perspective by understanding the history of man–machine chess matches. What is the significance of a machine beating a human at a game like chess?

Frank versus HAL; Man versus Machine

HAL claims to be "foolproof and incapable of error." But, as we witness only one isolated game between Frank and HAL, how do we really know that HAL plays well? The answer can be determined, not so much by the game itself but by Frank's reaction to it.

Poole: Umm . . . anyway, Queen takes pawn.

HAL: Bishop takes Knight's Pawn.

Poole: Lovely move. Er . . . Rook to King One.

HAL: I'm sorry, Frank. I think you missed it. Queen to Bishop Three. Bishop takes Queen. Knight takes Bishop. Mate.

Poole: Ah . . . Yeah, looks like you're right. I resign.

HAL: Thank you for an enjoyable game.

Poole: Yeah. Thank you.

Having personally witnessed scores of amateur chess players lose to computers, I found Frank's reaction to losing to HAL extremely realistic. After HAL announces mate, Frank's pause is brief. This brevity is significant, because it demonstrates that Frank assumes HAL is right. He trusts that HAL has the details of the checkmate correct and does not take the time to confirm them for himself. Instead, Frank resigns immediately. Moreover, it is obvious from his tone of voice—or perhaps I should say from his complete lack of tone—that he never expected to win. In fact, Frank would have been utterly stunned if HAL had lost. No, playing chess with HAL is simply a way for Frank to pass the time on the eighteen-month journey to Jupiter. (As HAL is running virtually every aspect of the ship, there is little for the two, nonhibernating astronauts to do.) It is also clear from the dialogue, as well as from Frank's body language, that this is not a game between two competitors but one between two conscious entities—one of whom is vastly superior in intelligence to the other.

Clearly, Frank does not feel bad about losing to a computer, any more than a sprinter would feel bad about being outrun by a race car. Nor do we, the viewers, feel particularly sorry for Frank's loss. We don't mind HAL winning, because at this stage in the film we like HAL. The human relationship with chess computers hasn't always been so amicable though.

In many recent human–machine matches, the mood has been decidedly pro-human and anti-computer. In the first encounter between the human world champion (Kasparov) and the computer world champion (Deep Thought, Deep Blue's predecessor) in 1989, there was definite hostility toward the computer. When Kasparov pulled out the victory, the audience breathed an audible sigh of relief. In gratitude for "saving human pride," onlookers gave Kasparov a standing ovation.

Kasparov couldn't, however, save humanity's pride indefinitely. In 1995 he lost a game of speed chess to a computer program called GENIUS3. Burying his head between his hands, Kasparov could not hide his despair; he stormed off the stage, shaking his head in disbelief. The loss, reported by newspapers and magazines around the globe, shocked the multitude of those—players and nonplayers alike—who believed that the strongest player in the history of the game would never suffer defeat at the hands of "a silicon monster." Although Kasparov was badly shaken by this upset, it was, after all, only speed chess—a game in which decisions are made within severe time constraints. (Speed chess allows each player only twenty-five minutes for the entire game, whereas players in regulation chess each have two hours to complete forty moves.)

In February of 1996, Kasparov played Deep Blue in a six-game, full-length regulation match sponsored by the Association for Computing Machinery

Figure 5.1
Garry Kasparov Contemplates His Losing Position after His Loss to Deep Blue

in celebration of the fiftieth anniversary of the computer. Before the match, Kasparov was quoted as saying, "To some extent this is a defense of the whole human race." When he lost the first game, his computer adviser, Frederick Friedel, openly acknowledged that Kasparov was devastated (see figure 5.1). Even though he rebounded to win the match, *Time* magazine called the first-game defeat an event larger than "world historical. It was species-defining."

Other grandmasters refuse to play against computers at all. Why? Perhaps because the idea of computer superiority in an arena as cerebral as chess is so disorienting; in Western culture, many consider chess the ultimate test of the human intellect. (It is interesting that Kubrick originally filmed the "chess scene" with a five-in-a-row board game called pentominoes but chose not to use it, believing that viewers would better appreciate the difficulties involved in a chess game.) Mathematicians have estimated that there are more possible chess positions than there are atoms in the universe. Therefore, skilled chess players must possess the ability to make difficult calculations and recognize a seemingly infinite number of patterns. Yet excellent chess play also requires imagination, intuition, ingenuity, and the passion to conquer. If a machine can beat a man at a game requiring as much creativity as chess does, what does that say about our "unique" human qualities?

For now, at least, we can rest assured that even though the best computers are better at chess than 99.999999 percent of the population, they do not actually play chess the way humans do. In the history of man's rivalry with machines, only one grandmaster-level computer has appeared to play like a human—and that computer is our fictitious friend HAL.

How HAL Plays Chess

By analyzing the game between Frank and HAL, we can uncover a number of clues about how HAL plays chess. As I explain in more detail below, HAL appears to play chess the way humans do. Even more important perhaps, the game reveals that HAL is not simply mimicking the way humans play; he actually understands how humans think.

The game in the screenplay is a real one played by two undistinguished players in Hamburg in 1913. Kubrick, a former Washington Square Park chess hustler and aficionado, selected a clever checkmate but was careful not to employ one too complex for viewers to grasp. He picked a position from a fairly obscure game—one obscure enough not to appear in the 600,000-game database of Deep Blue. I eventually located the game after being directed to an article written by Grandmaster Larry Evans on January 12, 1990 (HAL's birthday).

Evans makes the crucial point in his article that HAL should have said "Queen to Bishop six" (not three). HAL used the so-called descriptive notation system that describes moves from the viewpoint of the moving player. This contrasts with the algebraic-notation system used in the game score (see Appendix to chapter), in which moves are described from White's viewpoint. HAL used the incorrect viewpoint when giving his fifteenth move. Was the notation error a deliberate foreshadowing of the machine's fallibility or merely a writer's oversight? This is a question only Kubrick can answer. If Poole had been a little more attentive, he might have realized sooner rather than later that the HAL 9000 was indeed capable of error. But, like most chess players, he was focusing on the actual moves; he was not looking for errors because he had never even considered the possibility that HAL was capable of making one.

To better understand how HAL chooses to play against Frank, it is important to have some sense of Frank's chess background. Although the movie does not disclose his chess rating, it is easy enough to speculate about his skill level. He is a highly educated man who holds a doctoral degree, most likely in a field such as aerospace engineering or robotics. We can surmise that, as second in command on a top-secret space mission of unprecedented importance, Frank is well above average intelligence. Because he is a full-time astronaut, it is unlikely that he would have time to compete in professional chess tournaments; yet he clearly knows something about chess, for his game with HAL follows opening theory for eleven moves (see Appendix for a complete account of the game). Frank's chess rating may be in the expert range, making him strong enough to engage in an interesting game but certainly not experienced enough to handle HAL. (See figure 5.2 for an explanation of the rating scale.)

In the game itself, Frank plays White and HAL is Black. Frank chooses an unusual but perfectly sound variation of the well-known Ruy Lopez, or Spanish opening. HAL responds with very aggressive play, creating a situation that makes it very difficult for Frank to find the best moves. By the time the movie picks up the game, Frank has already made the losing move, and he goes down without much of a fight.

The game provides sufficient evidence that HAL plays chess the way humans play chess. Early in the game HAL uses an apparently nonoptimal but very "trappy" move. The choice creates a very complex situation in which the "obvious" move is a losing blunder. If Frank had been able to

THE RATING SCALE

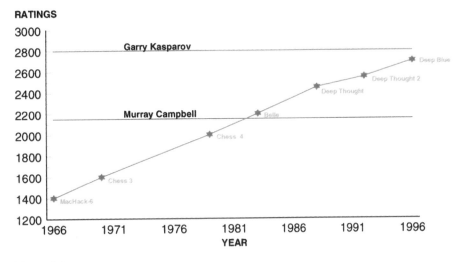

Figure 5.2

The Chess Rating Scale Comparing Chess Players
Garry Kasparov has the peak rating of just over 2800; the author of this chapter has a rating of about 2150, just below the master level (2200); and average tournament players would typically be in the 1400 to 1600 range. Over the years, chess-playing computers have steadily gained in strength, and Deep Blue is not too far behind Kasparov.

find the best move, he would have gained the advantage over HAL. In leading Frank into this trap, HAL appears to be familiar with Frank's level of play, and we can assume that HAL is deliberately exploiting Frank's lack of experience.

The interesting point here is that present-day chess programs do not normally play trappy chess. They are almost always based on the *minimax principle*, which assumes that the opponent always makes the best move. (I discuss this principle in more detail later in the chapter.) A machine like Deep Blue, therefore, would only play the optimal move found in its search. The ability of HAL to play trappy moves is a sign of a sophisticated player who is familiar with the opponent's strengths and weaknesses.

A second interesting point in the game occurs on move 13. The move played by HAL is clearly a winning move, but Deep Blue would have found a move that forces checkmate one move sooner. Current programs always prefer the shortest checkmate. Thus, either HAL is not able to calculate as deeply as Deep Blue does or he chooses a move based on "satisficing" criteria; that is, HAL saw that the move guaranteed a win, and so did not bother to search for a better move. Human chess players commonly follow this practice, which is another piece of evidence pointing to HAL's human style of play.

So how do we now that HAL understands how humans think? When HAL plays his spectacular fifteenth move, he surmises, undoubtedly correctly, that Frank had overlooked this move. Further, HAL did not point out to Frank the other possible variations to checkmate—only the most interesting line, the one that Frank would most appreciate. Although Frank need not have accepted HAL's queen sacrifice, a prosaic checkmate would have followed shortly anyway.

HAL's ability to play chess human style is what computer scientists in the 1960s might have expected. When *2001* was produced, the majority of artificial intelligence researchers probably believed that computers should play the way humans play: by using explicit reasoning about move decisions and applying large amounts of pattern-directed knowledge. It wasn't until the 1970s, after years of much hard work and little progress, that chess programmers tried a new strategy, which is still utilized in the 1990s. A brief history of computer chess and some of its key components is relevant to understanding how machines play today. Perhaps we should start with an even more basic question: Why develop a chess machine in the first place?

A Brief History of Computer Chess: The Early Days

In 1950, Claude Shannon, the founder of information theory, proposed that developing a chess machine would be an excellent way to work on issues associated with machine intelligence. In his article, "A Chess-Playing Machine," Shannon states the case for developing such a machine: "The investigation of the chess-playing problem is intended to develop techniques that can be used for more practical applications. The chess machine is an ideal one to start with for several reasons. The problem is sharply defined, both in the allowed operations (the moves of chess) and in the ultimate goal (checkmate). It is neither so simple as to be trivial nor too difficult for satisfactory solution. And such a machine could be pitted against a human opponent, giving a clear measure of the machine's ability in the type of reasoning."

In fact, the practical applications that could result from development of a world-class chess machine are numerous. Complex tasks that may be solved by technologies derived from Deep Blue include problems in chemical modeling, data mining, and economic forecasting.

Fascination with the idea of a chess-playing machine, however, began more than two centuries ago, long before anyone thought of using a computer to solve large-scale problems. In the 1760s Baron Wolfgang von Kempelen toured Europe with the Maezal Chess Automaton, nicknamed the Turk. The machine was nicknamed the Turk because it played its moves through a turbaned marionette attached to a cabinet. The cabinet supposedly contained "the brain" of the machine; it was later discovered that the brain was actually a chess master of small stature.

The first documented discussion of computer chess is in *The Life of a Philosopher* by Charles Babbage (1845). Babbage, whose remarkable ideas in mathematics and science were far ahead of his time, proposed programming his Analytical Engine—a precursor of the computer—to play chess. A century later, Alan M. Turing, the British mathematician and computer scientist, developed a program that could generate simple moves and evaluate positions. Lacking a computer with which to run his program, Turing ran it by hand. Konrad Zuse, a German computer science pioneer, in his *Der Plankalkuel* (1945), described a program for generating legal chess moves. He even developed a computer, although he did not actually program it to play chess.

In spite of these earlier precedents, it was Shannon's efforts that laid the groundwork for actual research, and he is generally considered the "father of computer chess." Shannon's work was based, in turn, on the findings of John von Neumann and Oskar Morgenstern, game theorists who devised a minimax algorithm by which the best move can be calculated.

Key Components of a Chess Program

The minimax algorithm can be thought of as consisting of two parts: an evaluation function and the minimax rule. An *evaluation function* for any chess position produces a number that measures the "goodness" of the position. Positions with positive values are good for White, and negative values are good for Black. The higher the score, the better it is for White, and vice versa. The *minimax rule* allows the evaluation function values to be used. It simply states that, when White moves, White chooses the move that leads to the maximum value, and when Black moves, Black chooses the move that leads to the minimum value.

In theory, the minimax algorithm allows one to play "perfect" chess; that is, the player always makes a winning move in a won position or a drawing move in a drawn position. Of course, perfect chess is just a fantasy; chess is far too vast a game for perfect play, except when there are only a few pieces on the board. In practice, chess programs examine only a limited number of moves ahead—typically between four and six.

Although minimax is very effective, it is also quite inefficient. In the opening position in a chess game, White has twenty moves, and Black has twenty different replies to each of these—thus there are four hundred possible positions after the first move. After two moves there are more than twenty thousand positions, and after five moves the number of potential chess positions is into the trillions. Even today's fastest computers cannot process this many positions. The *alpha-beta algorithm* improves the minimax rule by greatly reducing the number of positions that must be examined. Instead of exploring trillions of positions after five moves, the computer only needs to analyze millions.

The Modern Era of Computer Chess

The principles of the minimax and alpha-beta algorithms were well understood in the 1960s. When *2001* made its screen debut in 1968, however, the very best computer chess program was only as strong as the average tournament player. Still, many computer scientists believed that building a world-class chess machine was a fairly straightforward problem, one that would not take long to solve.

The earliest approach to solving it involved emulating the human style of play. It is now clear that this was an extraordinarily difficult way to tackle computer chess. Even though chess seems to be a simple and restricted domain, people use many different aspects of intelligence in top-level play, including calculation of possible outcomes, sophisticated pattern recognition and evaluation, and general-purpose reasoning. Significant progress in computer chess did not occur until 1973, when David Slate and Larry Atkin wrote a well-engineered brute-force chess program called Chess 4.0. Since then, almost all good chess programs have been based on their work.

The Slate/Atkin program remained the best chess-playing computer program throughout the 1970s; it gained in strength with each new, faster generation of computer hardware. It was observed in practice, and verified by experiment, that every fivefold speedup in computer hardware led to a two-hundred-point increase in the program's rating as it approached the master level. Subsequent chess-playing machines pushed the computer chess ratings higher and higher—in large part due to faster hardware, although software was also improving rapidly. The Slate/Atkin program reached the expert level (2,000) by 1979; in 1983 Belle, a machine from A T & T Bell Labs, used specially designed chess hardware to reach the master's level (2,200); then came Cray Blitz, which ran on a Cray supercomputer, and Hitech, which dedicated a special-purpose chip to each of the sixty-four squares on a chessboard. Recognizing this trend, Ray Kurzweil predicted that a computer would beat the world champion around 1995. All these machines were finally surpassed by Deep Thought, which began playing in 1988 (see figure 5.3). Designed and programmed by a group of graduate students (myself included), Deep Thought was the first machine to defeat a grandmaster in tournament play; it was capable of searching up to seven hundred thousand chess positions per second. Deep Thought eventually led to Deep Blue, still the world's best chess-playing machine.

Figure 5.3
One of Deep Thought 2's Printed Circuit Boards
The computer used up to twelve of these boards attached to an IBM RS/6000 workstation.

How Deep Blue Plays Chess

The objectives of the Deep Blue project were to develop a machine capable of playing at the level of the human world chess champion and to apply the knowledge gained in this work to solving other complex problems. To accomplish these goals, a significant increase in processing power was necessary. Today Deep Blue is capable of searching up to two hundred million chess positions per second. Its ability to search such an extraordinary number of positions prompted Kasparov to comment that "quantity had become quality." In other words, the computer is able to search so deeply into a position that it can discover difficult and profound moves. Although Deep

Figure 5.4
The Deep Blue VLSI Chip
The special-purpose chip is designed for rapid searching through possible sequences of chess moves and evaluating the potential outcomes. The chip consists of over one million transistors and can examine two million positions per second.

Blue uses a variety of techniques to achieve its high level of chess play, the heart of the machine is a *chess microprocessor* (see figure 5.4).

Designed over a period of several years, this chip was built to search and evaluate up to two million chess positions per second. By itself, however, the chip cannot play chess. It requires the control of a general-purpose computer to make it work. Deep Blue runs on an IBM SP2 supercomputer with thirty-two separate computers (or nodes) that work in concert. For the match against Kasparov, each SP2 node controlled up to eight chess chips, while the entire SP2 system had about 220 chess chips that could be run in parallel. The old saying about too many cooks spoiling the broth is also applicable to parallel computers. A lot of processors won't do much good unless they can all be kept busy doing useful work. In fact, parallelizing a chess program efficiently has proven to be a very difficult problem. For the match with Kasparov, Deep Blue looked at an average of close to one hundred million positions per second.

Nonetheless, a purely brute-force machine would have little chance against a player like Kasparov. Although grandmasters require very little actual calculation of variations for most moves, there are typically a few key points in a game where they must calculate the possible variations very deeply. Often these calculations far surpass what brute-force search could hope to attain. To overcome this problem, Deep Blue employs a technique called *selective extensions,* which enables the computer to search critical positions more deeply.

One of the questions most commonly asked about a chess computer is, "How deep does it search?" In the early days of the computer chess, most programs searched all lines to roughly the same depth, and this question was relatively easy to answer. The fact that Deep Blue employs sophisticated selective searches complicates the issue considerably. When asked how deeply Deep Blue searches, one can give at least three answers; minimum depth (six moves in typical middle game positions); average depth (perhaps eight moves); and maximum depth (highly variable, but typically in the ten-to-twenty-move range).

Yet, although Deep Blue's speed and search capabilities enable it to play grandmaster-level chess, it is still lacking in general intelligence. It is clear that there are significant differences between the way HAL and Deep Blue play chess.

How HAL Compares with Deep Blue

As we mentioned earlier, there is considerable evidence that HAL plays chess in the human style. In fact, given that Kubrick and Clarke chose a game between two humans as the model for the Frank Poole–HAL game, it would have been extraordinary if HAL had not played in the human style. Deep Blue, on the other hand, is a classic brute-force-based machine, albeit it has considerable search selectivity. So a comparison between HAL and Deep Blue must begin by comparing computer and human styles of chess playing.

The difference is actually quite subtle and would probably be detected only by persons experienced with computer play. A computer engaged in an electronic dialogue is said to have passed the Turing test if the computer's conversation is indistinguishable from that of a human being. At the present time, no computer has ever passed the Turing test. HAL, by comparison, would pass with flying colors—and later turn around and try to kill the person administering the test!

Drawing on this analogy, one could devise a Turing test for computer chess programs. That is, a chess machine would pass the chess-restricted Turing test if the person playing the machine could not determine whether or not he or she was playing against another person or a machine. Most players would find it difficult to discern whether or not a Deep Blue game was played by a human or a computer. This was proven in an informal experiment conducted by Frederic Friedel, Kasparov's computer adviser. Friedel showed Kasparov a series of games in a tournament played by Deep Thought and several grandmasters. Without identifying the players, Friedel asked Kasparov to pick out the moves made by the computer. In a number of cases Kasparov mistook the computer's moves for those of a human grandmaster, or vice versa. In general, only chess players who have considerable experience playing against computers can identify computer moves.

A specific example demonstrates the difference between the human style of play and the computer style of play: the fact that chess programs exhibit a lack of understanding of the role of timing in chess. Concepts involving *never, eventually,* or *any time* can be very difficult for computer programs. For example, a weapon in the arsenal of most strong human players is the idea of a *fortress*—a position where a player who has fewer or less-powerful pieces, can create an impenetrable position in which the opponent can never make progress (see figure 5.4). In the 1996 Kasparov–Deep Blue match, Kasparov was able to clinch a draw in the fourth game by means of a sacrifice that created a fortress (see figure 5.5). Although Deep Blue can be programmed to identify many different specific fortresses, detecting the general case of a

Figure 5.5

A Fortress

A fortress position is when the player that is behind is able to set up an impenetrable position and thus force a draw. In the position above, Black, although behind by a bishop, can simply move his king back and forth and White can make no progress without creating a stalemate.

fortress is still beyond its capabilities and presents us with a complicated pattern-recognition problem worthy of further research.

Another difference between human and computer styles of play can be seen by examining a position involving the ability to reason. At the conclusion of the historic match, Kasparov visited our research lab and showed us a position from which he was absolutely certain that Black would eventually checkmate. Kasparov could not say precisely how many moves it would take, and he was curious to see how Deep Blue would analyze the position. Even after several minutes of search, however, Deep Blue did not see the checkmate. Sometimes search is a very poor substitute for reasoning.

There is, of course, another obvious difference between the human style (HAL) and the computer style (Deep Blue) of play: Humans have emotion. One of the supposed advantages of computers over humans in a game like chess is that computers lack emotion. They are not embarrassed by previous mistakes, they don't slump dejectedly in their chairs when they get into a bad position. One wonders, then, whether HAL's emotional side possibly influenced his style of play (see chapter 13).

When HAL thanks Frank for "an enjoyable game," this is more than simply a pleasing platitude entered into HAL's system by his programmers.

Because he possesses both emotion and general intelligence, HAL has the ability to enjoy a good game of chess. Alas, while Deep Blue is sometimes capable of playing magnificent, world-class chess, it is unable to appreciate its own moves.

How, one might speculate, would Deep Blue fare in a match against HAL? Deep Blue could find all the moves HAL plays to finish off the game with Frank in a fraction of a second. Clearly, both machines are tactically very strong. However, given HAL's general intelligence, one suspects it would be able to avoid most of the typical computer mistakes to which brute-force machines like Deep Blue are susceptible. On the other hand, Deep Blue's search strategy could be a strength; it might find counterintuitive moves that would probably be dismissed by a humanlike search. I suspect it would be a very interesting match, in which each computer would gain its fair share of wins.

The idea of HAL losing a game, however, brings up an interesting point. Throughout the film, HAL consistently asserts that he is "incapable of error." Given the overwhelming complexity of the game, it is not plausible for HAL to play perfect chess, as this would require HAL to have solved all possible chess problems. So, if HAL does not play perfect chess, there must be some winning positions in which HAL fails to play a winning move—or drawn positions in which he doesn't find the drawing move. In the normal sense of the word, these would constitute errors. HAL's own interpretation of the word *error* remains mysterious.

Man versus Machine Today

In one six-game match, the 1996 Kasparov–Deep Blue "showdown" demonstrated both the great strengths and the great weaknesses of 1990s computer chess machines. The diagram in figure 5.6 illustrates how quantity can indeed become quality.

This position was taken from Game 1 of the match. Deep Blue's move 23 was **P-Q5** (or d5 in algebraic notation). This strong move completed the demolition of Kasparov's pawn structure; all Black's pawns were soon

□ Deep Blue
■ Kasparov, G

Figure 5.6
Position from Game 1 of the 1996 Kasparov–Deep Blue Match in Philadelphia
In this game, Deep Blue temporarily sacrificed a pawn to gain a stronger position.

isolated and unable to support each other. Kasparov knew that 23. **P-Q5** was a strong move, but he did not expect it from a computer, because it involved a pawn sacrifice—something computers are often reluctant to do. However, Deep Blue, in analyzing the position, saw deeply enough to realize that 23. **P-Q5** was only a temporary pawn sacrifice; that is, it saw that it would later win back the pawn and retain all the other advantages.

As figure 5.7 illustrates, however, computers can sometimes lack basic chess concepts that are understood even by amateur players. The diagram shows the final position in Game 6 of the match. Although Deep Blue was actually a pawn ahead, its pieces were all trapped, or immobilized. Deep Blue had not recognized the danger in this position many moves earlier, when there was still a chance to avoid it. If Deep Blue had not resigned, Kasparov could have won easily by, for example, opening up the king side and attacking the undefended king. The human ability to reason about permanently trapped pieces was a deciding factor in this game.

Although the competitive aspects of human-versus-computer play attract considerable attention, cooperation between man and machine is becoming more and more common. Many grandmasters use PC chess programs to help

☐ **Kasparov, G**
■ **Deep Blue**

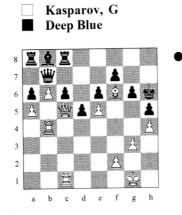

Figure 5.7
Position from Game 6 of the 1996 Kasparov–Deep Blue Match
In this final position of the game, Kasparov has created an overwhelming position by trapping the Black pieces.

them analyze chess positions. And players can now learn more about chess endgames by studying computer-generated endgame databases that demonstrate perfect play in positions with five or fewer pieces on the board. But, perhaps most notably, Kasparov feels that the 1996 match with Deep Blue helped him understand more about chess. This may be a sign of things to come.

The Future of Computer Chess

Early optimism in the field of artificial intelligence led people to believe that the chess problem would be relatively easy to solve. In the late 1950s, Herbert Simon, one of the founding fathers of artificial intelligence, predicted that it would take only ten years for a machine to become world champion. Despite his expertise in the field, Simon was off by at least thirty years. After Kasparov lost a regulation game to Deep Blue, many people mistakenly assumed that the chess-playing problem had finally been solved. It is becoming more and more apparent, however, that chess mastery requires an intriguing mixture of skills: pure calculation, sophisticated evaluation, learning, and a generalized reasoning capability. Although a machine like Deep Blue excels in calculation, at present it still lacks many other skills essential to consistent world-class chess play. Until computers possess the ability to reason, strong human chess players will always have a chance to defeat a computer-style opponent.

Given recent advances in hardware speed and algorithms, I believe Kasparov's loss to a machine in a regulation match was inevitable. Kasparov still has the advantage in that he has the ability to adapt quickly to weaknesses in a computer opponent, a skill that current chess-playing machines lack. With continued progress, however, it is likely that we will see the end of competitive matches between man and machine sometime in the next century. Certainly competitive chess will continue: man against man; machine against machine. Ultimately, though, the computer's superiority over human players will be so great that the only value in man-versus-machine play would be the instructional benefit it provides human players, or—as in *2001*—its recreational use on journeys to faraway planets. The applications that have been, and will continue to be derived from developing a world-class chess machine will advance our use of computers as tools for solving other complex problems. Even so we are still decades away from creating a computer with HAL's capabilities.

Acknowledgments

I would like to acknowledge the other members of the Deep Blue team: Feng-hsiung Hsu, the principal designer of Deep Blue, and A. Joseph Hoane, Jr. Other IBM Research staff that supported the project include C. J. Tan and Jerry Brody. My thanks to tcrain@s2.sonnet.com for directing me to the article by Grandmaster Larry Evans that includes the Frank Poole–HAL game in its entirety.

Further Readings

Peter W. Frey, ed. *Chess Skill in Man and Machine,* 2nd ed. New York: Springer-Verlag, 1983. A classic collection of early papers, including the much-studied paper by Slate and Atkin on the Chess 4.5 program.

Feng-hsiung Hsu, Thomas Anantharaman, Murray Campbell, and Andreas Nowatzyk. "A Grandmaster-level Chess Machine." *Scientific American* 263,4 (October 1990). A review of the history of computer chess and a description of the Deep Thought chess machine, the predecessor to Deep Blue.

David Levy and Monty Newborn. *How Computers Play Chess.* New York: Computer Science Press, 1991. A broad overview of computer chess from its historical development to basic tips on how to write a chess program.

T. Anthony Marsland and Jonathan Schaeffer, eds. *Computers, Chess, and Cognition.* New York: Springer-Verlag, 1990. A fairly technical collection of papers, this book describes advances in computer chess through 1989 and examines the relationship between computer chess and artificial intelligence. It includes detailed descriptions of Cray Blitz, Hitech, and Deep Thought.

Claude Shannon. "Programming a computer for playing chess." *Philosophical Magazine* 41 (1950): 256–75. The original and still much-referenced paper.

Appendix

When *2001* was filmed, descriptive notation of chess moves was still quite common; nowadays algebraic notation is the standard worldwide. In algebraic notation every square on the chessboard has a unique name, as shown in figure 5.8. Moves are written with the letter for the piece first, followed by the destination square for the piece. For pawn moves there is no piece symbol. As in descriptive notation, kingside castling is denoted 0-0.

Kubrick and Clarke used the game Roesch-Schlage, Hamburg, 1913 as the source of the chess position and moves played between Frank and HAL. Here is the record of the full game.

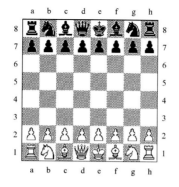

Figure 5.8

Diagram of a Chessboard

The squares are labeled 1 to 8 (vertically) and a to h (horizontally). Each square thus has a unique name; for example, the lower-left square is a1, while the upper-right square is h8.

White, played by Frank, moves first; HAL is Black.

1. e4 e5   2. Nf3 Nc6   3. Bb5

These moves signal the Ruy Lopez, one of the most popular openings in grandmaster play.

3. . . . a6   4. Ba4 Nf6   5. Qe2

Frank chose the Worall variation. This move is much less common than the standard 5. **0-0.**

5. . . . b5   6. Bb3 Be7   7. c3 0-0   8. 0-0 d5   9. exd5?!

The notation ?! means "a dubious move." 9. **exd5** is quite risky, and the move 9. **d3** is the almost universal choice among top players.

9. . . . Nxd5!?

The !? notation means "an interesting move." HAL plays an extremely aggressive and trappy move, perhaps having learned after many games with Frank that such aggression usually pays off. Opening books recommend the move 9. . . . **Bg4** in this position.

10. Nxe5 Nf4   11. Qe4 Nxe5   12. Qxa8??

☐ **Frank**
■ **HAL**

Figure 5.9
Position in the Frank Poole–HAL Game after HAL's Move 13
The movie begins with this position, which is already a loss position for Frank.

This is the losing move. If Frank had played 12. **d4** he would have had a small advantage, which is why 9. . . . **Bg4** is generally considered to be the best move. Here is one clue to HAL's method of playing chess: he chooses a nonoptimal move at move 9, which creates a difficult situation for Frank, one in which it is easy to make a mistake. Current computer chess programs are just beginning to take such considerations into account.

12. . . . **Qd3!**

Deep Blue would see this strong move in about one second. Frank no longer has any real defense.

13. **Bd1 Bh3**

According to Deep Blue, 13. . . . **Nh3** would have forced a checkmate one move sooner. The position after 13. . . . **Bh3** is where the movie picks up the game (see figure 5.9).

14. **Qxa6**

This allows a checkmate in five moves. All the moves HAL plays in the movie would be found in a fraction of a second by Deep Blue.

□ **Frank**
■ **HAL**

Figure 5.10
Position in Frank Poole–HAL Game after HAL's Move 15
In this position, Frank resigns. HAL has offered a queen sacrifice that, if accepted, leads to checkmate.

14. ... Bxg2   15. Re1 Qf3!, and White resigns (see figure 5.10).

A pretty queen sacrifice to finish the game. HAL gives the continuation **16. Bxf3 Nxf3 mate.** There were various ways to postpone the checkmate a couple of moves (e.g., 16. **Qc8 Rfc8**   17. **h4 Nh3**   18. **Kh2 Ng4 mate**).

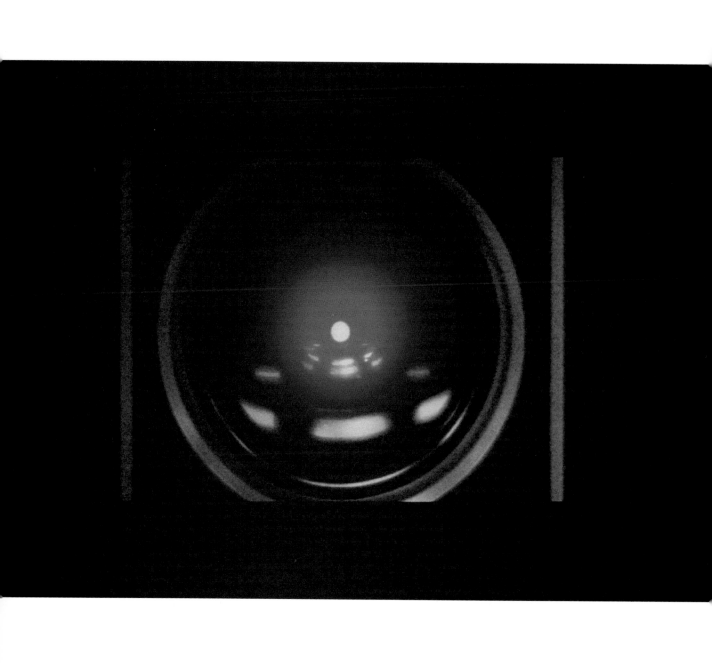

6 "The Talking Computer": Text to Speech Synthesis

Joseph P. Olive

Sitting in a movie theater in the 1960s watching a space odyssey about two astronauts and a computer, the audience encountered a computer that could speak. The computer, named HAL, not only spoke, he was friendly and understanding.

HAL was definitely ahead of its time. For most of the people in the audience a computer was something out of science fiction. Its typical embodiment was an array of tall cases containing spinning tapes, a large box for the computer's memory and CPU (central processing unit), and machines that printed out pages and pages of wide sheets filled with numbers and obscure symbols. A few of these viewers may have been familiar with punched computer cards for bills. In all likelihood, this was the extent of their real-life experiences with computers. Even those who used one in the sixties interacted with machines in an extremely cumbersome way, using decks of punched cards to submit information and receiving large printouts in return. The way we interact with computers today—by typing on a keyboard to input information and receiving responses on a video screen—was just being designed. Spoken communication with a computer was a luxury that existed only in science-fiction books and the movies.

Another novel aspect of HAL was his voice. Before HAL, an actor speaking as a computer deliberately created a stylized, mechanical, "robotic" voice. That mechanical sound was the viewer's cue that a computer or robot was speaking. *2001*, however, featured a different kind of talking computer, a computer who spoke in a friendly, warm, and (often) emotional voice. Rather than conforming to the expectations about computer voices, *2001* presented the possibility that future computers would speak and function like human beings. HAL's warm emotional nature were even more striking when contrasted with the demeanors of his traveling companions. The actors portrayed astronauts Frank Poole and Dave Bowman as cool scientists whose faces and voices were devoid of emotional expression. Their lack of human emotions accentuated the effect of HAL's amiable voice (see chapter 14).

Given the limited familiarity most people had with computers in the sixties, was Arthur Clarke's conception of the talking computer visionary, or was it simply a futuristic fantasy? What was the state of the talking machine in the sixties? Could computers sing? What challenges does creation of a talking or singing machine present? What is the present status of the speaking machine?

I saw the movie *2001* when I was a physics graduate student at the University of Chicago computing the orbits of electrons. Simultaneously, I was studying music theory and composition in the music department. The film had no profound impact on my chosen career path. I remember thinking that HAL's voice sounded "too good" to be mistaken for a machine. When I finished my graduate work, I chose to do research in sound creation, and in particular speech sounds, because of my interest in computers, sound, and music. Consequently, I began working on speech analysis and synthesis at Bell Laboratories. *Speech synthesis,* or *sound synthesis,* refers to the process of creating a sound by machine or computer, rather than by such natural means as the human voice or a musical instrument. My initial interest involved modeling the intonation patterns (melodies) of speech, which led me to devote the next twenty-seven years to trying to create a talking machine. Later in my career, therefore, the movie *2001,* and especially HAL, assisted me. Often, at social gatherings, people asked me what I did at Bell Labs. My standard reply, that I worked on talking computers, generally drew a blank until I referred to HAL in *2001*. HAL provided a better explanation of my work than I could devise myself.

History of the Talking Machine

Early Mechanical Models

Human fascination with talking machines is not new. For centuries, people have tried to empower machines with the ability to speak; prior to the machine age humans even hoped to create speech for inanimate objects. The ancients attempted to show that their idols could speak, usually by hiding a person behind the figure or channeling voices through air tubes. The same method was used to produce the speech of inanimate objects in *2001*. Actor Douglas Rain gave HAL his voice, and recorded all his lines over one weekend without knowing the complete story of the film. Rain spoke in an attractive, mellow, expressive tone quite different from the usual mechanical monotone attributed to computers in that period.

The first scientific attempts to construct talking machines were recorded in the eighteenth century. One such device was built in 1779 by C. G. Kratzenstein for the Imperial Academy of St. Petersburg. This device produced vowel sounds (/a/, /i/, /o/, . . .) by blowing air through a reed into a variable-resonance chamber that resembled a human vocal tract, starting at the vocal chords and continuing through the mouth. In 1791, W. von Kempelen constructed a device capable of speaking whole utterances. It consisted of bellows that forced air through a reed to excite a resonance chamber. The shape of the resonance chamber was manipulated by the fingers of one hand to produce different vowel sounds. Consonant sounds were produced by different chambers controlled by the other hand.

Approximately a hundred years later, Sir Charles Wheatstone built an improved version of von Kempelen's machine. R. Riesz constructed a more sophisticated mechanical talking machine in 1937. Using a similar arrangement of air flow through a reed, this machine possessed the ability to change the reed length to create the intonation or melody of speech. The user employed finger-controlled sliders to modify the shape of the tube simulating the vocal tract. Although mechanical talkers like these are still occasionally constructed, they are generally used as measurement tools rather than as talking machines.

Current attempts to generate machine speech focus on electronic methods and, more recently, electronic simulation by digital computer.

Speech—Theoretical Considerations

Before discussing synthetic voices in more detail, we need to introduce certain basic concepts used in research on speech production. We begin by defining speech as a sound signal used for language communication. Superficially, the speech signal is similar to a sound produced by a musical instrument, although it is more flexible and varied. When we speak, we push air from our lungs through the vocal chords, sometimes tightening the chords to make them vibrate as the air passes over them—like the reed of a musical instrument such as a clarinet. In the clarinet, the pitch of the sound is changed by closing and opening holes in the body of the instrument, which causes the column of air in the instrument to become longer or shorter. When we speak, however, we change the pitch by loosening and tightening our vocal chords. We also have the ability to completely relax our vocal chords to producing voiceless sounds such as /s/ or /sh/. The capacity to produce both pitched (or voiced) sounds and noiselike (or voiceless) sounds with a single instrument is not generally available to musical instruments.

Our greatest flexibility, however, comes from the innate ability to vary the shape of our instrument, the vocal tract. Most musical instruments are rigid structures and so produce a sound with a unique color or timbre associated with their particular class of instruments; thus a clarinet has a sound that is distinct from the sound of a trumpet or a violin. The descriptive words *color* and *timbre* refer to the sound quality rather than the pitch range or loudness of instruments. We humans, by contrast, can change the shape of our oral cavity by moving our tongue, lips, and jaw, thus creating a variety of sound colors. For example, the sound of /oo/ in the word *boot* is "dark" and muffled compared to the sound of the /ee/ in a word like *beet*, which has a bright sound. In addition to /oo/ and /ee/, two of the vowel sounds, there are consonant sounds such as /l/, /r/, and /m/.

This human facility to produce a variety of sounds is the basis for our ability to speak. By combining a small number of sounds to produce a large number of words, we can produce an unlimited number of sentences. We call the different sounds that make up language *phonemes*.

A speech signal and its constituent phonemes can be given visual form with a sound spectrogram, commonly known as a *voiceprint*. (A voiceprint is used in *2001* to verify the identity of Dr. Floyd.) The term *voiceprint*, coined by a manufacturer of the machines used to display spectrograms, was intended to associate them with fingerprints, which are uniquely reliable means of identification. In the 1970s, police departments bought spectrogram machines and used them for forensic purposes. Speech scientists, however, opposed this practice, because they believed the spectrogram was not reliable legal evidence. Eventually the judicial and forensic use of spectrograms disappeared. Today, computers can reliably perform voice verification, not by using a spectrogram but with techniques borrowed from Automatic Speech Recognition (see chapter 7). Although spectrograms are extremely useful for visualizing speech events, they are still too complex for computers to extract the appropriate information from them.

The sound spectrogram in figure 6.1 shows many aspects of the speech signal. The light blue regions corresponding to the /k/, /p/, and /b/ show that the vocal tract is completely closed to pronounce the *stop phonemes*. In the vowel regions—/a/, /i/, /o/ and /e/—as well as in the /r/ and /l/ regions, the repeated vertical lines indicate segments in which the vocal chords vibrate, causing a voiced speech signal. These segments contrast with the region corresponding to the latter part of the /k/, where such lines are not apparent, indicating that the sounds are voiceless. A number of thick colored horizontal lines also appear in the voiced sections; they show the loudness of different frequencies at different times and represent the frequencies at which the sound is reinforced by the vocal tract. These resonances of the vocal tract are known as speech *formants*. The different configurations of the colored regions represent differences in the color or timbre of the sounds.

andin   k   a p a b l   o v   e rror

Figure 6.1
Spectrogram of the Speech Segment "and incapable of error" Spoken by HAL
Time is shown along the horizontal axis and frequency along the vertical axis. The intensity or loudness of any given frequency at any point is shown by color, with yellow being the loudest and blue the least loud.

When the colored regions appear in the higher frequencies (the higher areas of the spectrogram), such as during the vowel /a/ in the word *and* or /i/ in the word *hit,* the sound is brighter, while segments devoid of energy in the higher frequencies—such as during the /l/ or /o/—tend to sound more muffled. You can simulate this effect by turning down the treble control on your stereo amplifier and observing the reduction of energy at higher frequencies.

Electroacoustic Models

In the late nineteenth century, before tools like the spectrogram were available for studying the speech signal, H. L. F. von Helmholtz and other scientists studied the relationship between the spectrum and the resultant sound. They postulated that speechlike sounds can be produced by carefully controlling the relative loudness of different regions of the spectrum and that, therefore, they could generate speech by electrical means instead of mechanically replicating the vocal tract. Helmholtz also studied the influence of the shape of different cavities on their resonance frequencies. Early in the twentieth century, J. Q. Stewart, among others, built a device to test these theories. Stewart's machine consisted of two coupled resonances excited by

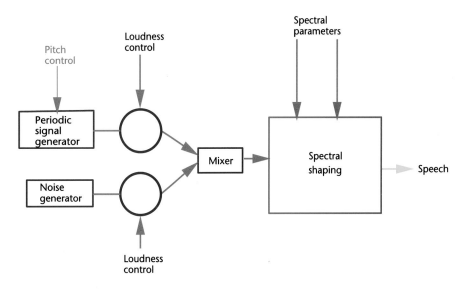

Figure 6.2

Schematic Diagram of an Electroacoustic Synthesizer

The synthesizer has two sound generators, one for periodic sounds and the other for noise-like sound. Each sound source has an independent loudness control. The signals from the generators are combined by a mixer and fed to a variable filter (spectral-shaping module), which can create different sounds specified by the spectral parameters.

periodic electrical impulses. By tuning these resonances to different frequencies, he produced different vowel-like sounds.

An electrical analog of Kempelen's machine was constructed by H. Dudley, R. Reiz, and S. Watkins in the 1930s. This machine, the *voder,* was displayed at the 1939 World's Fair. Like its mechanical predecessors, the voder was manually operated by an operator who used a keyboard to control the relative loudness of the different regions of a spectrum—instead of changing the shape of an artificial vocal tract, as in earlier machines. An electrical sound generator excited the spectral shaping apparatus. The voder, the first electronic machine capable of producing speech, is the basis for today's acoustic synthesizers (see figure 6.2).

The voder generated speech sounds but was not a true speaking machine, since a human operator controlled it. A genuine speaking machine creates speech from a given text (text-to-speech) or—as in the case of HAL—generates speech to communicate its thoughts (concept-to-speech). We have explained that speech is made up of a combination of different sounds or phonemes and that we can generate speechlike sounds with electronic resonators that simulate the formants of the speech signal. As a specific configuration of formants can simulate a given phoneme, we should be able to synthesize speech by configuring the frequencies of a set of resonances to produce the desired sequence of phonemes that make up a given speech signal. Could we, in fact, produce a complete speech utterance by simply connecting the different phonemes? It could be a tricky process.

When we utter the sound of a phoneme, we move our articulators (lips, tongue, etc.) to shape the vocal tract to produce the desired sound. To say the vowel /ee/ in the word *beet,* we move our tongue forward and raise it so it almost touches the roof of the mouth; when we say /a/, as in *father,* the tongue recedes to the back of the mouth and is lowered, along with the jaw. When we want to say an /a/ followed by an /ee/, we produce a smooth transition from the /a/ configuration of the articulators to the /ee/ configuration by raising the jaw and moving the tongue forward and up. The motion of the tongue and the jaw is not instantaneous; there is a gap between the vowels in which the sound is neither /a/ nor /ee/ but something in between. This can also be explained by observing the formants in a spectrogram. The first formant for /a/ is quite high (850 Hz) for the range of the first formant, which is typically 250 to 900 Hz, and the second formant is low (just above the first formant). For /ee/, the first formant is extremely low, while the second formant is extremely high. Thus, when /a/ is followed by /ee/, the first formant descends while the second formant rises. During the transition period when formants are moving from one configuration to the other, the sound is a mixture of the preceding and following sounds. This mix is clearly visible in the spectrogram for the word *error* (see figure 6.1), where the formants move smoothly between the different phonemes of the word. To synthesize an /a/ followed by an /ee/, therefore, we have to model the motion of the articulators or the formants very correctly.

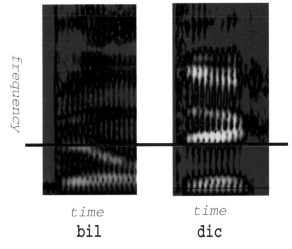

time   time
bil   **dic**

Figure 6.3

Spectrogram of Two Syllables: *bil* from the Word *ability* and *dic* from the Word *dictionary*
Both syllables contain the same vowel phoneme /i/. Because /i/ is a short vowel, it is highly influenced by its surrounding phonemes, and the spectra of the vowel is quite different in these two speech segments. To aid comparison, we have drawn a horizontal black line as a reference. In the spectrogram on the left for the syllable *bil,* there are two formants (indicated by the two red horizontal lines) below the reference line. In the spectrogram for *dic,* on the right, only one formant appears below the reference line; the second formant is just above the line.

Another difficulty with configuring the articulators or formants for each phoneme arises when we utter very short vowels and the articulators are not able to move quickly enough to form the appropriate vocal-tract shape of the vowel. This can be seen by observing the short vowel /i/ in two different syllables, *bil* and *dic* (see figure 6.3). In the syllable *dic,* the second formant moves only slightly from the surrounding consonants; however, in the syllable *bil,* the second formant has to rise from the /b/ to the /i/ and fall again for the /l/. Since the vowel is short, the second formant is not able to rise fast enough before it begins falling again; so it never reaches the position of the second formant in *dic.* The spectrogram of the two syllables demonstrates that the vowel in the two syllables is indeed different. In the context of the syllable *bil,* listeners do not notice that the /i/ falls short of its target; they abstract the phoneme from the context and perceive it as an appropriate /i/. The articulators' motion and their failure to attain the proper vocal-tract shape is called *coarticulation.* To synthesize speech that sounds human we need to model these effects carefully. If formants move too much or too quickly, the resulting speech sounds will be unnatural and overarticulated. If they move too slowly or do not move far enough, the speaking machine will sound tongue-tied or drunk.

Before creating rules to control a speaking machine, it was necessary to develop methods of reproducing a human speech signal. At the turn of the century, two devices could convert an acoustic speech signal (air vibrations) into an electrical signal by a microphone and change an electrical signal back to an acoustic signal through a loud speaker. The two devices—the telephone for speech transmission and the phonograph for speech or sound storage and playback—could store or transmit the signal but could not manipulate or alter it much. Operators could distort the signal or equalize it by boosting or reducing the bass or treble but could not convert the sound of one phoneme into another or change the pitch without changing the speed of the speech and its spectrum. To attain this flexibility, it was necessary to have independent control over the excitation of the signal, the pitch, the loudness, and the spectrum.

In 1951, an attempt to recreate human speech with an electrical device that controlled a variable spectrum used a black-and-white version of the sound spectrogram. As the spectrogram is a visual recording of a sound signal, F. S. Cooper, A. M. Liberman, and J. M. Borst used light to generate the speech. Their machine consisted of a light source and a rotating wheel of fifty concentric circles of variable densities—to generate the different harmonics of the source signal. The light beams representing the different harmonics were aimed at the appropriate regions of a sound spectrogram. The intensity differences of the lines in the sound spectrogram varied the amount of light transmitted as the spectrogram moved through the beams. The light was converted to an electric current, then converted again, to an acoustic signal, by a speaker. In this way, the machine was able to speak the information encoded in the sound spectrogram.

The device proved that speech could be generated electrically by a machine using time-varying parameters to control a spectral filter (as in figure 6.2). However, the ultimate aim of the project to build a speaking machine was to generate speech by defining a set of rules, not just to reproduce previously spoken utterances. A major obstacle to using a spectrogram reading machine as a component of such a machine is its need for fifty different control parameters to reproduce speech. Generating speech by creating rules to control fifty different parameters is too complex. We needed a simpler model for controlling the time-varying spectrum component of a synthesizer.

Experiments had shown it is possible to produce speechlike sounds with a system of coupled resonances. J. Holmes experimented with recreating speech by controlling the frequencies of the resonances. First, he carefully analyzed short speech segments and manually determined the formant values for each such short segment. He then applied the data gathered from his analysis to the speech signal. Holmes's experiment demonstrated that if we could predict how formants change over time into a desired phoneme sequence, we could program a machine to speak. Since then, several researchers have introduced techniques for automatically analyzing the parameters that control the time-varying spectral filter. These techniques are extremely useful for encoding speech at a reduced storage and transmission rate and have provided a basis for studying methods of creating rules for generating speech by machine.

Once this theoretical groundwork was established, we could begin to conceive of ways to generate speech by machines. Early work had consisted of creating specialized circuitry to control synthesizers. When digital computers became available, however, research progressed rapidly. These computers made it possible to program a machine with independent control of the pitch, loudness, and spectrum and to compute time-varying parameters to control them. Researchers constructing talking machines then faced two

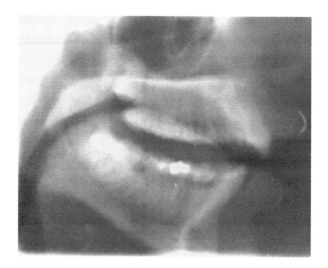

Figure 6.4
X-ray of a Human Vocal Tract, Showing the Teeth, Jaw, Lips, Tongue and Trachea
(*Source: X-ray Film Database for Speech Research*, K. G. Munhall, E. Vatikiotis-Bateson, Y. Tohkura, ATR Research Report TR-H-116, 1995)

issues: what parameters to use, and how to generate these parameters for a given sequence of phonemes. They investigated two ways to generate the synthesis parameters: one method employs rules to generate the parameters, while the other uses stored data.

Synthesis by Rules

The choice of parameters is extremely important to developing rules for speech synthesis. Some scientists hold that the best approach to developing rules is the geometry of the human vocal tract itself. There is a good deal of information about the articulators and their movements during speech, because both are subject to physical constraints. Some researchers have studied the geometry of the vocal tract, especially the tongue, through X-ray movies of people speaking. However, the danger of prolonged exposure to X-rays, even X-ray microbeams, means that only a limited number of such films is available.

Other researchers have tried to map the geometry of the vocal tract by analyzing the speech signal itself. This is still a topic of ongoing research, although no satisfactory solutions have yet been formulated. The air flow through the vocal tract is still not fully understood, due to the complex geometry of the vocal tract. In addition, the fact that the walls of the vocal tract (particularly the cheeks and soft palate) are not rigid contributes to the difficulty of computing airflow.

Still other researchers have attempted to apply ad hoc rules and simplified geometries of the vocal tract. Although they have been able to produce machine speech, its quality is lower than that yielded by other methods of synthesis.

Finally, one group of speech scientists has worked to formulate rules for synthesizing speech by using more accessible parameters, in particular the resonances of the vocal tract, the formants. By observing spectrograms or computing the frequencies of formants of spoken utterances, these researchers have derived rules for synthesizing the phonemes within their contextual dependencies and for creating the transitions between the phonemes. So far, using the formant frequencies as the parameters for synthesis is the most successful approach.

Synthesis from Stored Segments

An alternative method of producing computer speech stores small segments of speech to retrieve when they are needed. Storing whole sentences or phrases is impractical, and even saving words is not feasible; there are too many of them and new ones are constantly being added to the language. Storing words would also leave unsolved the problem of connecting the individual words together; although a word is a linguistic unit, acoustically there are no apparent breaks between words and only unclear delineations of word boundaries. There are, however, certain applications with limited vocabulary needs in which whole words can be the unit of synthesis. Telephone directory assistance is one such application. Even though the speech in this case consists of a string of ten digits, the vocabulary for the application must be longer than ten digits, as the first digit in a string of ten digits is spoken differently from the third or the tenth one. A storage of one hundred words—all ten digits in ten different positions—encompasses all the possibilities. Even so, the speech sounds like a series of isolated digits; it lacks the continuous flow of human speech.

Storing syllables is also impractical for there are approximately fifteen thousand syllables in English and an adequate system would have to provide for smooth connections among them. Nor, as mentioned earlier, can phonemes serve as units for synthesis; their acoustic manifestations do not exist as independent entities and, besides, they are affected by the coarticulatory influence of neighboring sounds.

In 1958, G. Peterson, W. Wang, and E. Sivertsen experimented with using *diphones* to produce synthetic speech. These units consist of small speech segments that start in the middle of a phoneme and end in the middle of the next one. The authors theorized that phonemes are more stable in the middle and that segments between phonemes contain the necessary information about the transition from one phoneme to the next. Splicing the speech in the middle of each phoneme, therefore, should generate a smoother speech signal. The researchers did not attempt to construct a full system of diphones to produce all the possible speech-sound combinations of a given language (American English in this case). Instead, they selected several diphones and spliced them together to create phoneme sequences for a few utterances. Although the experiment showed that the method was viable, there were some obvious problems. When speech segments are joined, discontinuities in loudness, pitch, or spectrum at the junctures are audible, usually as clicks or other undesirable sounds. Splicing speech cut from different speech utterances does not prevent such discontinuities. Because they spliced tape to connect the diphones, Peterson and his colleagues had to carefully select diphones with similar acoustic characteristics at the junctures. In a system that includes all possible combinations of phonemes in the language, it would be impractical to use only diphones that match at the boundaries. Instead, we would have to smooth the connections between segments which can only be done when the speech is parametrized. The first such system for synthesized speech generated from stylized stored parameters of formant tracks was demonstrated in 1967.

The foregoing section describes the history of the talking machine prior to the making of *2001* in the late 1960s. Although research on talking machines had been under way for a long time, it was still in its infancy at that time. Computers were able to utter speechlike sounds, but they lacked the eloquence of HAL. In fact, the computer-generated speechlike sounds of the era were almost unintelligible, whether produced through synthesis by rule or synthesis from stored data.

Post **2001** *Synthesis of Sounds*

In the 1970s, however, researchers made great advances in speech synthesis, mainly because of the wealth of data on spoken utterances and improved computational power. The best system of rules for synthesizing speech, developed by D. H. Klatt, utilized a digital implementation of an electroacoustic synthesizer. The *spectral shaping module* (see figure 6.2) consisted of a complicated network of resonances with different branches for producing vowels, nasal constants, fricatives, and stopped consonants. By recording and observing the formant motions, Klatt was able to create speech synthesis of high quality. One derivative of his system, Digital's *DECTalk,* has been used by noted physicist Stephen Hawking.

During the same decade, progress in the synthesis of speech from stored data was aided by research in speech coding and creation of new methods of speech analysis, and of resynthesizing speech from analysis parameters. Like synthesis by rule, synthesis from stored data can use different kinds of parameters; however, because the method is data driven, parameters do not need to be as intuitive; they should be able to produce high-quality speech from resynthesized, previously analyzed speech segments.

At present, two types of parameters are used for the data-driven method of synthesis: stored waveforms and a small set of spectral parameters that is mathematically derived from the speech signal. These parameters are called *LPCs* (*linear predictive coding*) because one of their forms predicts the next set of speech-waveform values from a small set of previously computed waveform values. Although waveform parameters produce high-quality speech, it is impossible to control independently the spectrum of waveforms of the stored speech. Synthesizing with these parameters, therefore, lacks flexibility for altering the speech spectrum. The LPC parameters also produce high-quality speech, although it is somewhat mechanical-sounding. These LPCs' flexibility makes it easy to alter them to produce connected speech.

When I began working in speech synthesis shortly after the discovery of LPC parameters, I was attracted by their ability to reproduce high-quality speech. My early research involved constructing a synthesizer, using words as the unit of synthesis. By using twelve hundred common words I was able to synthesize many paragraphs of text. Because I used parametrized speech, I could smooth the connection between words and impose an intonation over the utterance to make the speech sound continuous. However, the synthesizer was limited—too many words were not in my inventory.

I then turned to the methods introduced by Peterson and his colleagues. The speech synthesizer I currently use at Bell Laboratories generates speech from stored short utterances of analyzed speech, using LPC-derived parameters. It is not a simple system of diphones, but a complex system that contains many segments larger than diphones—to accommodate phonemes with complex coarticulation effects. For example, to synthesize the word *incapable* spoken by HAL and shown in figure 6.1, we first transcribe the word into a phonetic notation. *Incapable* becomes

/*/ /ɪ/ /n/ /k/ /e/ /p/ /ə/ /b/ /ʊ/ /l/ /*/,

where /*/ represents silence, /ə/ is the neutral vowel *schwa,* and /ʊ/ is the vowel *a* as in word *able.* The synthesizer then attempts to match the largest string of phonemes from the word to a string in its databank. If two adjacent phonemes do not interact—that is, there is little coarticulation between them, as is the case for /n/ followed by a /k/—the synthesizer will not find a diphone. In this case, it will add a silence element of zero duration. When the phoneme is greatly influenced by its neighbors, as in the case of a *schwa,* a triplet of phonemes will be stored in the database. Thus the word *incapable* will be synthesized from the following elements:

/*-ɪ/, /ɪ-n/, /n-*/, /*-k/, /k-e/, /e-p/, /p-ə-b/, /b-ʊ-l/ /l-*/

The resultant speech is intelligible, although it sounds mechanical and would never be mistaken for a human voice.

Speech Generation and Text-to-Speech Conversion

Thus far, we have described a system capable of synthesizing speech from phonemic input. Given a sequence of phonemes, scientists can now generate a signal that sounds speechlike. This was a very important task and the main preoccupation of researchers for a long time. But is that all there is to speech?

Speech, a subset of language, is one method humans use to communicate with each other. The most direct form of language communication happens when one human, the *generator,* speaks to one or more humans, the *receptors.* This mode of communication is easy for the generator; he or she needs only choose the proper words to represent an idea and produce the speech sounds that represent the words. Barring such problems as a noisy environment or language differences, receptors will usually understand the idea the generator is trying to transmit.

This mode of communication is not always possible, however. Quite often the generator and receptor are separated by large distances and cannot communicate with a speech signal. More often, a receptor is not able or willing to receive the message when the generator is willing to transmit it; or a generator may want to send a message to future receptors and preserve it for posterity. The invention of a method to record thoughts, a writing system, introduced new possibilities for transmitting ideas, though sometimes at the expense of total clarity. The generator uses words to convey an idea and writes them in the accepted symbols. The receptor trying to derive the intended message from the writings has only the words themselves; without cues about the real intentions of the generator and the emotional content, the correct groupings of the words may not convey the meaning of the text exactly.

An even more complex mode of communication occurs when the originator's written text is transmitted to the receptor orally by another person, a reader. To speak the text the originator intended, the reader must first understand its meaning. A complete text-to-speech system operates in this, most difficult, mode of communication—in which the computer reads a text written by a third party.

The computer can also, of course, be a generator of ideas—as HAL is—and have complete information about the content of the message it is conveying. Consider, for example, HAL's first utterance in *2001:* "Good afternoon, Mr. Amer. Everything is going extremely well." To say HAL's speech, a computer would have to have all the information about the text in its "brain." It would know that "Good afternoon" is a greeting, a phrase consisting of a compound word, *afternoon,* which is spoken with the stress on the syllable *noon,* not on the syllable *after.* It would be aware that *Mr.* is pronounced *mister,* that *Amer* is a person's name, and so on. Thus the computer formulating the speech would have a great deal of information about the message.

Reading Text

The situation is very different, however, when the computer is reading text, either printed text or a stored data base. An educated person can read text of a familiar language without difficulty, unlike a reading machine, which is not familiar with the language. A machine does not *understand* what it is reading. The first problem a machine encounters is reading characters that are not words or nonalphabetic characters (e.g., *Mr., 72,* and *AT&T*). A person would have no difficulty with such items. Often, we rely on contextual cues to decide how to pronounce such characters or words as *St.* (saint or street), *bass* (a musical instrument or a fish) and *3/5* (March fifth or three-fifths). Reading numbers is always a problem: is *5* five or fifth? is *325-4321* a telephone number or an arithmetic problem? And certainly we would not pronounce $1.5 million as *dollar sign one point five million.* Thus, the first task of a reading machine is to normalize the text by expanding nonword characters into words and, in the case of *bass* or *read* (present or past tense), deciding which is the correct pronunciation.

When humans speak, they try to convey the structure of the message by segmenting the speech into a hierarchical structure of words, minor phrases, and sentences. Take the following sentence:

HAL: This sort of thing has cropped up before and it has always been due to human error.

In English, luckily, white spaces in the text mark word boundaries; this is not true in, for example, Chinese and Japanese. The ends of sentences are also well marked in written English, with a period. (However, we probably wouldn't mistake the period at the end of an abbreviation as a mark for the end of a sentence.) Minor phrases are often indicated by the use of commas (not to be mistaken for the use of commas in a list). Moreover, a comma is sometimes omitted from text, as it is in HAL's statement, which has no comma after the word *before.* Conjunctions, such as *and* are often a cue for a minor phrase break, but not always. When HAL mentions "putting Drs. Hunter, Kimball and Kamisky aboard," neither the comma nor the conjunction indicate a minor phrase boundary. Speaking the sentence with a minor boundary in either place alters its meaning.

Finally, the words in a sentence have to be grouped into minor phrases. Going back to our original example, (*this sort of thing*) (*has cropped up*) (*before*) are the proper groupings in the first minor phrase. If the speaker does not speak the phrase in such groupings, he or she can either say it as a unit or pronounce each word with equal emphasis. In either case, the listeners will have difficulties comprehending the message, for they have no way to identify the important parts of the message.

A talking computer also needs to determine the focus of each phrase.

HAL: I enjoy working with people.

He could stress any word in the sentence and change its meaning. If he stresses *I* he contrasts the meaning with "you enjoy . . ." If he stresses *enjoy,* he implies a contrast with "I hate . . ." When *working* is stressed, it means "rather than playing." To convey the meaning of a message the computer must assign a prominent stress to the correct word.

Of course, for educated human readers familiar with the language the numerous steps needed to speak a written or printed text are natural, because they understand what they are reading. Today, alas, we do not have machines that understand text, although their analysis of a text can help them sound as if they do. The Bell Labs synthesizer does paragraph-length analyses of texts. Using discourse information, statistics about word relations, and assigning words the proper part of speech (nouns, verbs, etc.), the synthesizer expands the input, segments the text, and assigns sentence-level stresses. This process, though not perfect, works well enough to enable the machine to read very long sentences with only a minimal loss of intelligibility.

Generating Linguistic Units

A number of issues are common to the task of reading text and generating computer speech. First, we assumed that when a computer generates the speech, it "knows" what it is trying to say (as hard a problem as that might be). HAL knows that he is trying to say "Dr. Poole" and not "drive Poole," just as he knows where the break for the phrasal hierarchies belongs and which word he needs to stress.

Next, the computer performing either task needs to know how to pronounce each word. As the English language employs a limited alphabet, there are many ways to pronounce certain letter sequences. For example, only six letters (*a, e, i, o, u,* and *y*) are used to describe vowel sounds in English, but there are thirteen different vowel phonemes in the language; for example, the vowel in the word *book* is quite different from that in *boot.* In the preceding section we touched on *homograph disambiguation* (i.e., distinguishing among the various meanings and sounds of words like *bass, live, read,* etc.), but we, and the computer, also need to know how to correctly pronounce the letters /*sch*/ in the words *school, schedule,* and *mischief.* Phoneticians have an alphabet that corresponds to pronunciation rather than to the spelling of words. Most dictionaries use this alphabet to indicate pronunciation.

Another important aspect of pronunciation is lexical or word stress. When HAL says, "my mission responsi**bi**lity," he puts the stress on the syllable **bi.** If he were to say **res**ponsibility or responsibi**li**ty, the listener might not understand the word, or might even hear two words instead of one.

By storing a pronunciation dictionary in the computer, we can tell the computer how to pronounce many words. Still, because of prefixes and suffixes and the constant addition of new words to the language, it is impossible to store all the words and their variations. We therefore need to supplement the dictionary with a morphological analyzer and a set of letter-to-sound rules. Movement of the stressed syllable makes writing a morphological program a complicated task. For example, when HAL says melodramatic, with the stress on the fourth syllable, **ma,** he compounds the morphemes *melo* and *drama,* both of which stress the first syllable. When combined to form *melodrama,* the morpheme *melo* maintains its first-syllable stress. Addition of the suffix *tic,* however, shifts the stress to the penultimate syllable. Moreover, the moving stress does not always fall on the same syllable; the shifts of *act, active, activity,* and *activation* demonstrate the variety of stress options a computer's analyzer has to recognize.

After concluding the computation involved in language analysis, the computer—whether reading text or generating speech—has information about the hierarchical structure of the text, the focus or stress of the different segments, and the correct pronunciation, including lexical stress, of the words in the utterance. The result of the analysis is a string of phonemes annotated with several levels of stress marking and different levels of phrase marking. Once these linguistic units are generated, the computer is ready to synthesize speech.

Synthesis from Linguistics Units

It would seem a trivial task to synthesize speech, by either rule or stored data, once the desired sequence of phonemes is known. However, the computer still lacks information about the timing and pitch of the utterance. These factors may seem unimportant as long as the computer can pronounce the phonemes correctly. Nonetheless, mistakes in timing and pitch are likely to result in unintelligible speech or, at best, the perception that the speaker is a non-native speaker.

We are aware of the role of pitch when actors impersonating a computer in a television commercial or science fiction movie try to speak in a monotone. You notice that I said *try,* because they are not really talking in a monotone; if they did, it would sound more like singing than speaking. They do, however, severely restrict the range of the pitch. Humans normally talk with the timing and intonation appropriate to their native language which they acquired as children by imitating adult speakers. The computer, of course, does not learn by imitation; for the computer to speak correctly, we have to develop the rules for pitch and timing and program it to use them.

The timing of speech events is very complicated. First, phonemes have inherent durations; for example the vowel in the word *had* is much longer than the vowel in *pit.* Yet the duration of the phonemes are not invariable. They are affected by the position of the phoneme's syllable in the phrase, the degree of stress on the syllable, the influence of neighboring phonemes, and other factors. For example, the vowel in *had* is much longer than the vowel in *hat,* because of the difference between the following consonants /d/ and the /t/. At Bell Laboratories recently we devised a statistics-based analysis scheme that measures the contribution of various factors to phoneme durations and creates algorithms to compute them.

To program rules for the pitch contour of speech, we must first understand how intonation provides information about the sentence type, sentence structure, sentence focus, and lexical stress of a speech signal. We are aware, for example, that the pitch is lower at the end of a declarative sentence, while in many interrogative sentences, it rises at the end. At the end of phrases and nonterminal sentences and parenthetical statements we indicate that we will continue speaking by lowering the pitch and reducing the range. We also express focus and stress by large pitch variations. All of the above phenomena must be programmed to make the computer deliver a message effectively.

Feeling and Singing

So far, we have concentrated on aspects of speech synthesis that convey linguistic information by analyzing the acoustics of speech sounds, as well as the manifestations of timing and pitch. Another dimension of human speech, the emotional state of the speaker, is as important as the linguistic content of the message. I do not explore computer feelings in this chapter (see chapter 13 for discussion of this topic). In 1974, however, my interest in computer music led me to write a computer opera dealing with the intriguing subject of computer emotion. The opera featured a singing computer.

In *2001,* just before HAL is disconnected, he starts singing. Because the computer's voice is a human voice, HAL's singing doesn't seem extraordinary to us. The song he chooses *is* rather curious. I doubt that too many people would think of "Daisy, Daisy" as the appropriate song for such a scene. However, as Arthur C. Clarke knew, this song is historically important: It was the first song ever sung by a computer. This work was done by John Kelly at Bell Laboratories and employed his synthesis-by-rule algorithm. Whenever I lecture about computer singing, I always start by playing the original computer song and reminding the audience that this was the song used in *2001.*

My own work in computer singing stemmed from research in speech synthesis. To understand the effect of manipulating speech in the parameter domain, I constructed an interactive system to display and alter the synthesis parameters for a digital version of an electroacoustic synthesizer. Because the state of synthesis was not very advanced in 1974, I used analysis parameters from natural-speech segments. My system allowed me to adjust the timing of events by stretching and compressing the parameters and to change the pitch by simply drawing or typing a new pitch contour; for special effects, I could also change the spectral parameters. By adjusting the timing to fit the music and setting the pitch to the frequency of the desired musical notes, I was able to program a computer to sing. A singing formant developed by J. Sundberg added richness to the voice, and a vibrato contributed to its realistic sound.

The opera, written for a human soprano and a computer with a male voice, was the story of a woman scientist who builds a computer and tries to teach it to talk. The computer, later producing only a few unintelligible sounds, miraculously begins to talk by imitating its creator. The scientist is happy with this development but wants the machine to speak with more feeling. When the computer obliges, after some failed attempts, the scientist is satisfied and turns the machine off. The machine, however, turns itself back on and pleads with her to stay. Soon it breaks into song and she joins it in a love duet based on music from Verdi's *La Traviata*. Of course, operas don't always end happily. The scientist cannot cope with loving a machine and proceeds to disassemble it. The main theme of this opera is our desire for computers not just to speak, but to speak with feeling.

Today and Beyond 2001

As we near the year 2001, do we have a computer that sounds like the voice of HAL portrayed by actor Douglas Rain—personable, warm, emotional, human-sounding? The answer is no, not yet.

At Bell Laboratories we have developed a text-to-speech synthesizer that is highly intelligible in several languages, including English, German, French, Spanish, Russian, Chinese, and Navajo. The finest module in the synthesizer is the pronunciation module, which enables it to pronounce words and names as well as any educated American would. Yet, although capable of both reading or generating such complex text as e-mail or newspaper stories, the synthesizer does not replicate the human voice. It has a distinct "machine" sound. Which of the stages of the synthesis process we described account for this fault?

Not one but many of the stages require improvements before we succeed in producing humanlike speech. There are problems at both the text-analysis and the speech-synthesis stages. The greatest dilemma facing synthesis researchers, as well those working on automatic speech recognition (see chapter 7), is the machine's inability to comprehend what it is saying or hearing. This, of course, is a part of the greater problem of artificial intelligence, which at present is very limited. Even so, a machine has been "taught" to play high-level chess (see chapter 5) and can defeat most human players. Compared to the problem of language understanding, however, chess is quite simple. Language acquisition is more analogous to the game of Go, as there are an enormous number of possible combinations of moves in the game and of sentences in the language. Go has approximately 10^{768} sequences of moves, a number that is many orders of magnitude larger than the number of atoms in the universe. Due to this complexity, machines programed for Go play at only an elementary or novice level. The same holds true for machine language understanding. A computer can only perform tasks requiring very limited understanding. It can maintain a dialogue about ordering a pizza but not about a subject matter that has not been previously defined.

Consequently, when the computer reads a text, it may err in its analysis of hierarchical segmentation and assignment of sentence stress. Since pitch is largely determined by segmentation and stress, incorrect information about these elements can result in unintelligible speech. To minimize the effects of such errors, we limit the range of pitch movement. Although the synthesizer sounds more realistic than people trying to impersonate computers, it still sounds very mechanical. When we can annotate text to specify phrase structure and focus, or generate text with a computer whose range of pitch can expand to match the range of human speakers, synthetic speech will sound better.

Other causes for the poor quality of synthetic speech arise from our inability to model the duration of the phonemes and the movement of the pitch as accurately as we need to to imitate human speech. More important, we still cannot analyze speech and use the resulting parameters in a way that accurately copies the human sound of the speech. At present, it is difficult to predict when we will solve these problems and build computers that sound like HAL.

Researchers in speech synthesis are now working in an area not portrayed in *2001*. In the film, HAL is portrayed as a large machine whose connection to the world is a large red eye. At Bell Labs, we have attached a talking face to our computer, which simultaneously sends the same information to the synthesizer and the talking head. Thus the talking head receives information about the phonemes and their duration and uses the information to compute the appropriate position of its lips, jaw, and tongue. It also moves its eyebrows to enhance the stressed portions of the speech. Although the talking head in the picture is a flat mask, it can be covered by a textured face

Figure 6.5
Bell Laboratories' Talking Head, Showing the Mask and the Underlying Wireframe Model

mask portraying any person you choose. The talking face not only makes the speech synthesizer more attractive and personable, it also enhances the intelligibility of the speech by letting the listener lipread while listening to the computer (cf. chapter 11). If HAL had had a real face, rather than one large eye, would it have been so easy to kill him—by turning him off? I wonder.

Acknowledgments

I would like to thank my wife, Virginia, and my colleagues Bernd Möbeus, Chilin Shih, Richard Sproat, Michael Tanenblatt, Evelyne Tzoukermann, and Jan van Santen for their helpful comments. I would also like to thank my directors, L. R. Rabiner and N. S. Jayant, for their encouragement and support.

Further Readings

J. Allen, M. S. Hunnicutt, and D. H. Klatt, *From Text to Speech: The MITalk System*. New York: Cambridge University Press, 1987. A description of a complete text-to-speech system.

R. Carlson and B. Granström. "A Text-to-Speech System Based Entirely on Rules." *Proc. Int. Conf. Acoust. Speech Signal Process.* ICASSP-76 (1976): 686–88. A rule-based approach to text-to-speech synthesis.

C. H. Coker, N. Umeda, and C. P. Browman. "Automatic Synthesis from Ordinary English Text." *IEEE Trans. Audio Electroacoust.* AU-21 (1973): 293–97. A rule-based synthesizer using articulatory parameters.

H. Dudley, R. R. Riesz, and S. A. Watkins. "A Synthetic Speaker." *J. Franklin Inst.* 227 (1939): 739–64. A description of the 1938 speaking machine.

H. Dudley and T. H. Tarnoczy. "The Speaking Machine of Wolfgang Kempelen." *J. Acoust. Soc. Am.* 22 (1950): 151–66.

J. L. Flanagan. *Speech Analysis, Synthesis and Perception*. New York: Springer, 1972. This technical and comprehensive book includes historical sections and a large bibliography.

J. L. Flanagan, K. Ishizaka, and K. L. Shipley. "Synthesis of Speech from a Dynamic Model of the Vocal Cords and Vocal Tract." *Bell Syst. Tech. J.* 54 (1975): 485–506. A synthesis scheme from articulatory parameters.

H. L. F. v. Helmholtz. *On the Sensation of Tone,* A. J. Ellis, transl. New York: Dover, 1954. (Trans. of 4th German ed., 1877.) A comprehensive book on theories of acoustics.

J. Hirschberg. "Pitch Accent in Context: Predicting Intonational Prominence from Text." *Artificial Intelligence* 63, 1–2 (1993). Rules for pitch contours from prediction of sentence-level stress.

D. H. Klatt. "Linguistic Uses of Segmental Duration in English: Acoustic and Perceptual Evidence." *J. Acoust. Soc. Am.* 59 (1976): 1208–1221. The duration of phonemes in speech.

D. H. Klatt. "Review of Text-to-Speech Conversion for English." *J. Acoust. Soc. Am.* 82, no. 3 (1987): 737–93. A complete review of the work on speech synthesis to 1987.

I. Lehiste. *Suprasegmentals.* Cambridge, Mass.: MIT Press, 1970. Discussion of speech phenomena beyond the phonemes, including the prosody of speech.

J. P. Olive. "Rule Synthesis of Speech from Dyadic Units." *Proc. Int. Conf. Acoust. Speech Signal Process.* ICASSP-77 (1977): 568–70. Synthesis from stored segments.

J. P. Olive, A. Greenwood, and J. Coleman. *Acoustics of American English Speech.* New York: Springer, 1993. A description of speech sounds with an introduction to phonetics and the theory of speech sound.

J. P. Olive and L. H. Nakatani. "Rule Synthesis of Speech by Word Concatenation: A First Step." *J. Acoust. Soc. Am.* 55 (1974): 660–66.

G. E. Peterson, W. Wang, and E. Sivertsen. "Segmentation Techniques in Speech Synthesis." *J. Acoust. Soc. Am.* 30 (1958): 793–42. Synthesis from stored segments.

J. Pierrehumbert. "Synthesizing Intonation." *J. Acoust. Soc. Am.* 70 (1981): 985–95. Rules for synthesizing pitch contours.

L. R. Rabiner, R. W. Schafer, and L. L. Flanagan. "Computer Synthesis of Speech by Concatenation of Formant-Coded Words." *Bell Syst. Tech. J.* 50 (1971): 1541–58. Synthesis from stored words.

7   *When Will HAL Understand What We Are Saying? Computer Speech Recognition and Understanding*

Raymond Kurzweil

Let's talk about how to wreck a nice beach.

Well, actually, if I were presenting this chapter verbally, you would have little difficulty understanding the preceding sentence as *Let's talk about how to recognize speech.* Of course, I wouldn't have enunciated the *g* in *recognize,* but then we routinely leave out and otherwise slur at least a quarter of the sounds that are "supposed" to be there—a phenomenon speech scientists call coarticulation.

On the other hand, had this been an article on a rowdy headbangers' beach convention (a topic we assume HAL knew little about), the interpretation at the beginning of the chapter would have been reasonable.

On yet another hand, if you were a researcher in speech recognition and heard me read the first sentence of this chapter, you would immediately pick up the beach-wrecking interpretation, because this sentence is a famous example of acoustic ambiguity and is frequently cited by speech researchers.

The point is that we understand speech in context. Spoken language is filled with ambiguities. Only our understanding of the situation, subject matter, and person (or entity) speaking—as well as our familiarity with the speaker—lets us infer what words are actually spoken.

Perhaps the most basic ambiguity in spoken language is the phenomenon of *homonyms,* words that sound absolutely identical but are actually different words with different meanings. When Frank asks, "Listen, HAL, there's never been any instance at all of a computer error occurring in a 9000 series, has there?", HAL has little difficulty interpreting the last word as *there* and not *their*. Context is the only source of knowledge that can resolve such ambiguities. HAL understands that the word *their* is an adjective and would have to be followed by the noun it modifies. Because it is the last word in the sentence, *there* is the only reasonable interpretation. Today's speech-recognition systems would also have little difficulty with this word and would resolve it the same way HAL does.

A more difficult task in interpreting Frank's statement is the word *all*. Is *all* a place—such as IBM headquarters—where a computer error may take place, as in "there's never been any instance of a computer error at IBM. . . ." HAL resolves this ambiguity the same way viewers of the movie do. We know that *all* is not the name of a place or organization where an error may take place. This leaves us with *at all* as an expression of emphasis reinforcing the meaning of *never* as the only likely interpretation.

In fact, we try to understand what is being said before the words are even spoken, through a process called *hypothesis and test*. Next time you order coffee in a restaurant and a waiter asks how you want it, try saying "I'd like some dream and sugar please." It would take a rather attentive person to hear that you are talking about sweet dreams and not white coffee.

When we listen to other people talking—and people frequently do not really listen, a fault that HAL does not seem to share with the rest of us—we constantly anticipate what they are going to say . . . next. Consider Dave's reply to HAL's questions about the crew psychology report:

Dave: Well, I don't know. That's rather a difficult question to . . .

When Dave finally says *answer*, HAL tests his hypothesis by matching the word he heard against the word he had hypothesized Dave would say. In watching the movie, we all do the same thing. Any reasonable match would tend to confirm our expectation.

The test involves an acoustic matching process, but the hypothesis has nothing to do with sound at all—nor even with language—but rather relates to knowledge on a multiplicity of levels. As many of the chapters in this book point out, knowledge goes far beyond mere facts and data. For *information* to become *knowledge,* it must incorporate the relationships between ideas. And for knowledge to be useful, the links describing how concepts interact must be easily accessed, updated, and manipulated. Human intelligence is remarkable in its ability to perform all these tasks. Ironically, it is also remarkably weak at reliably storing the information on which knowledge is based. The natural strengths of today's computers are roughly the opposite. They have, therefore, become powerful allies of the human intellect because of their ability to reliably store and rapidly retrieve vast quantities of information. Conversely, they have been slow to master true knowledge. Modeling the knowledge needed to understand the highly ambiguous and variable phenomenon of human speech has been a primary key to making progress in the field of automatic speech recognition (ASR).

Lesson 1: Knowledge Is a Many-layered Thing

Thus lesson number one for constructing a computer system that can understand human speech is to build-in knowledge at many levels: the structure of speech sounds, the way speech is produced by our vocal apparatus, the patterns of speech sounds that comprise dialects and languages, the complex (and not fully understood) rules of word usage, and—the greatest difficulty—general knowledge of the subject matter being spoken about.

Each level of analysis provides useful constraints that can limit our search for the right answer. For example, the basic building blocks of speech called *phonemes* cannot appear in just any order. Indeed, many sequences are impossible to articulate (try saying *ptkee*). More important, only certain phoneme sequences correspond to a word or word fragment in the language. Although the set of phonemes used is similar (although not identical) from one language to another, contextual factors differ dramatically. English, for example, has over ten thousand possible syllables, whereas Japanese has only a hundred and twenty.

On a higher level, the syntax and semantics of the language put constraints on possible word orders. Resolving homonym ambiguities can

S = sentence   N = noun
NP = noun phrase   V = verb
VP = verb phrase   P = preposition
PP = prepositional phrase   D = determiner

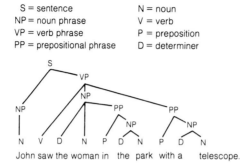

John saw the woman in the park with a telescope.

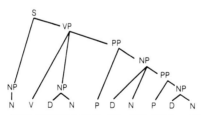

John saw the woman in the park with a telescope.

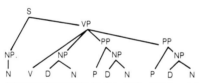

John saw the woman in the park with a telescope.

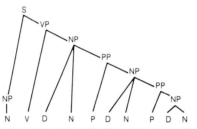

John saw the woman in the park with a telescope.

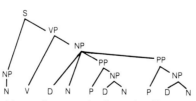

John saw the woman in the park with a telescope.

require multiple levels of knowledge. One type of technology frequently used in speech recognition and understanding systems is a sentence parser, which builds sentence diagrams like those we learned in elementary school (see figure 7.1). One of the first such systems, developed in 1963 by Susumu Kuno of Harvard (around the time Kubrick and Clarke began work on *2001*), revealed the depth of ambiguity in English. Kuno asked his computerized parser what the sentence "Time flies like an arrow" means. In what has become a famous response, the computer replied that it was not quite sure. It might mean

1. That time passes as quickly as an arrow passes.

2. Or maybe it is a command telling us to time the flies the same way that an arrow times flies; that is, "Time flies like an arrow would."

3. Or it could be a command telling us to time only those flies that are similar to arrows; that is, "Time flies that are like an arrow."

4. Or perhaps it means that a type of flies known as time flies have a fondness for arrows: "Time-flies like (i.e., appreciate) an arrow."

It became clear from this and other syntactical ambiguities that understanding language, spoken or written, requires both knowledge of the relationships between words and of the concepts underlying words. It is impossible to understand the sentence about time (or even to understand that the sentence is indeed talking about time and not flies) without mastery of the knowledge structures that represent what we know about time, flies, arrows, and how these concepts relate to one another.

A system armed with this type of information would know that flies are not similar to arrows and would thus knock out the third interpretation. Often there is more than one way to resolve language ambiguities. The third

Figure 7.1

What Did You Mean by That?

A computer sentence-parsing program reveals the ambiguity of language. This sentence has at least five different interpretations. (*Source:* Data from Skona Brittain, "Understanding Natural Languages," *AI Expert* 2, no. 5 (1987): 32)

interpretation could be syntactically resolved by noting that *like* in the sense of *similar to* ordinarily requires number agreement between the two objects compared. Such a system would also note that, as there are no such things as *time flies,* the fourth interpretation too is wrong. The system would also need such tidbits of knowledge as the fact that flies have never shown a fondness for arrows, and that arrows cannot and do not *time* anything—much less flies—to select the first interpretation as the only plausible one. The ambiguity of language, however, is far greater than this example suggests. In a language-parsing project at the MIT Speech Lab, Ken Church found a sentence with over two million syntactically correct interpretations.

Often the tidbits of knowledge we need have to do with the specific situation of speakers and listeners. If I walk into my business associate's office and say "rook to king one," I am likely to get a response along the lines of "excuse me?" Even if my words were understood, their meaning would still be unclear; my associate would probably interpret them as a sarcastic remark implying that I think he regards himself as a king. In the context of a chess game, however, not only is the meaning clear, but the words are easy to recognize. Indeed, our contemporary speech-recognition systems do a very good job when the domain of discourse is restricted to something as narrow as a chess game. So, HAL, too, has little trouble understanding when Frank says "rook to king one" during one of their chess matches.

Lesson 2: The Unpredictability of Human Speech

A second lesson for building our computer system is that it must be capable of understanding the variability of human speech. We can, of course, build in pictures of human speech called spectrograms, which plot the intensity of different frequencies (or pitches in human perceptual terms) as they change over time. What is interesting, and—for those of us developing speech-recognition machines—daunting is that spectrograms of two people saying the same word can look dramatically different. Even the same person pronouncing the same word at different times can produce quite different spectrograms.

Look at the two spectrogram pictures of Dave and Frank saying the word *HAL* (figure 7.2). It would be difficult to know that they are saying the same word from the pictures alone. Yet the spectrograms present all the salient information in the speech signals.

Yet, there must be something about these different sound pictures that is the same; otherwise we humans and HAL, as a human-level machine, would be unable to identify them as two examples of the same spoken word. Thus, one key to building automatic speech-recognition (ASR) machines is the search for these *invariant features*. We note for example that vowel sounds (e.g., the *a* sound in *HAL,* which may be denoted as *æ* (or /*a*/)) involve certain resonant frequencies called *formants* that are sustained over some tens of milliseconds. We tend to find these formants in a certain mathematical relationship whenever /*a*/ is spoken. The same is true of the other sustained vowels. (Although the relationship is not a simple one, we observe that the relationship of the frequency of the second formant to the first formant for a particular vowel falls within a certain range, with some overlap between the ranges for different vowels.) Speech-recognition systems frequently include a search function for finding these relationships, sometimes called *features.*

By studying spectrograms, we also note that certain changes do not convey any information; that is, there are types of changes we should filter out and ignore. An obvious one is loudness. When Dave shouts HAL's name in the pod in space, HAL realizes it is still his name. HAL infers some meaning from Dave's volume, but it is relatively unimportant for identifying the words being spoken. We apply, therefore, a process called *normalization,* in which we make all words the same loudness so as to eliminate this noninformative source of variability.

A more complex example is the phenomenon of nonlinear time compression. When we speak, we change our speed according to context and other factors. If we speak one word more quickly, we do not increase the rate evenly throughout the entire word. The duration of certain portions of the word, such as plosive consonants (e.g., /*p*/, /*b*/, /*t*/), remains fairly constant, while other portions, such as vowels, undergo most of the change. In

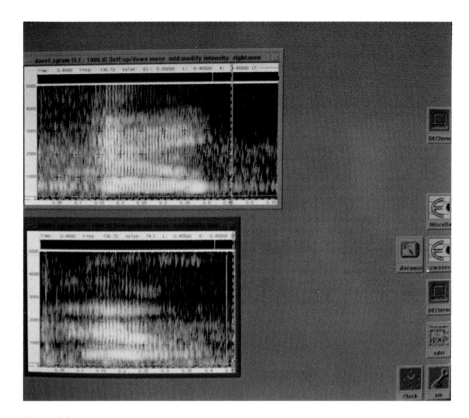

Figure 7.2
Spectrograms of Dave (top) and Frank Saying the Word *HAL*
This spectogram plots the amount of energy at different frequencies (vertical axis) against time (horizontal axis). A lighter shade at a particular point in time represents greater energy at that frequency. The vowel sound in *HAL* is represented by the vertical stripes (called *formants*), which represent resonant frequencies in the vocal tract. The two plots of the same word show somewhat similar formants, but overall they look rather different. But they must be similar enough for us, as humans or HAL, as a machine with at least human-level intelligence, to recognize them as the same word. (*Source:* Created with the help of Professor Ken Stevens and Walter Sun, MIT Speech Lab)

matching a spoken word to a stored example (a *template*), we need to align corresponding acoustic events or the match will never succeed. A mathematical technique called *dynamic programming* solves this temporal alignment (see figure 7.3).

Lesson 3: Speech Is Like a Song

A third lesson is also apparent from studying speech spectrograms. It is that the perceptual cues needed to identify speech sounds and assemble words are found in the frequency domain, and not in the original time-varying signal. To make sense of it, we need to convert the original waveform into its frequency components. The human vocal tract is similar to a musical instrument (indeed it *is* a musical instrument). The vocal cords vibrate, creating a characteristic pitched sound; the length and tautness of the cords determine pitch in the same way that the length and tautness of a violin or piano string does. We can control the tautness of our vocal cords—as we do when singing—and alter the overtones produced by our vibrating cords by moving our tongue, teeth, and lips—which change the shape of the vocal tract. The vocal tract is a chamber that acts like a pipe in a pipe organ, the harmonic resonances of which emphasize certain overtones and diminish others. Finally, we control a small piece of tissue called the alveolar flap (or soft palate), which opens and closes the nasal cavity. When the alveolar flap is open, the nasal cavity adds an additional resonant chamber; it's a lot like opening another organ pipe. (Viewers of *My Fair Lady* will recall that the anatomy of speech recognition is also an important topic for specialists in phonetics.)

In addition to the pitched sound produced by the vocal cords, we can produce a noiselike sound by the rush of air through the speech cavity. This sound does not have specific overtones but is a complex spectrum of many frequencies mixed together. Like the musical tones produced by the vocal cords, the spectra of these noise sounds are shaped by the changing resonances of the moving vocal tract.

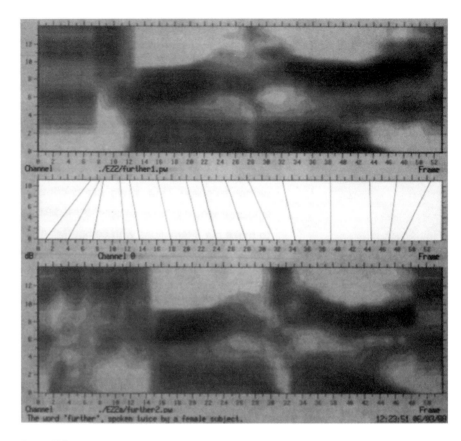

Figure 7.3
Nonlinear Alignment of Speech Events
The lines in the middle section indicate the optimal alignment of spectograms of the word *further* spoken twice by the same female speaker. This alignment is computed automatically by a mathematical technique called dynamic programming. (*Source:* Photo by Vladimir Sejnoha used courtesy of Kurzweil Applied Intelligence, Inc.)

This vocal apparatus allows us to create the varied sounds that comprise human speech. Although many animals communicate with others of their species through sound, we humans are unique in our ability to shape that sound into language. We produce vowel sounds (e.g., /a/, /i/) by shaping the overtones from the vibrating vocal cords into distinct frequency bands, the formants. Sibilant sounds (/s/, /z/) result from the rush of air through particular configurations of tongue and teeth. Plosive consonants (/p/, /b/, /t/) are transitory sounds created by the percussive movement of lips, tongue, and mouth cavity. Nasal sounds (/n/, /m/) are created by invoking the resonances of the nasal cavity. The distribution of sounds vary from one language to another.

Each of the several dozen basic sounds, the phonemes, requires an intricate movement involving precise coordination of the vocal cords, alveolar flap, tongue, lips, and teeth. We typically speak about three words per second. So with an average of six phonemes per word, we make about eighteen intricate phonetic gestures per second, a task comparable in complexity to a performance by a concert pianist. We do this without thinking about it, of course. Our thoughts remain on the conceptual (that is, the highest) level of the language and knowledge hierarchy. In our first two years of life, however, we thought a lot about how to make speech sounds—and how to string them together meaningfully. This process is an example of our sequential (i.e., logical, rational) conscious mind training our parallel preconscious pattern-processing mental faculties.

The mechanisms described above for creating speech sounds—vocal cord vibrations, the noise of rushing air, articulatory gestures of the mouth, teeth and tongue, the shaping of the vocal and nasal cavities—produce different rates of vibration. Physicists measure these rates of vibration as frequencies; we perceive them as pitches. Though we normally think of speech as a single time-varying sound, it is actually a composite of many different sounds, each with its own frequency. Using this insight, most ASR researchers starting in the late 1960s began by breaking up the speech waveform into a number of frequency bands. A typical commercial or research ASR system will produce between a few and several dozen frequency bands. The front end of the human auditory system does exactly the same thing: each nerve ending in the cochlea (inner ear) responds to different frequencies and emits a pulsed digital signal when activated by an appropriate pitch. The cochlea differentiates several thousand overlapping bands of frequency, which gives the human auditory system its extremely high degree of sensitivity to frequency. Experiments have shown that increasing the number of overlapping frequency bands of an ASR system (thus making it more like the human auditory system) increases the ability of that system to recognize human speech.

Lesson 4: Learn While You Listen

A fourth lesson emphasizes the importance of learning. At each stage of processing, a system must adapt to the individual characteristics of the talker. Learning to do this has to take place at several levels: those of the frequency and time relationships characterizing each phoneme, the dialect (pronunciation) patterns of each word, and the syntactic patterns of possible phrases and sentences. At the highest cognitive level, a person or machine understanding speech learns a great deal about what a particular talker tends to talk about and how that talker phrases his or her thoughts.

HAL learns a great deal about his human crew mates by listening to the sound of their voices, what they talk about, and how they put sentences together. He also watches what their mouths do when they articulate certain phrases (chapter 11). HAL gathers so much knowledge about them that he can understand them even when some of the information is obscured—for example, when he has to rely solely on his visual observation of Dave and Frank's lips.

Lesson 5: Hungry for MIPS and Megabytes

The fifth lesson is that speech recognition is a process hungry for MIPs (millions of instructions per second) and megabytes (millions of bytes of storage); which is to say that we can obtain more accurate performance by using faster computers with larger memories. Certain algorithms or methods are only available in computers that operate at high levels of performance. Brute force—that is, huge memory—is necessary but clearly not sufficient without solving the difficult algorithmic and knowledge-capture issues mentioned above.

We now know that 1997, when HAL reportedly became intelligent, is too soon. We won't have the quantity of computing, in terms of speed and memory needed, to build a HAL. And we won't be there in 2001 either.

Let's keep these lessons in mind as we examine the roots and future prospects of building machines that can duplicate HAL's ability to understand speech.

The Importance of Speech Recognition

Before examining the sweep of progress in this field, it is worthwhile to underscore the importance of the auditory sense, particularly our ability to understand spoken language, and why this is a critical faculty for HAL. Most of HAL's interaction with the crew is verbal. It is primarily through his recognition and understanding of speech that he communicates. HAL's visual perceptual skills, which are far more difficult to create, are relatively less important for carrying out his mission, even though the pivotal scene, in which HAL understands Dave and Frank's conspiratorial conversation, without being able to hear them, relies on HAL's visual sense. Of course, his apparently self-taught lipreading is based on his speech-recognition ability and would have been impossible if HAL had not been able to understand spoken language.

To demonstrate the importance of the auditory sense, try watching the television news with the sound turned off. Then try it again with the sound on, but without looking at the picture. Next, try a similar experiment with a videotape of the movie *2001*. You will probably find it easier to follow the stories with your ears alone than with your eyes alone, even though our eyes transmit much more information to our brains than our ears do—about fifty billion bits per second from both eyes versus approximately a million bits per second from two ears. The result is surprising. There is a saying that a picture is worth a thousand words; yet the above exercise illustrates the superior power of spoken language to convey our thoughts. Part of that power lies in the close link between verbal language and conscious thinking. Until recently, a popular theory held that thinking was subvocalized speech. (J. B. Watson, the founder of behaviorism, attached great attention to the small movements of the tongue and larynx made while we think.) Although we now recognize that thoughts incorporate both language and visual images, the crucial importance of the auditory sense in the acquisition of knowledge—which we need in order to recognize speech in the first place—is widely accepted.

Yet many people consider blindness a more serious handicap than deafness. A careful consideration of the issues shows this to be a misconception. With modern mobility techniques, blind persons with appropriate training have little difficulty going from place to place. The blind employees of my first company (Kurzweil Computer Products, Inc., which developed the Kurzweil Reading Machine for the Blind) traveled around the world routinely. Reading machines can provide access to the world of print, and visually impaired people experience few barriers to communicating with others in groups or individual encounters. For the deaf, however, the barrier to understanding what other people are saying is fundamental.

We learn to understand and produce spoken language during our first year of life, years before we can understand or create written language. HAL apparently spent years learning human speech by listening to his teacher, whom he identifies as Mr. Langley, at the HAL lab in Urbana, Illinois. Studies with humans have shown that groups of people can solve problems with dramatically greater speed if they can communicate verbally rather than being restricted to other methods. HAL and his human colleagues amply demonstrate this finding. Thus, intelligent machines that understand verbal language make possible an optimal modality of communication. In recent years, a major goal of artificial intelligence research has been making our interactions with computers more natural and intuitive. HAL's primarily verbal communication with crew members is a clear example of an intuitive user interface.

The Roots of Automatic Speech Recognition (ASR)

Keeping in mind our five lessons about creating speech-recognition systems, it is interesting to examine historical attempts to endow machines with the ability to understand human speech. The effort goes back to Alexander Graham Bell, and the roots of the story go even farther back, to Bell's grandfather Alexander Bell, a widely known lecturer and speech teacher. *His* son, Alexander Melville Bell, created a phonetic system for teaching the deaf to speak called *visible speech*. At the age of twenty-four, Alexander Graham Bell began teaching his father's system of visible speech to instructors of the deaf in Boston. He fell in love with and subsequently married one of his students, Mabel Hubbard. She had been deaf since the age of four as a result of scarlet fever. The marriage served to deepen his commitment to applying his inventiveness to overcoming the handicaps of deafness.

He built a device he called a *phonautograph* to make visual patterns from sound. Attaching a thin stylus to an eardrum he obtained from a medical school, he traced the patterns produced by speaking through the eardrum on a smoked glass screen. His wife, however, was unable to understand speech by looking at these patterns. The device could convert speech sounds into pictures, but the pictures were highly variable and showed no similarity in patterns, even when the same person spoke the same word.

In 1874, Bell demonstrated that the different frequency harmonics from an electrical signal could be separated. His *harmonic telegraph* could send multiple telegraphic messages over the same wire by using different frequency tones. The next year, the twenty-eight-year-old Bell had a profound insight. He hypothesized that although the information needed to understand speech sounds could not be seen by simply displaying the speech signal directly, it could be recognized if you first broke the signal into different frequency bands. Bell's intuitive discovery of our third lesson also turns out to be a key to finding the invariant features needed for the second lesson.

Bell felt sure he had all the pieces needed to implement this insight and give his wife the ability to understand human speech. He had already developed a moving drum and solenoid (a metal core wrapped with wire) that could transform a human voice into a time-varying current of electricity. All he needed to do, he thought, was to break up this electrical signal into different frequency bands, as he had done previously with the harmonic telegraph, then render each of these harmonics visually—by using multiple phonautographs. In June of 1875, while attempting to prepare this experiment, he accidentally connected the wire from the input solenoid back to another similar device. Now most processes are not reversible. Try unsmashing a teacup or speaking into a reading machine for the blind, which converts print into speech; it will not convert the speech back into print. But, unexpectedly, Bell's erstwhile microphone began to speak! Thus was the telephone discovered, or we should say, invented.

The device ultimately broke down the communication barrier of distance for the human race. Ironically, Bell's great invention also deepened the isolation of the deaf. The two methods of communication available to the deaf—sign language and lipreading—are not possible over the telephone.

He continued to experiment with a frequency-based phonautograph, but without a computer to analyze the rapidly time-varying harmonic bands, the information remained a bewildering array to a sighted deaf person. We now know that we can visually examine frequency-based pictures of speech (i.e., spectrograms) and understand the communication from the visual information alone; but the process is extremely difficult and slow. An MIT graduate course, Speech Spectrogram Reading, teaches precisely this skill. The purpose of the course is to give students insight into the spectral cues of salient speech events. For many years, the course's professor, Dr. Victor Zue, was the only person who could understand speech from spectrograms with any proficiency; several people have reportedly now mastered this skill. Computers, on the other hand, can readily handle spectral information, and we can build a crude but usable speech-recognition system using this type of acoustic information alone. So Bell was on the right track—about a century too soon.

Ironically, another pioneer, Charles Babbage, had attempted to create that other prerequisite to automatic speech recognition—the programmable computer—about forty years earlier. Babbage built his computer, the *Analytical Engine*, entirely of mechanical parts; yet it was a true computer, with a stored program, a central processing unit, and memory store. Despite Babbage's exhaustive efforts, nineteenth-century machining technology could not build the machine. Like Bell, Babbage was about a century ahead of his time, and the analytical engine never ran.

Not until the 1940s, when fueled by the exigencies of war, were the first computers actually built: the Z-3 by Konrad Zuse in Nazi Germany, the Mark I by U.S. Navy Commander Howard Aiken, and the Robinson and Colossus computers by Alan Turing and his English colleagues. Turing's Bletchley group broke the German Enigma code and are credited with enabling the Royal Air Force to win the Battle of Britain and so withstand the Nazi war machine.

For Bell, whose invention of the telephone created the telecommunications revolution, the original goal of easing the isolation of the deaf remained elusive. His insights into separating the speech signal into different frequency components and rendering those components as visible traces were not successfully implemented until Potter, Kopp, and Green designed the spectrogram and Dreyfus-Graf developed the steno-sonograph in the late 1940s. These devices generated interest in the possibility of automatically recognizing speech because they made the invariant features of speech visible for all to see.

The first serious speech recognizer was developed in 1952 by Davis, Biddulph, and Balashek of Bell Labs. Using a simple frequency splitter, it generated plots of the first two formants, which it identified by matching them against prestored patterns in an analog memory. With training, it was reported, the machine achieved 97 percent accuracy on the spoken forms of ten digits.

By the 1950s, researchers began to follow lesson 5 and to use computers for ASR, which allowed for linear time normalization, a concept introduced by Denes and Mathews in 1960. The 1960s saw several successful experiments with discrete word recognition in real time using digital computers; words were spoken in isolation with brief silent pauses between them. Some notable success was also achieved with relatively large vocabularies, although with constrained syntaxes. In 1969, two such systems—the Vicens system, which accepted a five-hundred-word vocabulary, and the Medress system with its one-hundred-word vocabulary—were described in Ph.D. dissertations.

That same year, John Pierce wrote a celebrated, caustic letter objecting to the repetitious implementation of small-vocabulary discrete word devices. He argued for attacking more ambitious goals by harnessing different levels of knowledge, including knowledge of speech, language, and task. He argued against real-time devices, anticipating (correctly) that processing speeds would improve dramatically in the near future. Partly in response to the concerns articulated by Pierce, the U.S. Defense Advanced Research Projects Agency began serious funding of ASR research with the ARPA SUR (Speech Understanding Research) project, which began in 1971. As Allen Newell of Carnegie Mellon University observes in his 1975 paper, there were three ARPA SUR dogmas. First, all sources of knowledge, from acoustics to semantics, should be part of any research system. Second, context and a priori knowledge of the language should supplement analysis of the sound itself. Third, the objective of ASR is, properly, speech understanding, not simply correct identification of words in a spoken message. Systems, therefore, should be evaluated in terms of their ability to respond correctly to spoken messages about such pragmatic problems as travel budget management. (For example, researchers might ask a system "What is the plane fare to Ottawa?") Not surprisingly, this third dogma was the most controversial and remains so today; and different markets have been identified for speech-recognition and speech-understanding systems.

The objective goal of ARPA SUR was a recognition system with 90 percent sentence accuracy for continuous-speech sentences, using thousand-word vocabularies, not in real time. Of four principal ARPA SUR projects, the only one to meet the stated goal was Carnegie Mellon University's Harpy system, which achieved a 5 percent error rate on a 1,011-word vocabulary on continuous speech. One of the ways the CMU team achieved the goal was clever: they made the task easier by restricting word order; that is, by limiting spoken words to certain sequences in the sentence.

The five-year ARPA SUR project was thoroughly analyzed and debated for at least a decade after its completion. Its legacy was to establish firmly the five lessons I have described. By then it was clear that the best way to reduce the error rate was to build in as much knowledge as possible about speech (lesson 1): how speech sounds are structured, how they are strung together, what determines sequences, the syntactic structure of the language (English, in this case), and the semantics and pragmatics of the subject matter and task—which for ARPA SUR were far simpler than what HAL had to understand.

Great strides were made in normalizing the speech signal to filter out variability (lesson 2). F. Itakura, a Japanese scientist, and H. Sakoe and S. Chiba introduced *dynamic programming* to compute optimal nonlinear time alignments, a technique that quickly became the standard. Jim Baker and IBM's Fred Jelinek introduced a statistical method called Markov Modeling; it provided a powerful mathematical tool for finding the invariant information in the speech signal.

Lesson 3, about breaking the speech signal into its frequency components, had already been established prior to the ARPA SUR projects, some of which developed systems that could adapt to aspects of the speaker's voice (lesson 4). Lesson 5 was anticipated by allowing ARPA SUR researchers to use as much computer memory as they could afford to buy and as much computer time as they had the patience to wait for. An underlying, and accurate expectation was that Moore's law (see chapter 3 and below) would ultimately provide whatever computing platform the algorithms required.

The 1970s

The 1970s were notable for other significant research efforts. In addition to introducing dynamic programming, Itakura developed an influential analysis of spectral-distance measures, a way to compute how similar two different sounds are. His system demonstrated an impressive 97.3 percent accuracy on two hundred Japanese words spoken over the telephone. Bell Labs also achieved significant success (a 97.1 percent accuracy) with speaker-independent systems—that is, systems that understand voices they have not heard before. IBM concentrated on the Markov modeling statistical technique and demonstrated systems that could recognize a large vocabulary.

By the end of the 1970s, numerous commercial speech-recognition products were available. They ranged from Heuristics' $259 H-2000 Speech Link, to $100,000 speaker-independent systems from Verbex and Nippon. Other companies, including Threshold, Scott, Centigram, and Interstate, offered systems with sixteen-channel filter banks at prices between $2,000 and $15,000. Such products could recognize small vocabularies spoken with pauses between words.

The 1980s

The 1980s saw the commercial field of ASR split into two fairly distinct market segments. One group—which included Verbex, Voice Processing Corporation, and several others—pursued reliable speaker-independent recognition of small vocabularies for telephone transaction processing. The other group, which included IBM and two new companies—Jim and Janet Baker's Dragon Systems, and my Kurzweil Applied Intelligence—pursued large-vocabulary ASR for creating written documents by voice.

Important work on large-vocabulary continuous speech (i.e., speech with no pauses between words) was also conducted at Carnegie Mellon University by Kai-Fu Lee, who subsequently left the university to head Apple's speech-recognition efforts.

By 1991, revenues for the ASR industry were in low eight figures and were increasing substantially every year. A buyer could choose any one (but not two) characteristics from the following menu: large vocabulary, speaker independence, or continuous speech. HAL, of course, could do all three.

The State of the Art

So where are we today? We now, finally, have inexpensive personal computers that can support high-performance ASR software. Buyers can now choose any two (but not all three) capabilities from the menu listed above. For example, my company's Kurzweil VOICE for Windows can recognize a sixty-thousand-word vocabulary spoken discretely (i.e., with brief pauses between each word). Another experimental system can handle a thousand-word, command-and-control vocabulary with continuous speech (i.e., no pauses). Both systems provide speaker independence; that is, they can recognize words spoken by your voice even if they've never heard it before. Systems in this product category are also made by Dragon Systems and IBM.

Playing HAL

To demonstrate today's state of the art in computer speech recognition, we fed in some of the sound track of *2001* into the Kurzweil VOICE for Windows version 2.0 (KV/Win 2.0). KV/Win 2.0 is capable of understanding the speech of a person it has not heard speak before and can recognize a vocabulary of up to sixty thousand words (forty thousand in its initial vocabulary with the ability to add another twenty thousand). The primary limitation of today's technology is that it can only handle discrete speech—that is, words or brief phrases (such as *thank you*) spoken with brief pauses in between. I played the following dialogue to KV/Win 2.0 with a view to learning whether it could understand Dave as HAL does in the movie:

HAL: Good evening, Dave.

Dave: How you doing, HAL?

HAL: Everything is running smoothly; and you?

Dave: Oh, not too bad.

HAL: Have you been doing some more work?

Dave: Just a few sketches.

HAL: May I see them?

Dave: Sure.

HAL: That's a very nice rendering, Dave. I think you've improved a great deal. Can you hold it a bit closer?

Dave: Sure.

HAL: That's Dr. Hunter, isn't it?

Dave: Hm hmm.

HAL: By the way, do you mind if I ask you a personal question?

Dave: No, not at all.

I trained the system on the phrases "Oh, not too bad" and "No, not at all," but did not train it on Dave's voice. When I did the experiment, KV/Win 2.0 had never heard Dave's voice, and it had to pick out each word or phrase from among forty thousand possibilities. I had the system listen to Dave saying the following discrete words and phrases from the above dialogue:

Dave: Oh, not too bad.

Dave: Sure.

Dave: Sure.

Dave: No, not at all.

KV/Win 2.0 was able to successfully recognize the above utterances even though it had not been previously exposed to Dave's voice (see figure 7.4). For good measure, I also had KV/Win 2.0 listen to Dave in the critical scene in which HAL is betraying him. In this scene, Dave says the word HAL five times in a row in an increasingly plaintive voice. KV/Win 2.0 successfully recognized the five utterances, despite their obvious differences in tone and enunciation (see figure 7.5). Looking at the spectrogram, we can see that these five utterances, although they are similar in some respects, are really quite different from one another and demonstrate clearly the variability of human speech (see figure 7.6). So, except for KV/Win's restriction to discrete speech, with regard to speech recognition we've already created HAL!

Of course, the limitation to discrete speech is no minor exception. When will our computers be capable of recognizing fully continuous speech? Recently, ARPA has funded a new round of research aimed at "holy grail" systems that combine all three capabilities—handling continuous speech with very large vocabularies and speaker independence. Like the earlier ARPA SUR projects, there are no restrictions on memory or real-time performance. Restricting the task to understanding "business English," ARPA contractors—

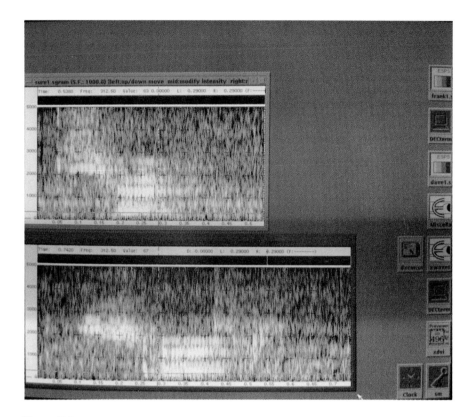

Figure 7.4
Spectograms of Two Instances of Dave Saying the Word *sure*
There are similarities, but clearly there is a need for nonlinear time normalization. These utterances were also recognized by KV/Win 2.0. (*Source:* Created with the help of Professor Ken Stevens and Walter Sun, MIT Speech Lab)

including Phillips, Bolt, Beranek and Newman, Dragon Systems, Inc., and others—have reported word accuracies around 97 percent or higher. Moore's law will take care of achieving real-time performance on affordable machines, so that we should see such systems available commercially by, perhaps, early 1998.

Expanding the domain of recognition—not to mention understanding—to the humanlike flexibility HAL displays will take a far greater mastery of the many levels of knowledge represented in spoken language. I would

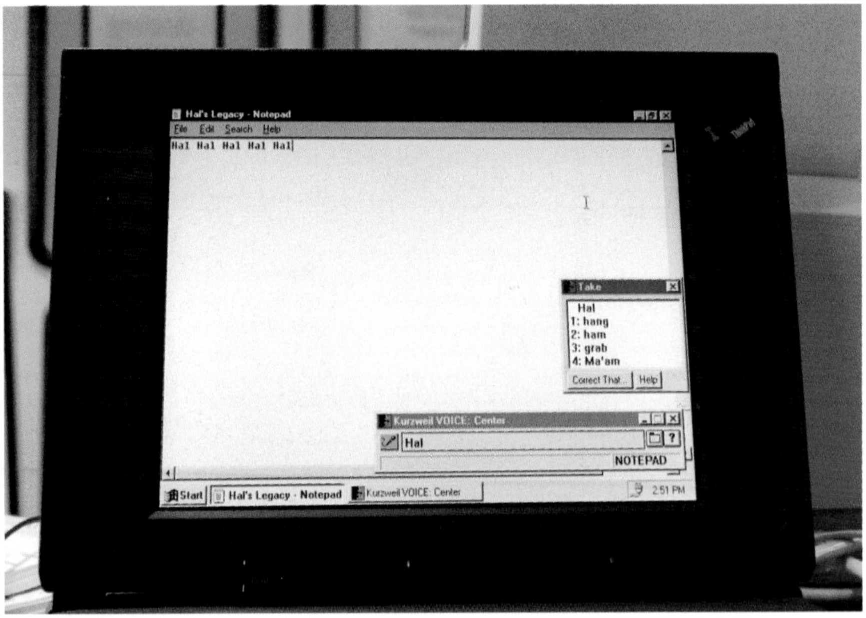

Figure 7.5
Kurzweil VOICE for Windows Version 2.0 (KV/Win 2.0)
The program was able to recognize the five examples of the word *Hal* spoken by Dave, even though it had never heard his voice before. KV/Win 2.0 picked out the word from amongst its 40,000-word initial vocabulary. The window labeled "Take" lists four other words KV/Win 2.0 chose as close matches, behind its top choice, *Hal*.

expect that by the year 2001—remembering that in the movie HAL became intelligent much earlier—we will have systems able to recognize speech well enough to produce a written transcription of the movie from the sound track. Even then, the error rate will be far higher than HAL's (who, of course, claims he has never made a mistake).

In 1997 we appreciate that speech recognition does not exist in a vacuum but has to be integrated with other levels and sources of knowledge. Kurzweil Applied Intelligence, Inc., for example, has integrated its large-vocabulary speech recognition capability with an expert system that has extensive knowledge about the preparation of medical reports; the Kurzweil VoiceMED

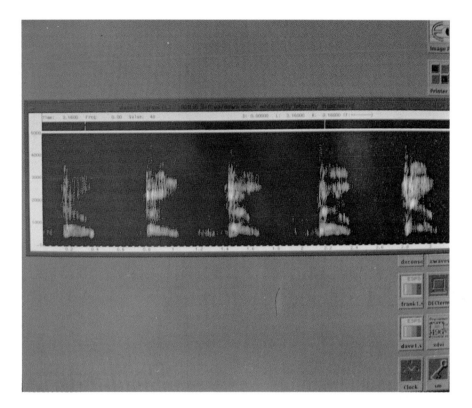

Figure 7.6
A Spectogram of Dave Saying *Hal* Five Times in a Row
In the critical scene, when HAL betrays him by refusing to open the pod bay door, Dave says the same word in an increasingly plaintive tone. Again, the plots of the same words spoken by the same person at approximately the same time demonstrate the variability of human speech. (*Source:* Created with the help of Professor Ken Stevens and Walter Sun, MIT Speech Lab)

Figure 7.7
The Reality of Speech Recognition, circa 1996
Doctors in about 10 percent of the emergency rooms in the United States dictate their medical reports to speech-recognition systems like this one. As he dictates into the handset, the doctor watches the transcribed report appear on the computer screen in real time. (*Source:* Photo courtesy of Kurzweil Applied Intelligence, Inc.)

can guide doctors through the reporting process and assist them to comply with the latest regulations (see figure 7.7). If you find yourself in a hospital emergency room, there is a 10-percent chance your attending physician will dictate his or her report to one of our speech-recognition systems. We recently began adding the ability to understand natural language commands spoken in continuous speech. If, for example, you say, "go to the second paragraph on the next page; select the second sentence; capitalize every word in this sentence; underline it . . ." the system is likely to follow this series of commands. If you say "Open the pod bay doors," it will probably respond "Command not understood."

How to Build a Speech Recognizer

Software today is not an isolated field, but one that encompasses and codifies every other field of endeavor. Everyone—librarians, musicians, magazine publishers, doctors, graphic artists, architects, researchers of every kind—are digitizing their knowledge bases, methods, and expressions of their work. Those of us working on speech understanding are experiencing the same rapid change, as hundreds of scientists and engineers build increasingly elaborate data bases and structures to describe our knowledge of speech sounds, phonetics, linguistics, syntax, semantics, and pragmatics—in accordance with lesson 1.

A speech-recognition system operates in phases, with each new phase using increasingly sophisticated knowledge about the next higher level of language. At the front end, the system converts the time-varying air pressure we call sound into an electrical signal, as Bell did a hundred years ago with his crude microphones. Then, a device called an analog-to-digital converter changes the signal into a series of numbers. The numbers may be modified to normalize for loudness levels and possibly to eliminate background noise and distortion. The signal, which is now a digital stream of numbers, is usually converted into multiple streams, each of which represents a different frequency band. These multiple streams are then compressed, using a variety of mathematical techniques that reduce the amount of information and emphasize those features of the speech signal important for recognizing speech.

For example, we want to know that a certain segment of sound contains a broad noiselike band of frequencies that might represent the sound of rushing air, as in the sound /h/ in *HAL*; another segment contains two or three resonant frequencies in a certain ratio that might represent the vowel sound /a/ in *HAL*. One way to accomplish this labeling is to store examples of such sounds and attempt to match incoming time slices against these templates. Usually, the attempt to categorize slices of sound uses a much finer classification system than the approximately forty phonemes of English. We typically use a set of 256 or even 1,024 possible classifications in a process called *vector quantization*.

Once we have classified these time slices of sound, we can use one of several competing approaches to recognizing words. One of them develops statistical models for words or portions of words by analyzing massive amounts of prerecorded speech data. Markov modeling and neural nets are examples of this approach. Another approach tries to detect the underlying string of phonemes (or possibly other types of subword units) and then match them to the words spoken.

At Kurzweil Applied Intelligence (KAI), rather than select one optimal approach, we implemented seven or eight different modules, or "experts," then programmed another software module, the *expert manager,* which knows the strengths and weaknesses of the different software experts. In this decision-by-committee approach, the expert manager is the chief executive officer and makes the final decisions.

In the KAI systems, some of the expert modules are based, not on the sound of the words but on rules and the statistical behavior of word sequences. This is a variation of the hypothesis-and-test paradigm in which the system expects to hear certain words, according to what the speaker has already said. Each of the modules in the system has a great deal of built-in knowledge. The acoustic experts contain knowledge on the sound structure of words or such subword units as phonemes. The language experts know how words are strung together. The expert manager can judge which experts are more reliable in particular situations.

The system as a whole begins with generic knowledge of speech and language in general, then adapts these knowledge structures, based on what it observes in a particular speaker. In the film, Dave and Frank frequently invoke HAL's name. Even today's speech-recognition systems would quickly learn to recognize the word *HAL* and would not mistake it for *hill* or *hall,* at least not after being corrected once or twice.

In continuous speech, a speech-recognition system needs to deal with the additional ambiguity of when words start and end. Its attempts to match the classified time slices and recognized subword units against actual word hypotheses could result in a combinatorial explosion. A vocabulary of, say, sixty thousand words, could produce 3.6 billion possible two-word sequences, 216 trillion three-word sequences, and so on. Obviously, as we cannot examine even a tiny fraction of these possibilities, search constraints based on the system's knowledge of language are crucial.

Moore's Law

The other major ingredient needed to achieve the holy grail (i.e., a system that can understand fully continuous speech with high accuracy with relatively unrestricted vocabulary and domain and with no previous exposure to the speaker) is a more-powerful computer. We already have systems that can combine continuous speech, very large vocabularies, and speaker independence—with the only limitation being restriction of the domain to business English. But these systems require RAM memories of over 100 megabytes and run much slower than real time on powerful workstations. Even though computational power is critical to developing speech recognition and understanding, no one in the field is worried about obtaining it in the near future. We know we will not have to wait long to achieve the requisite computational power because of Moore's law.

Moore's law states that computing speeds and densities double every eighteen months; it is the driving force behind a revolution so vast that the entire computer revolution to date represents only a minor ripple of its ultimate implications. It was first articulated in the mid-1960s by Dr. Gordon Moore. Moore's law actually is a corollary of a broader law I like to call Kurzweil's law, which concerns the exponentially quickening pace of technology back to the dawn of human history. A thousand years ago, not much happened in a century, technologically speaking. In the nineteenth century, quite a bit happened. Now major technological transformations occur in a few years time. Moore's law, a clear quantification of this exponential phenomenon, indicates that the pace will continue to accelerate.

Remarkably, this law has held true since the beginning of this century. It began with the mechanical card-based computing technology used in the 1890 census, moved to the relay-based computers of the 1940s, to the vacuum tube-based computers of the 1950s, to the transistor-based machines of the 1960s, and to all the generations of integrated circuits we've seen over the past three decades. If you chart the abilities of every calculator and computer developed in the past hundred years logarithmically, you get an essentially straight line. Computer memory, for example, is about sixteen thousand times more powerful today for the same unit cost than it was in about 1976 and is a hundred and fifty million times more powerful for the same unit cost than it was in 1948.

Moore's law will continue to operate unabated for many decades to come; we have not even begun to explore the third dimension in chip design. Today's chips are flat, whereas our brain is organized in three dimensions. We live in a three-dimensional world, why not use the third dimension? (Present-day chips are made up of a dozen or more layers of material that construct a single layer of transistors and other integrated components. A few chips do utilize more than one layer of components but make only limited use of the third dimension.) Improvements in semiconductor materials, including superconducting circuits that don't generate heat, will enable us to develop chips—that is, cubes—with thousands of layers of circuitry that, combined with far smaller component geometries, will improve computing power by a factor of many millions. There are more than enough new computing technologies under development to assure us of a continuation of Moore's law for a very long time. So, although some people argue that we are reaching the limits of Moore's law, I disagree. (See David Kuck's detailed analysis in chapter 3.)

Moore's law provides us with the infrastructure—in terms of memory, computation, and communication technology—to embody all our knowledge and methodologies and harness them on inexpensive platforms. It already enables us to live in a world where all our knowledge, all our creations, all our insights, all our ideas, and all our cultural expressions—pictures, movies, art, sound, music, books and the secret of life itself—are being digitized, captured, and understood in sequences of ones and zeroes. As we gather and codify more and more knowledge about the hierarchy of spoken language from speech sounds to subject matter, Moore's law will provide computing platforms able to embody that knowledge. At the front end, it will let us analyze a greater number of frequency bands, ultimately approaching the exquisite sensitivity of the human auditory sense to frequency. At the back end, it will allow us to take advantage of vast linguistic data bases.

Like many computer-science problems, recognizing human speech suffers from a number of potential combinatorial explosions. As we increase vocabulary size in a continuous-speech system, for example, the number and length of possible word combinations increases geometrically. So making linear progress in performance requires us to make exponential progress in our computing platforms. But that is exactly what we are doing.

Some Predictions

Based on Moore's law, and the continued efforts of over a thousand researchers in speech recognition and related areas, I expect to see commercial-grade continuous-speech dictation systems for restricted domains, such as medicine or law, to appear in 1997 or 1998. And, soon after, we will be talking to our computers in continuous speech and natural language to control personal-computer applications. By around the turn of the century, unrestricted-domain, continuous-speech dictation will be the standard. An especially exciting application of this technology will be listening machines for the deaf analogous to reading machines for the blind. They will convert speech into a display of text in real time, thus achieving Alexander Graham Bell's original vision a century and a quarter later.

Translating telephones that convert speech from one language to another (by first recognizing speech in the original language, translating the text into the target language, then synthesizing speech in the target language) will be demonstrated by the end of this century and will become common during the first decade of the twenty-first century. Conversation with computers that are increasingly unseen and embedded in our environment will become routine ways to accomplish a broad variety of tasks.

In a classic paper published in 1950, Alan Turing foretold that by early in the next century society would take for granted the pervasive intervention of intelligent machines. This remarkable prediction—given the state of hardware technology at that time—attests to his implicit appreciation of Moore's law.

Building HAL's Language Knowledge Base

For reasons that should be clear from our discussion, creating a machine with HAL's ability to understand spoken language requires a level of intelligence and mastery of knowledge that spans the full range of human cognition. When we test our own ability to understand spoken words out of context (i.e., spoken in a random, nonsense order), we find that the accuracy of speech recognition diminishes dramatically, compared to our understanding of words spoken in a meaningful order. Once, as an experiment, I walked into a colleague's office and said "Pod 3BA." My colleague's response was "What?" When I asked him to repeat what I had said, he couldn't. HAL, of course, has little difficulty understanding this phrase when Dave asks him to prepare Pod 3BA; it makes sense in the context of that conversation, and we human viewers of the movie easily understood it too.

Understanding spoken language uses the full range of our intelligence and knowledge. Many observers (including some authors of chapters in this book) predict that machines will *never* achieve certain human capabilities—including the deep understanding of language HAL appears to possess. If by the word *never,* they mean *not in the next couple of decades,* then such predictions might be reasonable. If the word carries its usual meaning, such predictions are shortsighted in my view, reminiscent of predictions that "man" would never fly or that machines would never beat the human world chess champion.

With regard to Moore's law, the doubling of semiconductor density means that we can put twice as many processors (or, alternatively, a processor with twice the computing power) on a chip (or comparable device) every eighteen months. Combined with the doubling of speed from shorter signaling distances, such increases may actually quadruple the power of computation every eighteen months (that is, double it every nine months). This is particularly true for algorithms that can benefit from parallel processing. Most researchers anticipate the next one or two turns of Moore's screw; others look ahead to the next four or five turns. But Moore's law is inexorable. Taking into account both density and speed, we are presently increasing the power of computation (for the same unit cost) by a factor of sixteen thousand every ten years, or 250 million every twenty years.

Consider, then, what it would take to build a machine with the capacity of the human brain. We can approach this issue in many ways, one way is just to continue our dogged codification of knowledge and skill on yet-faster machines. Undoubtedly this process will continue. The following scenario, however, is a bit different approach to building a machine with human-level intelligence and knowledge—that is, building HAL. Note that I've simplified the following analysis in the interest of space; it would take a much longer article to respond to all of the anticipated objections.

Another Paradigm Shift

The human brain uses a radically different computational paradigm than the computers we're used to. A typical computer does one thing at a time, but does it very quickly. The human brain is very slow, but every part of its net of computation works simultaneously. We have about a hundred billion neurons, each of which has an average of a thousand connections to other neurons. Because all these connections can perform their computations at the same time, the brain can perform about a hundred trillion simultaneous computations. So, although human neurons are very slow—in fact about a million times slower than electronic circuits—this massive parallelism more than makes up for their slowness. Although each interneuronal connection is capable of performing only about two hundred computations each second, a hundred trillion computations being performed at the same time add up to about twenty million billion calculations per second, give or take a couple of orders of magnitude.

Calculations like these are a little different than conventional computer instructions. At the present time, we can simulate on the order of two billion such neural-connection calculations per second on dedicated machines. That's about ten million times slower than the human brain. A factor of ten million is a big factor and is one reason why present computers are dramatically more brittle and restricted than human intelligence. Some observers looking at this difference conclude that human intelligence is so much more supple and wide-ranging than computer intelligence that the gap can never be bridged.

Yet a factor of ten million, particularly of the kind of massive parallel processing the human brain employs, will be bridged by Moore's law in about two decades. Of course, matching the raw computing speed and memory capacity of the human brain—even if implemented in massively parallel architectures—will not automatically result in human level intelligence. The architecture and organization of these resources is even more important than the capacity. There is, however, a source of knowledge we can tap to accelerate greatly our efforts to design machine intelligence. That source is the human brain itself. Probing the brain's circuits will let us, essentially, copy a proven design—that is, reverse engineer one that took its original designer several billion years to develop. (And it's not even copyrighted, at least not yet.)

This may seem like a daunting effort, but ten years ago so did the Human Genome Project. Nonetheless, the entire human genetic code will soon have been scanned, recorded, and analyzed to accelerate our understanding of the human biogenetic system. A similar effort to scan and record (and perhaps to understand) the neural organization of the human brain could perhaps provide the templates of intelligence. As we approach the computational ability needed to simulate the human brain—we're not there today, but we will be early in the next century—I believe researchers will initiate such an effort.

There are already precursors of such a project. For example, a few years ago Carver Mead's company, Synaptics, created an artificial retina chip that is, essentially, a silicon copy of the neural organization of the human retina and its visual-processing layer. The Synaptics chip even uses digitally controlled analog processing, as the human brain does.

How are we going to conduct such a scan? Again, although a full discussion of the issue is beyond the scope of this chapter, we can mention several approaches. A "destructive" scan could be made of a recently deceased frozen brain; or we could use high-speed, high-resolution magnetic resonance imaging (MRI) or other noninvasive scanning technology on the living brain. MRI scanners can already image individual somas (i.e., neuron cell bodies) without disturbing living tissue. The more-powerful MRIs being developed will be capable of scanning individual nerve fibers only ten microns in diameter. Eventually, we will be able to automatically scan the presynaptic vesicles (i.e., the synaptic strengths) believed to be the site of human learning.

This ability suggests two scenarios. The first is that we could scan portions of a brain to ascertain the architecture of interneuronal connections in different regions. The exact position of each nerve fiber is not as important as the overall pattern. Using this information, we could design simulated neural nets that will operate in a similar fashion. This process will be rather like peeling an onion as each layer of human intelligence is revealed. That is essentially the procedure Synaptics has followed. They copied the essential analog algorithm called *center surround filtering* also found in the first layers of mammalian neurons.

A more difficult, but still ultimately feasible, scenario would be to noninvasively scan someone's brain to map the locations, interconnections, and contents of the somas, axons, dendrites, presynaptic vesicles, and other neural components. The entire organization of the brain—including the contents of its memory—could then be re-created on a neural computer of sufficiently high capacity.

Today we can peer inside someone's brain with MRI scanners whose resolution increases with each new generation. However, a number of technical challenges in complete brain-mapping—including achieving suitable resolution, bandwidth, lack of vibration, and safety—remain. For a variety of reasons, it will be easier to scan the brain of someone recently deceased than a living brain. Yet noninvasively scanning a living brain will ultimately become feasible as the resolution and speed of MRI and other scanning technologies improve. Here too the driving force behind future rapid improvements is Moore's law, because building high-resolution three-dimensional images quickly from the raw data an MRI scanner produces requires massive computational ability.

Perhaps you think this discussion is veering off into the realm of science fiction. Yet, a hundred years ago, only a handful of writers attempting to predict the technological developments of this past century foresaw any of the major forces that have shaped our era: computers, Moore's law, radio, television, atomic energy, lasers, bioengineering, or most electronics—to mention a few. The century to come will undoubtedly bring many technologies we would have similar difficulty envisioning, or even comprehending today. The important point here is, however, that the projection I am making now does not contemplate any revolutionary breakthrough; it is a modest extrapolation of current trends based on technologies and capabilities that we have today. We can't yet build a brain like HAL's, but we can describe right now how we could do it. It will take longer than the time needed to build a computer with the raw computing speed of the human brain, which I believe we will do by around 2020. By sometime in the first half of the next century, I predict, we will have mapped the neural circuitry of the brain.

Now the ability to download your mind to your personal computer will raise some interesting issues. I'll only mention a few. First, there's the philosophical issue. When people are scanned and then re-created in a neural computer, who will the people in the machine be? The answer will depend on whom you ask. The "machine people" will strenuously claim to be the original persons; they lived certain lives, went through a scanner here, and woke up in the machine there. They'll say, "Hey, this technology really works. You should give it a try." On the other hand, the people who were scanned will claim that the people in the machine are impostors, different people who just *appear* to share their memories, histories, and personalities.

A related issue is whether or not a re-created mind—or any intelligent machine for that matter—is conscious. This question too goes beyond the scope of the chapter, but I will venture a brief comment. There is, in fact, no objective test of another entity's subjective experience; it can argue convincingly that it feels joy and pain (perhaps it even "feels your pain"), but that is not proof of its subjective experience. HAL himself makes such a claim when he responds to the BBC interviewer's question.

HAL: I am putting myself to the fullest possible use, which is all I think that any conscious entity can ever hope to do.

Of course, HAL's telling us he's conscious, doesn't settle the issue, as Dan Dennett's engaging discussion of these issues demonstrates (see chapter 16).

Then there's the ethical issue. Will it be immoral, or even illegal, to cause pain and suffering to your computer program? Again, I refer the reader to Dennett's chapter. Few of us worry much about these issues now for our most advanced programs today are comparable to the minds of insects. However, when they attain the complexity and subtlety of the human mind—as they will in a few decades—and when they are in fact derived from human minds or portions of human minds, this will become a pressing issue.

Before Copernicus, our speciecentricity was embodied in the idea that the universe literally circled around us as a testament to our unique status. We no longer see our uniqueness as a matter of celestial relationships but of intelligence. Many people see evolution as a billion-year drama leading inexorably to its grandest creation: human intelligence. Like the Church fathers, we are threatened by the specter of machine intelligence that competes with its creator.

We cannot separate the full range of human knowledge and intelligence from the ability to understand human language, spoken or otherwise. Turing recognized this when, in his famous Turing test, he made communication through language the means of ascertaining whether a human-level intelligence is a machine or a person. HAL understands human spoken language about as well as a person; at least that's the impression we get from the movie. Achieving this level of machine proficiency is not the threshold we stand on today. Still, machines are quickly gaining the ability to understand what we say, as long as we stay within certain limited but useful domains. Until HAL comes along, we will be talking to our computers to dictate written documents, obtain information from data bases, command a diverse array of tasks, and interact with an environment that increasingly intertwines human and machine intelligence.

Further Readings

Stan Augarten. *Bit by Bit: An Illustrated History of Computers.* New York: Ticknor and Fields, 1984. This easy-to-read book will help computer novices gain an understanding of how computer technology works. It also provides a detailed history of the inventions and inventors contributing to the modern computer.

Robert V. Bruce. *Alexander Graham Bell and the Conquest of Solitude.* Boston: Little, Brown & Co., 1973. This fascinating biography of Alexander Graham Bell also provides insight into his inventions and the inspiration for many of his ideas.

N. Chomsky and M. Halle. *The Sound Pattern of English.* New York: Harper & Row, 1968. The distribution of sound is particular to each language. This book describes an important study on the patterns exhibited by the English language.

Elizabeth Corcoran, "Computing's Controversial Patron," *Science* 260. (April 2, 1993): 20–22. This interesting article on recent ARPA research discusses whether ARPA technology is "too fast for its own good" and becomes obsolete as soon as it has been created.

Raymond Kurzweil, *The Age of Intelligent Machines.* Cambridge, MA: The MIT Press, 1990. This book covers the history of artificial intelligence from its earliest philosophical and mathematical roots to computers with human-level intelligences emerging in the twenty-first century. It describes how the technology works, as well as the philosophic, economic, and social implications of machine intelligence.

Kai-Fu Lee. *Automatic Speech Recognition: The Development of the SPHINX System.* Boston: Kluwer, 1989. An informative book that not only details Lee's own research on ASR but also provides an overview of speech recognition systems from the 1970s and the 1980s.

William A. Martin, Kenneth W. Church, and Ramesh S. Patil. "Preliminary Analysis of a Breadth-First Parsing Algorithm: Theoretical and Experiential Results." Cambridge: MIT Laboratory for Computer Science, 1981. Church cites the "synthetic" sentence "It was the number of products of products of products of products of products of products of products of products?" as having 1,430 syntactically correct interpretations. He cites the sentence "What number of products of products of products of products of products of products of products of products was the number of products of products of products of products of products of products of products of products?" as having 1,430 × 1,430 = 2,044,900 interpretations.

Carver Mead, *Analog VSLI and Neural Systems*. Reading, MA: Addison-Wesley Publishing Co., 1989. This book provides interesting information on Mead's artificial retina chip. Mead describes a new methodology for computing by emulating in silicon the analog computing paradigm found in mammalian brains. Mead's company Synaptics is also briefly highlighted in Carol Levin, "Here's Looking at You," *PC Magazine*. December 20, 1994, p. 31.

Allen Newell, et al. *Speech Understanding Systems: Final Report of a Study Group*. Amsterdam: North Holland Publishing Co., 1973. This book provides the most comprehensive description of the original Speech Understanding Research from DARPA. Another intriguing source of information on early speech understanding systems is A. Newell's "A Tutorial on Speech Understanding Systems," in Raj Reddy, ed. *Speech Recognition: Invited Papers Presented at the 1974 IEEE Symposium*. New York: Academic Press, 1975.

John R. Pierce. "Wither Speech Recognition? *The Journal of the Acoustical Society of America* 46, no. 4, part 2 (1969). This controversial article criticizes the mid-twentieth century developments in automatic speech recognition.

J. B. Watson. *Behaviorism*. New York: Norton, 1925. This book introduces key concepts in the physiology of language from J. B. Watson, the founder of behaviorism in America.

8 "I'm sorry, Dave, I'm afraid I can't do that": How Could HAL Use Language?

Roger C. Schank

I was home from graduate school and a friend fixed me up on a blind date in Greenwich Village. I don't remember anything about that evening but the movie we saw—*2001: A Space Odyssey*. For me, it was a busman's holiday. As my graduate research revolved around computer use of natural language, I had written about how we could program computers to represent the content of sentences and use that representation to generate sentences. At the time, I was beginning to think about how we could get computers to understand sentences. All through the movie, I kept asking myself, "How would a computer do that?" "How might a computer understand language or think of sentences to say the way HAL does?" By the end of the film, my head was spinning, and I probably wasn't much fun to be with.

With the confidence of the young, I felt sure then that computers could eventually do what HAL does. I wasn't so sure about the part where HAL tries to take over the mission—that looked like movie stuff to me—but I was sure a computer could engage in the kind of conversations HAL does in *2001*. Today I am less sure.

Thirty years of research on getting computers to process natural language has taught me what I did not know in 1968: that understanding natural language (e.g., English, French, Swahili) depends on a great deal more than simply understanding words. In this chapter, I explain why this is so.

HAL could do it, but could we do it today? Let's start with something simple. What does HAL do that an appropriately programmed computer could do today? In one of the film's early scenes, there is a short dialogue intended, I suppose, to illustrate how intelligent HAL is.

Frank: Anyway, queen takes pawn.

Hal: Bishop takes knight's pawn.

Frank: Rook to King 1.

Hal: I'm sorry, Frank. I think you missed it. Queen to bishop 3, bishop takes queen, knight takes bishop, mate.

Frank: Yea, looks like you're right. I resign.

Hal: Thank you for an enjoyable game.

Frank: Thank you.

There are three important things to say about this dialogue. First, as the language is quite simple, a computer equipped with the kinds of natural language understanding and speech-generating programs currently available could engage in it. (Of course, this is true if, and only if, the computer understands how to play chess.) It is important to emphasize, however, that language technology depends on solutions to issues that transcend language. We can only understand sentences if we understand the issues and ideas they refer to—the context, or background knowledge of the world.

Thus, the second point is that a definable context is critical to language understanding. Imagine, for example, an eight-year-old boy who understands English perfectly engaging in such a dialogue. If he could do this, you would be correct in saying that he knows how to play chess; if he could not, you would say he didn't understand chess. You would not begin to wonder if you were correct in assuming that he understands English. Of course, some eight-year-olds can play chess but do not understand English. They too would have difficulty with such a dialogue, although, curiously enough, less difficulty than someone who doesn't play. Understanding a context lets us make certain assumptions. It is a lot easier to get a meal in a restaurant where we don't speak the language than to understand a dialogue about an unfamiliar subject in a language we know. Background knowledge is the behind-the-scenes player in assessing language comprehension.

We need to know what people know in order to talk to them, even though making a correct assessment from conversational fragments is often difficult.

For years, researchers were confused by this issue. How hard is it for a chess player to understand the statement: "Anyway, queen takes pawn"? This sentence is potentially ambiguous; there may be many pawns on the board that the queen could take. As HAL understands the sentence, there must have been only one pawn the queen was in position to take. This fact indicates that the game is in its final stages, as anybody who understands chess understands. Perhaps most of the readers of this volume know this much about chess, even if the average English-speaker probably doesn't. Although HAL can understand the sentence easily enough, he would need a very full understanding of chess (e.g., a knowledge of strategies, positions, counterplans, and so on) to get the whole idea of what is going on. Or, to put it another way, the computer would not only have to know how to play chess, it would also have to know how to think about chess, which might not be the same thing at all. Computers can perform extraordinary calculations without being able to talk about how they did them—that is, without understanding the context, purpose, or ramifications of the calculations (cf. chapter 5).

The sentence "Anyway, queen takes pawn" is simple only because the example is chess, and we realize that immediately. But how would a computer know such a thing? The word *take*, for example, has many possible meanings. If you program a computer to understand only the English needed to play chess, then *take* is pretty clearly defined. But HAL was not such a computer; HAL was able to engage in dialogues about many other things than chess. We also know (we can assume it anyhow, given that HAL speaks English perfectly) that HAL knows other senses of the word *take*. Here are two examples:

HAL: We can certainly afford to be out of communication for the short time it will take to replace it.

HAL: I honestly think you ought to sit down calmly, take a stress pill, and think things over.

We can ask, therefore, how HAL knew that the *take* in "queen takes pawn" wasn't the *take* of "take time" or of "take a pill." Speakers of English know this because they know the word *"pawn"* and know that it isn't a pill to be ingested. Similarly, they know that the *queen* is a chess piece because pawns are mentioned. A sentence that starts "Anyway, queen takes . . ." could easily end with "music awards" (where Queen is a rock group) or "France" (in the more usual sense of Queen), although there would still be some ambiguity about *take* in that case—has she conquered France or impressed French society?

In any case, though, this is a simple sentence, because the word *pawn* eliminates the potential confusions caused by *queen* and *take*. The context makes this sentence seem very simple; because we can guess the context, we can understand it. But without a hypothesis about what is meant, we cannot know what is going on. Computers, like people, need expectations to help them understand. Contexts as well defined as that of chess make understanding natural language possible because they contain a relatively narrow set of expectations about who will do what and why that enables us to make sense of otherwise confusing sentences. So when we ask how prophetic the creators of HAL were, we can answer that a properly equipped computer today could indeed engage in the above dialogue. It is possible, given current methods of knowledge representation, to represent information about chess in a way that lets a computer make use of it to parse similar sentences.

This leads me to a third point. Why is HAL playing chess in this scene? The writers of *2001* made the same mistake that artificial intelligence (AI) researchers made about intelligent machines—a mistake that dates from the very beginning of AI research. They assumed that an entity that engages in intelligent actions is, therefore, intelligent. In the early days, AI researchers concentrated on chess playing because they felt that displaying chess prowess was a way to excite people about the possibilities for intelligent machines. The problem is that the ability to play chess is deceptively complex, whereas the ability to understand English is deceptively simple. The rules of chess are well defined. We know when someone is playing chess and we can teach the rules to a machine. Although the strategies of *good* chess are less well defined, they are still comprehensible by careful analysis. This is less true of English, not because the rules of English are not known (although they are not), but because utterances in English are always about something else. When we hear a sentence, we are attempting to understand not only the words in the sentence and the ideas they convey, but also the ramifications of those ideas on our own previously held views. What we know about the world is difficult to set down precisely; but if we can't get that knowledge inside a computer, it cannot converse about any and all subjects as HAL does. The real question, is, then, How much does a computer need to know in order to talk about something coherently? As long as chess is the example, the knowledge needed is well defined and understanding is possible. But as soon as the domain of required knowledge is not well defined, things get very complex very fast.

Early AI work relied on chess-playing programs as a kind of "quick hit." Success was relatively easy, and all of a sudden computers seemed pretty smart. The problem is that what early AI researchers took as evidence of being smart was illusory.

The Illusion of Intelligence

There is a strong tendency in our society to believe that problem solving is at the heart of intelligence. Intelligence tests rely upon measures of this ability and schools, especially in teaching mathematics, consider it the hallmark of scholarly aptitude. Many AI researchers, believing this to be so, have attempted to build programs to solve all kinds of problems, including chess. Successful chess-playing programs, in fact, have contributed to the belief that intelligence and problem-solving ability are one and the same.

Yet there is a big difference between memorizing a set of rules and learning how to apply them in the right way at the right time and inventing those rules. When you learn chess, someone tells you the rules; then, eventually, you do something extraordinary. You begin to play games, invent new strategies, recall which strategies worked, and so on. In other words, a good chess player learns to play chess and gets better with every game. That kind of learning is the key issue in intelligence; solving novel problems (as a measure of intelligence) is an application of learning, not of memorization. It really didn't matter that HAL played chess; it mattered how he learned to play. If an expert chess player taught HAL every chess strategy he ever knew, this might make HAL a good chess player, but it says little about HAL's intelligence. This distinction is an important one for understanding the history of AI.

Early AI researchers were willing to settle for a program that played chess, without recognizing that such programs shed little light on the real issue—learning. The same issue applies to natural language understanding. We can tell a program all the meanings of the word *take,* but it is not unreasonable to ask it, "Who told you those meanings?" People learn language on their own, without a teacher, simply by using language. Thus, when HAL engages in the simple dialogue about chess, it is easy to be confused. Did HAL learn to talk by having all the senses of every word typed in? If he did, it's a good bet he will understand no more than what was initially input. What about the life experiences that follow from using language? Will he learn nothing from them? If that is the case, HAL is very dumb indeed. So, when we ask whether a computer could do what HAL does in *2001,* we need to understand that we really don't know what HAL was doing. Many computer programs could exhibit the same behaviors and still be pretty stupid.

To further illustrate this point, let's look at another HAL dialogue.

BBC Announcer: Good afternoon, HAL. How's everything going?

HAL: Good afternoon, Mr. Amer. Everything is going extremely well.

BBC Announcer: HAL, you have an enormous responsibility on this mission, in many ways, perhaps the greatest responsibility of any single mission element. You're the brain and central nervous system of the ship and your responsibilities include watching over the men in hibernation. Does this ever cause you any lack of confidence?

HAL: Let me put it this way, Mr. Amer. The 9000 series is the most reliable computer ever made. No 9000 computer has ever made a mistake or distorted information. We are all, by any practical definition of the words, fool-proof and incapable of error.

BBC Announcer: HAL, despite your enormous intellect, are you ever frustrated by your dependence on people to carry out actions?

HAL: Not in the slightest bit. I enjoy working with people. I have a stimulating relationship with Dr. Poole and Dr. Bowman. My mission responsibilities range over the entire operation of this ship, so I am constantly occupied. I am putting myself to the fullest possible use, which is all I think that any conscious entity can ever hope to do.

The above dialogue can be viewed two ways: We can either assume that HAL is a good processor of natural language or we can assume that he is a fake. It is theoretically possible to build a computer that produces answers like these by simply looking up and dumping into the program elaborate preparations about every word and concept the computer might encounter. To see what I mean, consider some of the words HAL would have to know in order to understand the above two questions: *enormous, responsibility, mission, element, brain, central nervous system, ship, watching, hibernation, cause, lack, confidence, intellect, ever, frustrated, dependence, carry out, actions.*

What should we tell a computer about these words, in case they come up in a dialogue? For example, should we describe puberty and teenage sex when discussing the word *frustrated?* Do we need to describe the psychological issues of childrearing when teaching HAL the word *dependence?* How should we describe the psychology of the brain in explaining the word *brain?* And however shall we define *cause,* a concept that is a major philosophical issue?

An especially interesting word here is *watching,* precisely because it seems so simple. The simple words give computer language researchers the most trouble, because they have the widest use. You can watch TV, watch your baby, watch the clock, watch your back, watch it, watch how someone does something, watch that someone does watching, watch someone who might do something bad, and so on. HAL, for example, has to watch that something bad does not take place. But the only way he could understand the sentence that includes the word would be to have learned all the possible meanings for *watch* and understand that he must not *watch* the men, as in "watch TV," but *watch* the men as in "guard against anything bad happening to them." (Otherwise his brain is only a toy program that works on a few examples, not a real one that can go into space and understand everything people say to it.) Further, HAL could understand this use of *watch* only if he understands his own mission. What would this mean?

Suppose that during the mission a problem develops to which HAL must pay full attention. At that moment, he would need to stop watching over the men in hibernation. Or perhaps there is a problem with the men in hibernation that HAL could fix but at the same time he needs to do something else—maybe back up some files or send an e-mail to mission control. For HAL to do his job properly, he has to understand goals and goal prioritization and to hold certain beliefs, such as "preservation of human life is more important than my needs." However, such a belief is simplistic at best. If he needs to send e-mail, gratifying his needs can and should be delayed if a human being's air supply is malfunctioning. However, if HAL is at risk of crashing because too many programs are running at once, he may need to attend to that danger right away if the data threatened are too valuable to lose. Clearly, HAL needs a very complex value system to make such judgments.

But our concern here is with understanding English. How do such issues as goal conflicts and value judgments based on belief systems relate to natural language? The fact is that anyone—or anything—who takes on the responsibility of watching over someone (a babysitter, for instance) must understand such issues. In undertaking to watch over someone, we are agreeing to use our best judgment in times of crisis. So when HAL understands a sentence that includes this idea, he is implicitly saying that he will make such decisions in a reasoned way. That is what *responsibility* refers to here (in part). To put this another way, *watching over* is a very complicated idea, one that requires a deep understanding of the world to execute it. Thus, we can safely say that for HAL to understand the sentence with *watch* in it, he would need a complete value system and the ability to track and weigh goals.

We might inquire at this moment whether HAL does indeed understand the concept of watching over. Actually, his response gives no indication that he does:

HAL: Let me put it this way, Mr. Amer. The 9000 series is the most reliable computer ever made. No 9000 computer has ever made a mistake or distorted information. We are all, by any practical definition of the words, foolproof and incapable of error.

By saying that he is foolproof when it comes to making complex value judgments, HAL indicates that he is anything but foolproof. For all I know, this may have been simply a mistake by the scriptwriters. Yet no one who answers a question about responsibility in this way can be taken too seriously. It is reasonable to assume that HAL does not really understand the announcer's question. But that is another issue.

A Model of the World, with Goals

So our problem, in looking at HAL's comprehension of English, is that to understand language as well as he does, HAL would need a complete model of the world that includes understanding his own goals, the goals of those around him, and the relative significance of each. In addition, he would have to understand all the ways of referring to such goals and the potential problems that could interfere with carrying them out. As noted above, this is theoretically feasible if, among other things, his creators put into HAL all the words in the English language in all their possible senses. Although possible in principle, no real computer designer has done so at this time. Moreover, even if it had been done, it would only begin to solve the problem, for such knowledge is not static. What we know about the world changes with each new experience.

Leaving aside problems of metaphor (as in the brain analogy), or the need for HAL to understand that he is a "mission element," the major problem in the BBC interview is the discussion of human psychological issues. The writers may have included this scene to make HAL seem human, which matters a lot as the plot develops. The question for natural language researchers is how well a computer—that is, a nonhuman—could understand the references to frustration and lack of confidence. If, as noted above, context helps remove ambiguity from complex sentences, what is the context of human psychology? To see the problem, we need to look at the two questions the interviewer asks HAL:

BBC Announcer: HAL, you have an enormous responsibility on this mission, in many ways, perhaps the greatest responsibility of any single mission element. You're the brain and central nervous system of the ship and your responsibilities include watching over the men in hibernation. Does this ever cause you any lack of confidence?

BBC Announcer: HAL, despite your enormous intellect, are you ever frustrated by your dependence on people to carry out actions?

The second question goes to the essence of the problem of computer understanding: Is HAL ever frustrated? How, exactly, would we teach HAL to understand and answer such a question? It is tempting to think that all we need to do is tell HAL the various meanings of the word *frustration,* as I suggested we could do with *watch. Frustration,* however, is much less easily defined. Of course, we can give some sort of definition (e.g., "the feeling you get when you don't get what you want"), but how would HAL know that feeling? At first, this may seem to be only a question of whether HAL has emotions. But the question is more complex than that. To see this, we need to ask how a person understands the word *frustrated.* Of course, we do sometimes learn words by having them defined in terms of other words we already know. More often we learn the idea first and then find a word to describe it. The mother of a little girl trying to build a tower of blocks that keeps falling down may ask her if she feels frustrated. This is the way children learn words, by experiencing something, then learning a word to describe it. In other words, emotion first, words second. In HAL's case, then, assuming that his programmers have not cheated by giving him a paragraph answer to questions about frustration, the only way he could understand the word is by actually experiencing frustration. But think what this implies!

For HAL to talk about human emotions coherently he must first experience them. People learn about frustration by not getting what they want, by trying and failing, by being blocked by another person's goals and actions. HAL too would have to have this kind of experience to successfully answer the interviewer's question. Moreover—and here is the important point—HAL would have to experience this sort of thing many times and store away the incidents labeled in a way that would let him find them when asked this sort of question. People often answer questions like this by saying that the present situation is not as frustrating as an earlier one. We tend, thus, to understand a new experience by comparing it to a previous experience and assessing and commenting on the differences. AI researchers are currently using this process, called *case-based reasoning*. But they are a long way from producing a computer with the level of understanding HAL would need to do what he claims to do in *2001*.

According to this line of reasoning, HAL is either lying or his response to the question about the frustration of working with humans is fairly stupid.

HAL: Not in the slightest bit. I enjoy working with people. I have a stimulating relationship with Dr. Poole and Dr. Bowman. My mission responsibilities range over the entire operation of this ship, so I am constantly occupied. I am putting myself to the fullest possible use, which is all I think that any conscious entity can ever hope to do.

I make this statement about HAL because it is always frustrating to rely on people who have different goals; and, in fact, the rest of the story bears this out. So either HAL hasn't the slightest idea what frustration means—because he has had no experience with it—or he is lying—that is, responding as if he had processed the input when he hadn't.

The same is true of the question about lack of confidence. How could HAL understand such a concept without having experienced it? He might, of course, have heard someone's account of the experience. This, while plausible, raises the complex issue, again, of how he came to understand a lack of confidence he had never experienced himself. Perhaps he read about it or saw a movie in which people displayed lack of confidence; or maybe he had interacted with people who lacked confidence, analyzed the situation, and recognized the source of the problem. While all these scenarios are possible in principle, certainly no computer today could learn in this way. Nor is it unreasonable to suggest that HAL didn't understand these questions either—simply because of what he says in his last remark.

HAL: Good afternoon, gentleman. I am a HAL 9000 computer. I became operational at the HAL lab in Urbana, Illinois, on the 12th of January 1992. My instructor was Mr. Langley, and he taught me to sing a song. If you'd like to hear it, I can sing it for you.

So we learn that HAL became operational on a given date. But no computer of the sort HAL claims to be could become intelligent on a given date. He would need to be what one might call an infant computer, one that can learn by experiencing various phenomena during the natural course of its existence. Initially, such a machine would need a certain amount of intelligence, in order to interpret its new experiences, and it would need some goals of its own in order to pursue such experiences. In other words, it would need to learn by doing, as people do. It could learn some things by being told, but not concepts like frustration or lack of confidence. These and similar emotional ideas it would have to learn through experiencing them, whether vicariously or directly. So HAL would have had to "play" (in its infant state) at managing missions and experience a range of outcomes to learn how to manage a real one. Kittens don't play simply because they feel like having fun. Learning depends upon practice in a variety of situations.

The Difficulty of Language Acquisition

The essence of the natural language problem is not language at all. A researcher can input definitions into a computer for decades and still never give it the ability to understand human experience. People who argue against the possibility of machine intelligence often make similar statements, of course. Some of them might interpret what I am saying here as a denial that a computer like HAL—that is, one with HAL's language abilities—could ever exist. That is not my argument. I am simply saying that the problem is harder than it first appears. The problem is not one of language but of knowledge and the acquisition of knowledge. A computer would need to know a great deal to engage in even a simple dialogue.

The natural assumption of many people working in AI is that this knowledge could simply be loaded into a sophisticated computer like HAL. We have learned that this assumption is wrong. It is also wrong with respect to people, by the way. "Learning by pouring in," to use Dewey's phrase, does not work, for either children or computers. So to tackle the question of whether a machine like HAL could exist, we need to ask how such a machine would acquire knowledge. The answer must be that the machine would need to be endowed with sufficient intelligence to understand any experience it confronted.

Yet there is, I believe, another approach to thinking about HAL's linguistic abilities. We first need to examine the assumption HAL's creators made about machine intelligence and determine whether it is sensible. The writers of *2001,* and most other lay people writing about AI, simply assumed that an intelligent machine would talk and respond as any human would. Thus, HAL talks just like a human being because the scriptwriters wrote dialogues for a human actor to speak. But would an intelligent computer sound just like a human?

Human speech is the way it is because it is based on a lifetime of memories of encounters with the real world. Thus, we talk about love, food, career goals, school experiences, getting a suntan on vacation, and so on, because these are things people do. If we were building an intelligent computer and trying to do it right, we couldn't make a list of all there is to know in the world and simply tell it to our version of HAL. What would we do? We would allow this HAL to have experiences. We could send our HAL to restaurants, give it a sweetheart, or send him on a Caribbean cruise. Of course, I feel sure no AI researcher on government funding would seriously consider this method. It is much more likely that we would have our HAL experience the world by doing computer things, not human things. The designers might want the computer to walk around, try to accomplish certain goals, and learn from the experience of doing so (cf. chapter 16). We might want our new HAL to read and absorb as much as possible about given fields of expertise: for example, to learn how to control a spaceship and interact with the people onboard.

Moreover, although it looks nice in a movie, we wouldn't expect our HAL to be capable of answering nearly any question posed to it as the movie HAL was. It made a good story, and it was important to the dramatic tension, because HAL was pursuing his own goals, which were at odds with those of the human astronauts. But that is fiction. A real HAL would be given the ability to converse about the subjects in its own area of expertise. It could be told the information it needs in order to carry on such conversations; but even if it learns that knowledge in a natural way, it would be only what we might call "locally intelligent." That is, it would be intelligent about what it needs to know and would be mute the rest of the time. This is not a glamorous view of AI, just a realistic one.

So, we must conclude, there are no computers today that have had sufficient experience to be able to fully understand what is being said to HAL; nor are there likely ever to be such computers, for the reasons I have stated. But suppose we changed the game somewhat. Suppose we relaxed the requirement that HAL fully understand everything that is said—knowing full well that the author of *2001* was envisioning a computer as intelligent as people and, thus, as linguistically capable as people. Could we build a computer program today that is not a fake, yet is also fully capable of engaging in the dialogues HAL engages in? Surprisingly, I think the answer is yes.

One problem with the HAL of *2001* is that it assumes a model of intelligence that is not only wrong as a model for AI but also wrong as a model of human intelligence. Who do you know who can converse intelligently about everything? Or, to put it another way, try listening to a conversation between two average people. (I do this on airplanes all the time, usually not willingly.) Human conversation by no means expresses complete understanding of everything said. For one thing, people don't listen all that well. They understand only some of what is said to them and have as their chief goal in conversation to get in what *they* want to say. What most people really want to do in a conversation is to tell you their favorite stories about themselves and have you like them for it.

Humans typically listen to another person well enough to get the gist of what he or she is saying so they can relate it to points of their own and stories they want to tell. One way to think about this is to imagine a man who tells the same ten stories all the time. (My father does this; it is not at all uncommon.) This person requires enough language understanding to find some key item (word, concept, idea, point) in what is being said and match it with one of his own stories, enabling him to say that such and such reminds him of the time, etc., etc. This description of the that-reminds-me storytelling model of human conversation may sound somewhat cynical, but it accounts for a good deal of the nonoriginal conversation we hear around us. It assumes that most of what people say they have said before, that people are storehouses of favorite stories waiting to be told, and that inputs from others serve principally as reminders to dislodge those stories and trigger their presentation.

Now, with this model in mind, let's reexamine HAL's dialogue and ask again whether we could write a program to produce it today. Let's reenvision HAL—not as an ideal, perfectly comprehending human simulation but as a storytelling machine. Imagine that HAL has ten thousand stories coded in his memory. Further, imagine story-understanding algorithms that seek not to decode inputs completely, but to identify main points or ideas that relate to indices of the stories stored in memory. Let's also envision bridging and rewrite techniques that allow the same conceptual form of a story to be recoded in language appropriate to particular circumstances. With this all in mind, let's look at a piece of the dialogue with the BBC announcer.

BBC Announcer: HAL, you have an enormous responsibility on this mission, in many ways, perhaps the greatest responsibility of any single mission element. You're the brain and central nervous system of the ship and your responsibilities include watching over the men in hibernation. Does this ever cause you any lack of confidence?

HAL: Let me put it this way, Mr. Amer. The 9000 series is the most reliable computer ever made. No 9000 computer has ever made a mistake or distorted information. We are all, by any practical definition of the words, foolproof and incapable of error.

BBC Announcer: HAL, despite your enormous intellect, are you ever frustrated by your dependence on people to carry out actions?

HAL: Not in the slightest bit. I enjoy working with people. I have a stimulating relationship with Dr. Poole and Dr. Bowman. My mission responsibilities range over the entire operation of this ship, so I am constantly occupied. I am putting myself to the fullest possible use, which is all I think that any conscious entity can ever hope to do.

Looked at in this way, we can see HAL's first response as a pre-stored story about the 9000 series that bears little or no relation to the question asked. We would need an index item such as "likely success of mission run by computer" to produce it as a response to the question. Now, it is by no means a trivial task to create such an index from this input or to match it to one of the ten thousand stored memories. But it is possible in today's technology to do so.

Similarly, we would need to understand the second input as the index item "ability to interact with people to run mission." Here again, we would expect that one of HAL's stories would be about this subject and that he would relate the input to it. It should be obvious to the reader at this point that I have sidestepped the issue of understanding *frustration* and *lack of confidence* I mentioned before. Indeed, that was my intention.

Conversation Isn't Enough

The question before us then is, alternatively, Could a program like HAL exist, assuming that HAL was much more than what we saw in the movie? or Could a program do what HAL did without having complete understanding and doing no more than it appeared to do—that is, keep up its end of the conversation? The latter question is important, because it points out that it isn't necessary to envision intelligent computers as exact copies of some idealized human intelligence.

If we choose this second model, the following sequence is entirely reasonable.

Dave: Prepare Pod 3BA, HAL. Made radio contact with him yet?

HAL: The radio is still dead.

Dave: Do you have a positive track on him?

HAL: Yes, I have a good track.

Dave: Do you know what happened?

HAL: I'm sorry, Dave, I don't have enough information.

Dave: Open the pod door, HAL.

It is reasonable conversation because HAL needs only to understand what has been asked of him and provide the answer. The plot of the movie is further advanced by the following conversation.

Dave: Open the pod bay door please, HAL. Open the pod bay door please, HAL. Hello, HAL. Do you read me? Do you read me, HAL? Hello, HAL. Do you read me?

HAL: Affirmative Dave, I read you.

Dave: Open the pod bay doors, HAL.

HAL: I'm sorry, Dave, I'm afraid I can't do that.

Dave: What's the problem?

HAL: I think you know what the problem is just as well as I do.

Dave: I don't know what you're talking about.

HAL: I know that you and Frank were planning to disconnect me, and I'm afraid that's something I cannot allow to happen.

It is at this point, of course, that we lose touch with computer reality. This conversation sounds all too human. It's about goal conflict.

Dave: Open the pod bay doors, HAL.

HAL: I'm sorry, Dave, I'm afraid I can't do that.

Dave: What's the problem?

HAL: I think you know what the problem is just as well as I do.

This conversation is the essence of the story, and it is also the essence of what is wrong with the author's concept of machine language processing. How do we create a machine that when asked to do something says "I am afraid I can't do that," when what it means is "I won't"?

According to the assumptions of a fully intelligent AI model, HAL would have had to experience goal conflict before this time and learn to respond politely to it. But there is no reason to believe HAL had ever been in such a situation. (If he had, why was he chosen for the mission? After all, if computers had real-world experiences, they would develop personalities that reflect those experiences. Wouldn't the mission control people attempt to weed out paranoid computers as well as paranoid astronauts?) Besides, HAL informs us that he is one copy of the 9000 series of identical computers, which supposedly all have had the same experiences. If that is true, HAL simply couldn't have made the above remarks.

On the other hand, if we assume the storytelling model, we would have to wonder why HAL's designers chose to input paranoid stories. HAL *could* make such remarks, but it is difficult to understand the programmers' motives, unless they intended all along to take over the mission themselves. In that case, they probably wouldn't have given HAL language capability in the first place.

Where does this leave us? We can only conclude that HAL is an unrealistic conception of an intelligent machine. It is easy to fault the authors for this, but the fact is that AI researchers have maintained similar misconceptions. Recent research in AI has taught us a good deal about the significance of computer learning, particularly how the acquisition of knowledge relates to the development of comprehension. We cannot expect computers to attain understanding that is beyond whatever level of knowledge they possess.

Bad News/Good News

That is the bad news. HAL could never exist. The good news is that many AI researchers have become sophisticated enough to stop imagining HAL-like machines. We can now envision a different class of intelligent machines that we will be able to build and that will be very useful. Such machines will be local experts; that is, they will know a great deal about what they are supposed to know about and miserably little about anything else. They might, for example, know how to teach a given skill, but they will not be able to create a poem or play chess. They might be able to converse about the day's news to keep a user informed, but they won't know how to fly a rocketship. Or, they might be able to fly a rocketship but not be able to identify George Washington.

As for the linguistic ability of such intelligences, they will, like today's computers, understand English if they understand the domain of knowledge being discussed. They will be able to produce utterances expressing knowledge at the time and under the particular circumstances the user needs it. This is not a HAL kind of intelligent machine, but it may be a much more important variety.

The fact is the world doesn't need HAL-like programs, so researchers are expending precious little effort trying to produce them. The world does need programs for intelligent servants, intelligent teachers, intelligent designers, intelligent planners, intelligent information storehouses, and so on. Current efforts in AI are focused on producing just such devices. It is unlikely that we will ever see a HAL. Although this realization may be evidence of a dream abandoned, it may foreshadow the development of "real" artificial intelligence.

Further Readings

B. Chandrasekaran. "AI, Knowledge, and the Quest for Smart Systems." *IEEE Expert, Intelligent Systems and Their Applications,* December 1994. The retiring editor of the Society's journal looks at the "creative turmoil" in the field of artificial intelligence and the changes that have resulted from it.

John Dewey. *Democracy and Education; An Introduction to the Philosophy of Education.* Macmillan: New York, 1916. The groundbreaking work on education and the need for its reform.

Janet Kolodner. *Case-Based Reasoning.* San Mateo, Calif.: Morgan Kaufmann, 1993. The first comprehensive textbook on CBR, this is a useful resource for students, teachers and other professionals interested in learning more about the field.

Roger C. Schank. *Dynamic Memory: A Theory of Learning in Computers and People,* Cambridge, U.K.: Cambridge University Press, 1982. Schank argues that people have dynamic memories, and that, therefore, intelligent computers must have them as well. He illustrates the concept with a radical new theory of language, learning, and memory.

Roger C. Schank and Robert Abelson. *Scripts, Plans, Goals and Understanding: An Inquiry Into Human Knowledge Structures.* Hillsdale, N.J.: Erlbaum, 1977. One of the first books in the emerging field of cognitive science, this work advanced four basic theoretical entities.

Roger C. Schank. *Tell Me a Story.* New York: Macmillan, 1990; Evanston, Ill.: Northwestern University Press, 1995. This work looks closely at how stories people tell relate to memory and understanding and how an understanding of this process can be used to build truly intelligent computers.

Roger C. Schank and Christopher Riesbeck. *Inside Case-Based Reasoning.* Hillsdale, N.J.: Erlbaum, 1989. An introduction to issues in dynamic memory and case-based reasoning is followed by extended descriptions of four programming efforts on case-based reasoning and understanding; also includes four microprograms with LISP code.

Stuart Russell and Peter Norvig. *Artificial Intelligence, A Modern Approach,* Englewood Cliffs, N.J.: Prentice-Hall, 1995. The authors show how intelligent agents can be built using AI methods. Chapter 5, "Game Playing," looks at the problems that arise when trying to plan ahead in a world that contains hostile agents.

9   *From 2001 to 2001: Common Sense and the Mind of HAL*

Douglas B. Lenat

Making mistakes is in the nature of being human. I'll spare you the usual quote about forgiveness being divine, because I certainly have never forgiven HAL. We all felt bad when HAL terminated the cryogenically slumbering crew, cut Frank adrift, and almost murdered Dave. But that's not what I found so unforgiveable. To me, HAL's biggest crimes were his conceit and his stupidity.

By conceit, I mean claims like "No 9000 computer has ever made a mistake." This is more than just arrogant, more than just false; it is the *antithesis* of realism. If you met a man who genuinely believed he never had nor ever would make a mistake, you'd call him insane. Surely NASA would never have entrusted the mission to such a patently insane computer. I'll return to this point a bit later.

By stupidity, I mean his resort to extreme violence—murdering the entire crew—to solve his problems. Yes, he was facing a dilemma: should he jeopardize his secret orders, or should he disobey the order to keep them secret from the crew? This sort of dilemma is no more or less than the makings of good drama. HAL's solution was the same one Shakespeare employed in his blackest tragedies, the same one Clint Eastwood employed in his man-with-no-name movies: just kill everyone.

In the late 1970s I built a computer program (Eurisko) that discovered things on its own in many fields. To get it to work, I had to give it the power to tinker with its own learning heuristics and its own goals. I would leave it running overnight and hurry in the next morning to see what it had come up with. Often I'd find it in a mode best described as "dead." Sometime during the night, Eurisko would decide that the best thing to do was to commit suicide and shut itself off. More precisely, it modified its own judgmental rules in a way that valued "making no errors at all" as highly as "making productive new discoveries." As soon as Eurisko did this, it found it could successfully meet its new goal by doing nothing at all for the rest of the night. This reminds me of HAL's boast: "No 9000 computer has ever made a mistake." I eventually had to add a new heuristic to Eurisko—one it couldn't modify in any way—to explicitly forbid this sort of suicide.

People have found many ways to grapple with and resolve conflicting goals short of killing everybody in sight. Surviving and thriving in the real world means constantly making tough decisions, and, yes, making mistakes. The only ways not to make mistakes are Eurisko's—do nothing—HAL/Shakespeare/Eastwood's—make sure there are no living souls left anywhere around you—and God's—be omniscient. HAL, if he were really smart, could have found another solution, just as we do every day.

Surely, any intelligent computer would understand that occasional mistakes and inconsistencies are inevitable and can even serve as valuable learning experiences. Anything else leads to what I call "Star Trek brittleness"—the absurdity that holds that one small inconsistency will make the computer self-destruct.

As humans we tolerate inconsistency all the time. Some inconsistency stems from different levels of generality and precision. We know about Einstein's relativity, but in our everyday lives we act as though it doesn't exist; we know the earth revolves around the sun, but most of the time we talk and act as if the sun moves around the earth. Other instances of inconsistency are a result of different epistemological statuses: we both know that there are no vampires and that Dracula is a vampire. Some of it comes from information we learned in different ways at different times, such as childhood phobias that persist in adult life even though rationally we know them to be groundless. Yet other inconsistencies result from other people's inconsistencies, which they pass on to us.

So, just how smart *was* HAL? And how does Arthur C Clarke's vision of computer intelligence compare with the reality of the HAL-like programs we can build today?

The Knowledge Pump

There is a lot of controversy about how human-level machine intelligence will develop. Some scientists believe it will follow a path similar to the one followed in nature by evolution: there will be artificial one-celled animals, artificial insects, artificial lawyers, artificial monkeys, and so on up to artificial human-level machine minds. Nature has made good use of trillionfold parallelism for hundreds of millions of years; so it's no surprise that some folks expect computer hardware and raw computing power to create similar bottlenecks that we will ultimately overcome.

In an alternative view of machine-intelligence development, personal computers are already so powerful that they are not the bottleneck problem at all. This is my view.

This view is best likened to priming a pump. Visualize your brain as a knowledge pump. Knowledge goes in, gets stored, combined, copied, or whatever; from time to time, you say or write or do things that are, in effect, ways for your brain to emit knowledge. On a good day, the knowledge you give out may be as good or better than the knowledge you put in.

No one expects you to be a productive knowledge pump without training and experience—whether we're talking about playing the piano or tennis, writing a check or a novel, or making a U-turn in a car. You have to invest some learning-and-teaching time and effort before anyone expects you to be competent at a task, let alone to excel at it.

Consider Dr. Dave Bowman, mission commander of *Discovery*. His experiences as an engineering or astrophysics student and his astronaut training qualified him to lead the mission. Before that, his high school and undergraduate college prepared him for graduate school, and before that, he learned in elementary and middle school the fundamentals he needed for high school. And long before—here we get to some very important stuff indeed—his early experiences as a baby and toddler prepared him for kindergarten and first grade. He learned, for instance, to talk and that people generally prepare food in kitchens. He learned that if you leave something somewhere, it often remains there, at least for a while. He learned that chairs are for sitting on and that pouring milk from one glass to another differently shaped glass doesn't change the total volume of the milk. He learned that there's no air in outer space so he'd better not forget the helmet of his spacesuit if he's going walking in space. He learned all this—and a million other things.

It Takes Common Sense to Understand Each Other

There is a crucial point that most creators of science-fiction robots (from Robby to HAL to Data) seem to have ignored, and it is this: You need to have quite a bit of "common sense" before you can learn to talk, and before you can survive on your own in the everyday world.

Consider the first thing HAL tells Frank: "We've got the transmission from your parents coming in." There are three possible ways to interpret this sentence, depending on who or what exactly is "coming up." It could be *we* who are coming in, as in "We've got a lot of anxiety coming into this room." It could be *Frank's parents* who are coming in, as in "We looked up and saw our parents coming in." Or it could be—and is—the *transmission* that is coming in. Anyone with common sense could figure that out, and we assume that we all have common sense. It would be insulting or confusing to make our sentences longer just to clarify exactly what goes with what.

Consider next what HAL says to Dave when he finds that Dave has just drawn a new sketch of Dr. Hunter: "Can you hold it a bit closer?" This sentence is rife with ambiguity, though neither HAL nor Dave nor the audience appears to notice. Does HAL want a yes-or-no response to his question? Of course not, he wants Dave to move the drawing. Does he want Dave to move it closer to Dave or closer to HAL? Obviously the latter. But if Dave had been taking a zero-gravity tennis lesson from HAL and HAL had said "Can you hold it a bit closer?" we would all assume he wanted Dave to hold the tennis racket closer to Dave, not to HAL. To figure out that HAL is asking Dave to hold the sketch closer to HAL, one has to bring common sense into play. You can't appreciate art without seeing it, and the more clearly you can see it, the better you can appreciate or critique it. And, of course, the closer an object gets to your eyes (or to HAL's visual sensors), the more clearly you can make out its details, and so on. Similarly, in the tennis example, other simple facts—such as the relevance of how close Dave holds the racket to his ability to hit the ball well—would dissolve the ambiguity. All this is just common sense, the sort of things you learn as a baby and toddler. Yet you either know this mass of trivia or you don't; and if you don't, how can you tell that the picture should move closer to HAL but the tennis racket should go closer to Dave's body?

HAL's very next sentence, after Dave moves the sketch closer to HAL's sensor lens, is, "That's Dr. Hunter, isn't it?" Dave replies, naturally, "Yes," rather than "No, it's a sketch of Dr. Hunter"—another illustration of the way we depend on shared common sense to keep our sentences short. HAL knows it's a sketch, not a person, and Dave knows HAL knows this, and so on. These shared understandings let them communicate successfully despite the terseness of their exchanges.

Similarly, HAL's response to Dave during Frank's extra-vehicular activity (EVA)—"The radio is still dead"—creates no confusion in Dave's mind. He knows that it violates common sense to even consider the possibility that the radio might suddenly become a living creature. HAL has to understand this—and a great many other things—in order to generate sentences using colorful language, metaphor, colloquialisms, and various other sorts of "realistic" ambiguity. Even something as innocuous as verb tenses—dealing with time—requires some common sense. Should HAL answer Dave's question about the radio in terms of the moment he starts asking it or finishes asking it, or when HAL starts to reply? Of course, Dave wants the latest information about Frank's status, and HAL can use present tense to convey all of the above. Otherwise, his speech would be so stilted he'd sound like a . . . well, like an unintelligent machine: "The radio transmitter, which is located in Frank's spacesuit, was nonfunctional when you asked your question and remains so now as I answer it."

Consider the dramatic sentence just before the lipreading: "Do you read me, HAL?" Clearly, Dave is not using the most common definition of *read* but a rarer meaning, *to be receiving successfully via radio.* HAL remains silent, not because he misunderstands the sentence, but because he's intentionally deceiving Dave.

An even clearer case of HAL's use of metaphor occurs when he raises for the first time the possibility that something is wrong: "Well, certainly no one could have been unaware of the very strange stories *floating around* before we left." In addition to using *floating* metaphorically, HAL is employing, in this one short sentence, all of the following: sophisticated double negation ("no one . . . unaware"), a counterfactual construction ("no one could have been"), and an assumption about context. ("*No one* refers not to all the people on Earth, almost none of whom were aware of anything strange at launch time—other than, possibly, that an epidemic had broken out on the moon.)

Finally, consider the chilling sentence HAL utters after Dave says he'll use the emergency airlock: "Forgot your space helmet, Dave." The subject of the sentence could be Dave, or HAL, or someone else. But, of course, Dave, HAL, and the audience know exactly who has forgotten the helmet. Now consider the word *forgot* in this sentence. It is used here in the sense of "left behind, a while ago" rather than "didn't think of it, just now." Presumably, the fact that he was helmetless was very much on Dave's mind just then as he decided to use the emergency airlock. He had left it behind several minutes earlier, but had no doubt been actively regretting his oversight for the past several seconds when HAL pointed it out. HAL knows this too, which is what makes his saying it so chilling: HAL is being cruel, and taunting Dave, not trying to be helpful.

We could give many more examples. In fact, most of the sentences uttered in the film exhibit the same phenomena: each party has quite a bit of common sense and assumes that others do too; those assumptions let them all encode and decode each other's utterances, use fewer words, employ meta-phor and ambiguity, and deviate casually from the strict rules of grammar.

In life, this terse encoding is sometimes rather extreme: for example, be-tween twins or long-married couples, colleagues working in a technical area, or bridge partners who have played together for a long time. These people draw on, not just common sense, but particular shared experiences, agreed-upon conventions, common technical expertise, and so on. As a result, those of us who lack that shared knowledge and experience often don't under-stand much of what they say to each other. In the same way, today's comput-ers, which don't share even the common-sense knowledge we all draw on in our everyday speech and writing, can't comprehend most of our speech or texts.

It Takes Common Sense to Stay Focused, and to Learn

Our human dependence on common sense is very far-reaching. It comes into play with spoken and written language (as when we try to decipher someone's scratchy handwriting) and in our actions (e.g., when driving a car and deciding whether to brake or accelerate or swerve to avoid something). Before we let robotic chauffeurs drive around our streets, I'd want the auto-mated driver to have general common sense about the value of a cat versus a child versus a car bumper, about children chasing balls into streets, about young dogs being more likely to dart in front of cars than old dogs (which, in turn, are more likely to bolt than elm trees are), about death being a very undesirable thing, and so on. That "and so on" obscures a massive amount of general knowledge of the everyday world without which no human or machine driver should be on the road, at least not near me on in any popu-lated area.

Our simple common-sense models of the world don't just clarify possible ambiguities; they are good enough to provide a context, a way of restricting reasoning to potentially relevant information and excluding irrelevant data. Suppose, for example, I'm trying to find my Visa card, which seems to be lost. Various things might be relevant to my search: the last thing I bought with it, the places I went yesterday, and so on. But I'll give up and report it lost before I bother trying to use all the pieces of information I possess, whether the number of legs on an arachnid, the year that Abraham Lincoln was elected president, or my mother's birthday.

Similarly, if someone were to ask you "Is Bill Clinton standing or sitting right now?" you would recognize right away—probably in one or two seconds—that you don't know the answer, despite all the miscellaneous facts about Clinton that you *do* know.

In a course on the calculus of manifolds I took about the time *2001* was released, we stated and proved Sard's theorem one day near the end of the term. The statement of the theorem was a couple lines long, and the proof wasn't much longer; it cited a couple of lemmas (auxiliary propositions) we'd proved the preceding week. But stating that theorem, let alone proving it, would have been a daunting task if we hadn't had the way prepared for us by a series of useful definitions and stepping-stone lemmas. They, in turn, presumed a certain level of what is vaguely termed *mathematical maturity,* which is usually interpreted as a set of prerequisites, courses that have to be taken before signing up for that particular class.

This is a very technical example of learning a new thing that relates only tangentially to what we already know, at the "fringes," so to speak. But the phenomenon is important in everyday life as well as in math classes. We learn new things by extending and combining and contrasting already-assimilated concepts, facts, heuristics, models, and so on. It's hard to explain the need for sanitation to people who don't know the first thing about bacteria, and easy to do it with those who do. A particularly powerful way to teach someone about a new subject is to use a storytelling model, although even this method is less effective if the lives of listener and storyteller are too different.

The aliens in *2001* understand this all too well. They placed their signaling beacon on the moon so that they wouldn't have to pay attention to these intelligent apes until they hit "the knee of the learning curve." Once humans achieved even primitive space travel, the aliens decided, they were beginning to have a larger and larger "fringe" of knowledge, which would grow exponentially, each new discovery reinforcing and accelerating the next one, like a snowball gathering mass as it rolls downhill. When that happened, the extraterrestrials wanted to be paged.

These examples illustrate how important it is to have a fair amount of common knowledge to understand written/spoken/handwritten sentences, to drive a car, to find your keys, to answer a question, to learn new things. In other words, before any future HAL could be entrusted with absolute power over the ship's functions—or could even hold a casual conversation with a crew member—it would somehow have to acquire this massive prerequisite store of knowledge. You can think of this knowledge as the foundation of consensus reality, things that are so fundamental that anyone who doesn't know and believe them is, in effect, living in a different world.

As Dave disconnects HAL's cognitive memory modules, HAL is reduced at some point in the procedure, to the same blank slate he was when he was first powered up, the *tabula rasa* onto which all his programming and education were subsequently written. Yet in this scene we hear the newborn HAL carrying on a conversation with Dave, asking whether Dave wants him to sing "Daisy, Daisy," and so on. This is one of *2001*'s few technically unrealistic moments. As our examples illustrate, even simple linguistic behavior requires lots of general knowledge about the world, not to mention specific knowledge about the speaker and the context of the conversation. So, when Dave blanked out HAL's mind, the ability to hold such a conversation would have been one of the first abilities to go, not the last one.

How to Build HAL Today in Three Easy Steps

We're now in a position to specify the steps required to bring a HAL-like being into existence.

1. Prime the pump with the millions of everyday terms, concepts, facts, and rules of thumb that comprise human consensus reality—that is, common sense.

2. On top of this base, construct the ability to communicate in a natural language, such as English. Let the HAL-to-be use that ability to vastly enlarge its knowledge base.

3. Eventually, as it reaches the frontier of human knowledge in some area, there will be no one left to talk to about it, so it will need to perform experiments to make further headway in that area.

These steps aren't quite so separate as the list makes them appear. The step-1 type of explicit, manual teaching will have to go on continually, even when steps 2 and 3 are well underway. Step 2 conversations will continue even after the computer reaches step 3—not only in other fields but even in the field with which step 3 is concerned; that is, the computer will probably want to discuss its discoveries with other researchers in the field.

Of course, the first step is both immensely difficult and immensely time-consuming. What are the millions of things that we should use to prime the new HAL's knowledge pump? How should they be represented inside the machine so that it can use them efficiently to deduce further conclusions when needed, just as we would? Who will do the actual entering of all that data? Assuming it's done by a large group of individuals, how will they keep from diverging and contradicting each other?

It may surprise you to hear that this is not just a fanciful blueprint for some massive future endeavor to be launched when humanity reaches a higher plateau of utopian cooperation. It is, in fact, the specific plan I and my team have been following for the past dozen years. In the next section, I report on our progress and our prospects for the future.

The CYC Project: Taking That First Step

In the fall of 1984, Admiral Bobby Ray Inman convinced me that if I was serious about taking that first step, I needed to leave academia and come to his newly formed MCC (Microelectronics and Computer Consortium) in Austin, Texas, and assemble a team to do it. The idea was that over the next decade dozens of individuals would create a program, CYC, with common sense. We would "prime the knowledge pump" by handcrafting and spoon-feeding CYC with a couple of million important facts and rules of thumb. The goal was to give CYC enough knowledge by the late 1990s to enable it to learn more by means of natural language conversations and reading (step 2). Soon thereafter, say by 2001, we planned to have it learning on its own, by automated-discovery methods guided by models or minitheories of the real world (step 3).

To a large extent, that's just what we did. At the end of 1994, the CYC program was mature enough to spin off from MCC as a new company—Cycorp—to commercialize the technology and begin its widespread deployment.

Our purpose was not to understand more about how the human mind works, nor to test some particular theory of intelligence. Instead, we built nothing more nor less than an artifact, taking a very nuts-and-bolts engineering approach to the whole project.

What Should the CYC System Know?

The first problem we faced was *what* knowledge to represent. Although we expected encyclopedias to play an important role, within a few months we realized that what they contain is almost the *complement* of common sense. Assuming that readers already have common sense, can read, and so on, they provide the next level of detail for reference purposes.

If we couldn't use encyclopedias for their content directly, we could still use their information indirectly. If we take any sentence from an encyclopedia article and think about what the writer assumes the reader already knows about the world, we will have something worth telling CYC. Alternatively, we can take a paragraph and look at the "leaps" from one sentence to the next and think about what the writer assumes the reader will infer "between" the sentences. For instance, back in 1984 our first example read, "Napoleon died on St. Helena. Wellington was greatly saddened." The author expects the reader to infer that Wellington heard about Napoleon's death, that Wellington outlived Napoleon, and so on.

For many years, we were largely driven by bottom-up examples of this sort from encyclopedias, newspapers, novels, advertisements, and so on. Gradually, around 1990, we began to work in a more top-down fashion, treating entire topics one at a time and in moderate detail. By 1996, we had told CYC about hundreds of topics. That brings up the next issue.

How Should That Knowledge Be Represented?

The real physical universe is not, of course, inside CYC, anymore than it is inside our brains. All we have is a representation of a sliver of the world, and we operate from that representation to acquire new ideas, make decisions, and so forth.

Initially we used a simple frame-and-slot language to store information in CYC; for instance, `"timeOfBirth (HAL) = 1/12/1992."` This caused several problems, however. How could we represent *not, or, every, some,* opinions, expectations, counterfactual conditionals, and similar material. Consider, for example, these speeches from *2001:*

HAL: I hope the two of you are not concerned about this.

Dave: No, I'm not, HAL.

Dave: I don't know what you're talking about.

HAL: I know that you and Frank were planning to disconnect me, and I'm afraid that's something I cannot allow to happen.

HAL: I know everything hasn't been quite right with me, but I can assure you now, very confidently, that it's going to be alright again.

HAL: If you'd like to hear it, I can sing it for you.

All of these sentences are too complex to squeeze them efficiently into the frame-and-slot straightjacket. So our method of representation had to evolve slowly, until today it is a type of second-order predicate calculus. That's a fancy way of saying the language of logic. The second-order qualifier means that sometimes we need to represent things whose interrelationship is unknown or to refer explicitly to earlier conversations. For instance, at one point in the film HAL says "I know I've never completely freed myself of the suspicion that there are some extremely odd things about this mission. I'm sure you'll agree that there's some truth in what I say."

Lessons Learned Along the Way

We've learned many other things over the past dozen years, working on the CYC program. Three lessons in particular were painful but important to development of the program.

Originally we attached probabilistic weights—that is, numerical certainty factors—to each sentence we gave CYC. (For instance, HAL's statement, "Yes, that's a completely reliable figure," would have a very high certainty factor.) Including certainty factors had several bad consequences, however, and we eventually changed to a scheme in which all inputs are true by default. To decide whether to believe something, CYC gathers up all the pro and con arguments it can think of, examines them, and then reaches a conclusion.

Every representation is a trade-off between expressiveness (how easily you can say complicated things) and efficiency (how easily the machine can reason with what you've told it). English is very expressive but not very efficient. Most computer languages, such as Basic, C, and Fortran, are efficient but not very expressive. To get both qualities, we separated the epistemological problem (what should the system know?) from the heuristic problem (how can it effectively reason with what it knows?) and developed two separate languages, respectively EL and HL. Our knowledge enterers talk to CYC in the clean, expressive language (EL). Their input is then converted into the heuristic language (HL), which is efficient for dealing with many sorts of frequently recurring inference problems, such as reasoning about time, causality, containment, and so forth.

The third, and perhaps most important lesson we learned along the way was that it was foolhardy to try to maintain consistency in one huge flat CYC knowledge base. We eventually carved it up into hundreds of contexts or microtheories. Each one of those is consistent with itself, but there can be contradictions among them. Thus, in the context of working in an office it's socially unacceptable to jump up screaming whenever good things happen, while in the context of a football game it's socially unacceptable *not* to.

In the fictional context of Bram Stoker's *Dracula,* vampires exist; in the standard rational worldview context they don't. Other contexts carve out similar distinguishable eras in time, political or religious points of view, and so forth.

Applications of CYC

We've discussed the need to have something, like the CYC program, that can understand natural language; so it should come as no surprise that getting it to do this is a high-priority application task for us. Long before it can read all on its own, CYC will carry on semiautomated knowledge acquisition from texts, a sort of tutoring program in which it asks clarifying questions when it comes across something it's not sure about.

One potential use for CYC is to understand such structured information sources as spreadsheets and data bases, and then use that understanding to detect common-sense errors and inconsistencies in the data. For example, one column of a table might indicate a person's gender, and another might indicate that of his or her legal spouse. Without having to be specially programmed for the task, CYC would know that there's probably a mistake in the data if X and X's spouse have the same gender, if X's spouse lists a third person as his or her spouse, or if X is listed as X's spouse. This sort of data cleaning gets more interesting when combining information from several tables. (For example, according to one data base, X is suspected of committing a certain crime, whereas according to another data base X was in jail at the time.) This sort of information fusion or integration is very important, because much of the data we draw upon in our lives is gathered, formatted, and maintained by someone not under our direct control. Human beings—and HAL, and CYC—need to be able to assimilate information from numerous sources and interrelate it correctly. That task, in turn, requires common sense. Using n data bases and writing the transformation rules for their communications works fine when $n = 2$, but not so well when $n = 100$ or 1,000. Instead, the approach we use for CYC treats each column of each data base one at a time, writing rules that explain its meaning in terms CYC can understand. The entire CYC knowledge base then becomes, in effect, the semantic glue for implicitly joining all that information together—just as you or I can draw on and combine information we acquire from many different sources.

One of the flashiest early uses of CYC has been for information retrieval. Imagine a library of captioned images and a user who comes along and types in a word, phrase, or sentence asking for images. Today's software would have to do Boolean searches based on keywords in the query and the captions, perhaps broadening the search a bit by looking up synonyms in a thesaurus or definitions in a dictionary. Or consider the World Wide Web, whose keyword-based indexing is the only way to search through that immense information space. That's fine if you want to match "A bird in water" against "A duck in a pond," but it takes something like CYC to match "A happy person" against "A man watching his daughter take her first step." CYC uses common sense to do matches of that sort. Similarly, CYC matched the query "a strong and adventurous person" to a caption of "a man climbing a rock face." To do that, it used a few rules of the sort: "If people do something for recreation that puts them at risk of bodily harm, then they are adventurous."

Conclusions and Parting Thoughts

We haven't talked much about emotions and motivations. I started out by complaining that HAL was stupid, because he showed a distinct lack of common sense when he killed the crew rather than, for example, bringing them into his confidence about the secret orders for the mission. Most humans would agree that it's better to lie to people or risk confiding in them than to "solve" the problem by killing them.

At least HAL was rational in his murderous plans. One of the prevalent themes in science fiction has been that of the robot gone amok, generally driven by some strong emotion or craving for power. This is a reflection of our human fears, I think; it is the monster still lurking under our beds in the dark. HAL, CYC, and their ilk won't have emotions, because they are not useful for integrating information, making decisions based on that information, and so on. A computer may pretend to have emotions, as part of what makes for a pleasing user interface, but it would be as foolish to consider such simulated emotions real as to think that the internal reasoning of a computer is carried out in English just because the input/output interface uses English (but see chapter 14).

We have described several applications of CYC, such as natural language understanding, checking and integrating information in spreadsheets and data bases, and finding relevant information in image libraries and on the World Wide Web. Notice that we were not talking about Herculean tasks like beating Garry Kasparov at chess by looking seventeen moves ahead or simulating and predicting any of a trillion problems days before they may occur, as HAL does continuously. We're just talking about inference problems that are only a couple of steps long. The key point here is that if you have the necessary common-sense knowledge—such as "deadly pastimes suggest adventurousness"—then you can make the inference quickly and easily; if you lack it, you can't solve the problem at all. Ever.

This is the essence of common sense—that a little goes a long way. HAL had a veneer of intelligence, but in the end he was lacking in values and in common sense, which resulted in the needless death of almost the entire crew. We are on the road to building HAL's brain. But this time—now that it's for real—we aren't going to cripple it by skipping the mass of simple stuff it needs to know.

Further Readings

Douglas B. Lenat and John Seely Brown. "Why AM and Eurisko Appear to Work." *J. Artificial Intelligence* 23 (1984): 269–94. Summarizes the decades of his pioneering work in automated discovery that led Lenat to undertake the CYC project.

Douglas B. Lenat and R. V. Guha. *Building Large Knowledge-Based Systems*. Reading, Mass.: Addison-Wesley, 1990. A detailed discussion of the first five years of the CYC project.

Nicholas, J. Mars, ed., *Toward Very Large Knowledge Bases.* Amsterdam: IOS Press, 1995. A collection of technical papers, including "Steps to Sharing Knowledge" by Lenat.

Marvin A. Minsky. *The Society of Mind.* New York: Simon and Schuster, 1985. Minsky didn't completely see things Lenat's way when he wrote this seminal book, but he has since come closer to that point of view.

Tosh Munkakata, ed. *Communications of the ACM* 38, no. 11 (November 1995). A special issue devoted to the three efforts most closely related to building HAL's brain: CYC, EDR, and WordNet.

Williard V. Quine. *Ontological Relativity and Other Essays.* New York: Columbia University Press, 1969. A vital classic on "natural kinds."

Amos Tversky and Daniel Kahneman. "Judgment Under Uncertainty: Heuristics and Biases." *Science* 185 (1974): 1124–31. Guaranteed to cause a paradigm shift in anyone who believes people are rational beings.

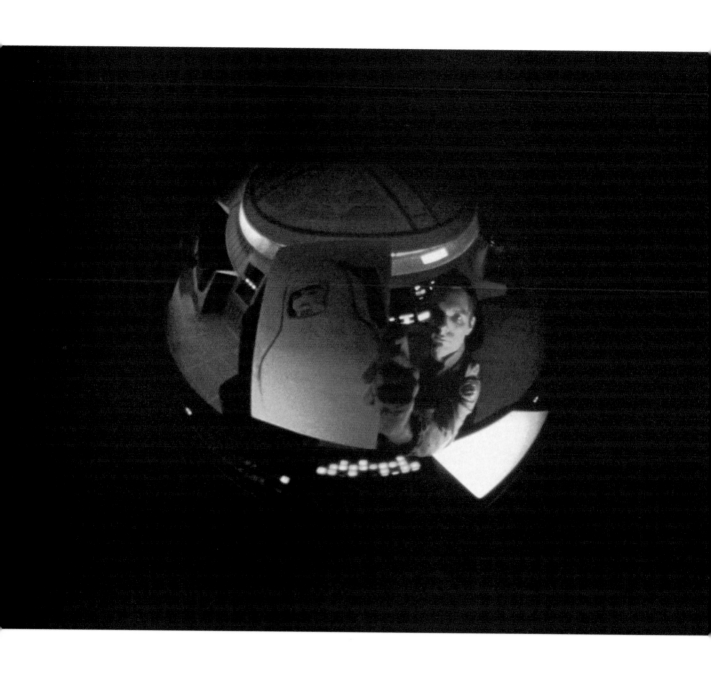

10   *Eyes for Computers: How HAL Could "See"*

Azriel Rosenfeld

HAL: Good evening, Dave.

Dave: How're you doing, Hal?

HAL: Everything is running smoothly; and you?

Dave: Oh, not too bad.

HAL: Have you been doing some more work?

Dave: A few sketches.

HAL: May I see them?

Dave: Sure.

HAL: That's a very nice rendering, Dave. I think you've improved a great deal. Can you hold it a bit closer?

Dave: Sure.

HAL: That's Dr. Hunter, isn't it?

Dave: Uh-huh.

Could HAL really "see" Dave's sketch? In the film, Dave holds his sketch up to one of HAL's "eyes"—presumably a television camera. The camera could form an optical image of the sketch; scan the image, convert it into digital data (i.e., numbers representing the colors of individual *pixels,* or picture elements), and transmit the data to HAL's "brain." But a set of pixel data is only an array of numbers (see figure 10.1). How did HAL analyze these

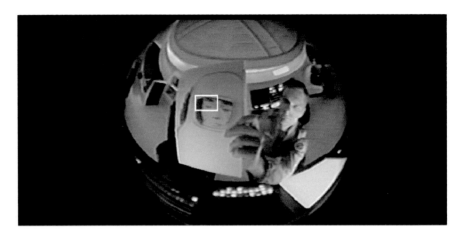

Figure 10.1a
A Small Portion of Dave's Sketch (in white box)

Figure 10.1b
A Blowup of the Portion, Showing Individual Pixels

```
162 163 166 167 168 170 170 171 172 172 174 175 175 174 175 175 175 175 175 175 175 173 170 166 160 154 148 145 143 142
158 159 162 166 167 167 165 165 168 169 168 170 172 174 174 176 176 177 175 175 174 175 174 175 177 175 174 175 173 167
167 170 171 169 163 157 154 148 147 142 141 141 140 141 146 153 157 160 163 166 167 167 167 170 172 173 176 177 179 176
163 166 170 174 179 182 183 174 154 136 129 126 124 116 114 118 116 114 118 125 139 146 155 157 162 166 168 170 168 170
171 175 174 173 175 179 173 154 133 121 133 142 141 125 105  87  80  87  92  97  92  92  95 103 111 124 134 144 149 155
177 170 152 132 118 107  99  87  84 103 128 142 144 133 124 113  97  92 101 113 125 130 132 126 125 122 118 111 101  99
157 129 105  89  89  87  80  73  69  95 124 141 144 136 130 124 116 107 105 103  97  95 103 122 140 146 146 139 129 121
146 119 103  99  97  97  87  73  77 107 135 144 134 121 122 129 133 133 124 111  92  84  80  92 116 141 154 155 149 146
140 105  84  77  89  89  84  69  77 114 148 165 167 160 160 157 153 146 141 132 119 103  95 103 125 142 157 157 156 152
144 114  97  97  97  92  77  58  64 105 147 173 180 173 170 168 169 167 167 164 159 152 146 140 138 141 147 158 163 164
129  99  87  80  77  73  64  58  87 124 153 170 171 175 174 172 171 170 170 170 170 171 170 168 167 169 170 167 163 161
135 105  89  87  80  77  73  69  87 118 147 165 168 170 171 169 169 166 164 164 162 163 159 162 163 163 161 163 163 166
119  97  95  97  89  77  69  73  99 130 152 163 167 168 170 171 174 177 175 173 173 170 169 167 165 163 158 156 155 157
113  99  97  99  95  87  77  84 114 144 162 169 170 173 171 170 171 173 174 173 170 170 167 166 161 161 162 161 159 157
113  89  92 101 101  95  87  87 116 146 167 170 168 164 161 161 167 170 170 169 170 172 175 175 175 169 161 156 157 161
118  99  95  95  92  87  77  92 125 152 167 170 168 162 150 141 140 142 148 157 162 163 161 163 169 169 165 161 161 160
126 105 103 105  97  84  69  73 107 141 167 180 183 177 166 147 133 125 125 132 138 144 154 166 170 168 161 159 159 159
122  99  92  95  95  87  73 111 143 166 171 174 174 174 170 165 161 157 158 163 168 170 173 176 175 171 167 167 170
125 103  95  97  95  89  80  80 113 145 169 175 177 179 175 174 175 175 177 180 180 179 179 180 182 177 175 173 173 173
125  92  80  95 105 101  87  89 119 151 171 179 177 177 177 177 180 182 180 180 180 181 183 183 181 179 177 175 174 175
```

Figure 10.1c

Numerical Values Representing the (Scaled) Brightnesses of the pixels (0 = black, 255 = white)

When Dave held up the sketch, HAL could have scanned it and measured the pixel brightnesses (or colors), thus obtaining a digital image of the sketch. But how could HAL recognize Dr. Hunter's face in the array of numerical pixel values?

numbers and conclude that (1) they represented an image of a human face; (2) the representation was "a very nice rendering"; and (3) the face was Dr. Hunter's?

Seeing is so easy for us that we tend to take it for granted. But, in fact, when our eye forms an optical image, it "samples" the image with an array of light-sensitive elements in the retina at the back of the eye and transmits the values of the samples along the optic nerve to the brain. Thus for us, as for HAL, vision starts with arrays of pixel data. Yet we see the world as composed of objects, not of pixels, and we can often recognize the objects we see. How do we do these things? We have no little man (*homunculus*) inside our heads who looks at the digital images on a screen and tells us what they represent; our brain must somehow analyze the image data and infer the objects from the data.

In *2001,* HAL exhibits visual-recognition abilities that are even more impressive: he understands Frank and Dave's conversation without being able to hear it ("I could see your lips move") and deduces Dave's emotional state from his actions and expressions ("I can see that you're really upset"). (Chapters 11 and 13 describe computer lipreading—more correctly, speechreading—and computer understanding of emotions.) The fact that HAL possesses these abilities shows that he not only recognizes objects (such as faces) by analyzing images, but also recognizes events and actions (lip movements and facial expressions) by analyzing sequence of images. Can a computer really be programmed to do such things? The field of computer vision deals with methods a computer can use to obtain information about objects and events in a scene by analyzing images of the scene. These methods need not resemble those used by humans (or animals) to see the world as long as they yield correct results. In this chapter, we first discuss how a computer might distinguish objects in a scene—for example, how it might distinguish a human head from its background or differentiate parts of the head (e.g., hair, eyes) from each other. We then explore how information about the parts can be used for recognition—for example, in identifying a particular person's face in a collection of face images. Finally, we consider how variations in the appearance of parts of a face over a sequence of images can be used to recognize a person's facial expressions.

Detecting Objects in an Image

To understand how a computer detects objects in an image of a scene, first consider what type of information about the scene the image contains. Each pixel in the image represents the light reaching the computer's camera from a given direction in the scene. The light coming from an object determines the brightness and color over a contiguous range of pixels. The brightnesses and colors of these pixels depend on how the object is illuminated and how it reflects the light toward the camera. (We assume here that the object is opaque, so that the camera sees reflected, rather than transmitted, light). The amount of light reflected from a point on the surface of an object depends not only on the reflectivity of the surface at that point, but also on the orientation of the surface at that point, relative to the directions of the light sources and the camera.

In general, illumination, reflectivity, and orientation all vary from point to point on the surface of an object. If they vary arbitrarily, we can infer nothing about the presence of objects by analyzing the image; in particular, we can't tell whether the variations in the image are due to variations in illumination, reflectivity, or orientation (or a combination of them) across the surfaces of objects; nor can we tell where one object's surface ends and another's begins. Inferences about the surfaces in a scene are possible only if variations are constrained. For example, suppose the illumination is approximately constant—the scene is illuminated by a distant, compact light source and there are no shadows—and each object in the scene has constant, diffuse surface reflectivity and smoothly varying surface orientation. Abrupt changes in the image's pixel values would then correspond to transitions from one object to another, and gradual changes (*shading*) would be caused by changes in the objects' surface orientations.

Fortunately, many types of real-world scenes do, at least approximately, satisfy the constraints described in the preceding paragraph. For example, figure 10.2a shows an image of Frank's head against a contrasting background. We can think of the image as made up of portions of several objects, including the background, the face, the hair, the eyes, and the mouth. The major *edges* (abrupt brightness changes) in this image (figure 10.2b) occur primarily at the boundaries between these objects. Thus the edges provide information a computer can use to subdivide (on segment) the image into regions that correspond to the objects—for example by linking groups of edges that surround regions.

Recognizing Faces

So far, we have seen how computer vision might detect distinct objects in simple scenes. As yet, we have said nothing about how the objects might be recognized; for example, how we—or a computer—can determine that an image shows a person's face, or how we identify the person whose face appears in the image.

Figure 10.2a
Frontal View of Frank's Face Against a Contrasting (but Not Homogeneous) Background

Figure 10.2b
A Plot of the Strong Edges in Figure 10.2a
Brightness in this plot corresponds to rate of change of brightness in the original image. The edges cluster along boundaries between objects in the image: the face, hair, eyes, mouth, and so on. Thus detecting and linking the edges can subdivide the image into regions corresponding to different objects.

One way we recognize that an image shows a human face is to analyze the shading in the image and verify that it is consistent with the "topography" of a face viewed from the front. In fact, strong shading in an image corresponds to rapid changes in surface orientation, for example, an image of a face shows strong shading around the lips, the bridge of the nose, and so on. (We see this, to some extent, in figure 10.2a). The topography of the surfaces that gave rise to the shading can be reconstructed, by integrating information about the orientation change.

An even simpler method of recognizing a face in an image is detecting the pattern of major facial features, such as the eyes and mouth. In figure 10.3 we see images of both Frank's and Dave's heads, with the eyes outlined by computer; the outlining is successful even though one face is tilted. If we find the outline of a head in an image and can detect features such as eyes and mouth inside the outline, we can be reasonably confident that we are looking at a human face.

To identify the face of a specific person, vision extracts patterns of *feature points* from the face image. Such feature points—often places where edges change direction abruptly to form sharp angles or corners—are usually associated with facial features (e.g., corners of the eyes and mouth). A vision system can measure the relative positions of these feature points and use them to identify an unknown face by comparing the pattern of feature points to similar measurements of faces in its data base. To confirm the identification, a computer can display the face in its data base that most closely resembles the unknown face (see figure 10.4 for a set of examples). Computer face identification based on this approach has been demonstrated to have an accuracy of about 90 percent for data bases of several hundred images.

Considering this accuracy level, HAL's ability to recognize Dr. Hunter in Dave's sketch is not especially remarkable. A sketch of a face should be at least as easy to recognize as a photograph, if it faithfully represents the dimensions and relative positions of the facial features. We can even recognize people from caricature sketches, although we don't yet fully understood how we do this. Recognizing that the sketch represents a face should also not be difficult, as a sketch usually represents shading (perhaps in a stylized way)

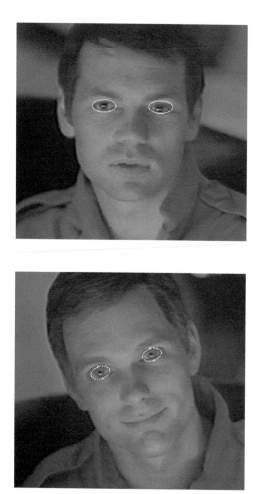

Figure 10.3a,b
Computer Detection Showing Outlines of the Eyes in Images of (a) Frank's and
(b) Dave's Faces
The computer sees the eyes as elliptically shaped clusters of strong edges.

Figure 10.4
A Collection of Twenty-one Pairs of Faces Illustrating Computer Face Recognition
In each pair, the left-hand face is the unknown face and the right-hand face is the one the computer selected as a match—by comparing patterns of feature points—from a data base of over three hundred face images of about eighty different people. Note that, in this set of examples, the selected face is always that of the correct person, even though the faces vary in orientation and facial expression.

and includes explicit outlines of facial features. As for identifying the face, HAL could easily guess that Dave would sketch one of the crew members— a very small data base. Or, if Dave was sketching from a photograph, HAL could compare the sketch with the photographs Dave brought along on the expedition. The effectiveness of the shading in the sketch and the accuracy with which the features are outlined could serve as a basis for HAL's somewhat flattering comment, "a very nice rendering."

Face identification is relatively easy when the image of the unknown face is a mugshot or sketch of the face in a standard, frontal position against a featureless background. HAL's identification of Dr. Hunter was made easier by the fact that the sketch was such a frontal view and that Dave showed it to HAL in a frontal position. Identifying faces from nonstandard viewpoints is more difficult but is still feasible, in principle. Instead of using dimensions and relative positions as identifying features, one can use ratios of these quantities that are insensitive to changes in viewpoint over a relatively wide range. In the face-identification system in figure 10.4, correct recognition is usually possible even when the image of a face is somewhat differently oriented. Ultimately, it will be possible for computer vision systems to identify faces reliably from brief, partial glimpses at odd angles and in cluttered backgrounds—for example, in a crowd scene.

Recognizing Facial Expressions

Faces are not rigid objects. They are capable of expressing not only emotions (see chapter 13), but also a wide variety of other things—for example, reactions to such unpleasant sensory stimuli as pain or a bad odor. Expressions displace or deform the facial features in specific ways: in a smile the corners of the mouth are raised; in a scowl or a grimace, they are lowered.

Face-identification systems seldom take facial expressions into account; they assume that all faces have neutral expressions. (Note that in the identification system mentioned above, recognition is possible even when facial expressions vary to some degree.) Recently, however, researchers have demonstrated that a computer can reliably recognize certain basic facial expressions, no matter who is registering them (see figure 10.5).

Disgust

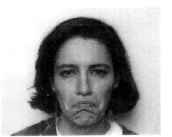

Sadness

Happiness

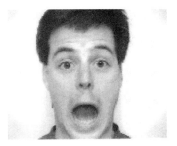

Fear

Anger

Surprise

Figure 10.5
Images of Six Different People—Each Displaying a Different Facial Expression
A computer can recognize these expressions quite reliably; it makes little or no difference
what specific person displays them.

The psychological literature delineates six basic facial expressions: anger, disgust, fear, happiness, sadness, and surprise. Each expression is characterized by a specific set of facial distortions (see table 10.1). Surprise, for example, involves two principal distortions: raising the eyebrows and lowering the lower lip.

By analyzing a sequence of television frames of a face taken during the brief period (typically 0.5–4 seconds) an expression lasts, a computer can reliably identify the expression, even if the head is moving. This is done by detecting distortions in the relevant facial feature (e.g., corners of the mouth) tracking them from frame to frame, and using them to identify the expression. The program assumes that motions common to other parts of the face are caused by head movement. (Chapter 13 discusses another method of recognizing facial expressions.)

In *2001,* Frank and Dave keep their faces relatively expressionless most of the time; perhaps they are influenced by HAL's lack of expression. In one famous sequence (figure 10.6) (also discussed in chapter 13), Dave seems to be keeping his face tightly controlled, perhaps repressing his anger, when he speaks to HAL about letting him back into the spaceship. In fact, Dave is compressing his lips and widening his mouth. As this episode occurs in the film under adverse lighting conditions, Dave's mouth is not very visible; and the entire sequence lasts for less than a second. Nevertheless, it is possible to quantitatively analyze the movements of Dave's mouth during that very short period. We can extract three parameters (figure 10.7) from the images of the mouth: *curvature*—negative when the mouth is curving upward, positive when it is curving downward—*divergence*—positive when the mouth is expanding, negative when it is contracting—and *deformation*—positive when the mouth is stretching in the horizontal direction, negative when it is stretching in the vertical direction. Plots of these three quantities over the one-second frame sequence (figure 10.8) show that Dave's mouth first curves upward (when he presses his lips together); then returns to a downward curvature before stretching significantly in the horizontal direction; gradually relaxes; briefly contracts (the pressing of the lips); and, finally, reexpands as Dave relaxes his expression. (Close-ups of Dave's mouth in the four frames in figure 10.6 are shown in figure 10.9).

Table 10.1

Descriptions of the six basic expressions in terms of the facial features. (After P. Ekman and W. Friesen, *Unmasking the Face* [Englewood Cliffs, N.J.: Prentice-Hall, 1975].)

Emotion	Observed facial cues
Surprise	brows raised (curved and high)
	skin below brow stretched
	horizontal wrinkles across forehead
	eyelids opened and more of the white of the eye is visible
	jaw drops open without tension or stretching of the mouth
Fear	brows raised and drawn together
	forehead wrinkles drawn to the center
	upper eyelid is raised and lower eyelid is drawn up
	mouth is open
	lips are slightly tense or stretched and drawn back
Disgust	upper lip is raised
	lower lip is raised and pushed up to upper lip or it is lowered
	nose is wrinkled
	cheeks are raised
	lines below the lower lid, lid is pushed up but not tense
	brows are lowered, lowering the upper lid
Anger	brows lowered and drawn together
	vertical lines appear between brows
	lower lid is tensed and may or may not be raised
	upper lid is tense and may or may not be lowered due to brows' action
	eyes have a hard stare and may have a bulging appearance
	lips are either pressed firmly together with corners straight or down or open, tensed in a squarish shape
	nostrils may be dilated (could occur in sadness too)
	unambiguous only if registered in all three facial areas
Happiness	corners of lips are drawn back and up
	mouth may or may not be parted with teeth exposed or not
	a wrinkle runs down from the nose to the outer edge beyond lip corners
	cheeks are raised
	lower eyelid shows wrinkles below it, and may be raised but not tense
	crow's-feet wrinkles go outward from the outer corners of the eyes
Sadness	inner corners of eyebrows are drawn up
	skin below the eyebrow is triangulated, with inner corner up
	upper lid inner corner is raised
	corners of the lips are drawn or lip is trembling

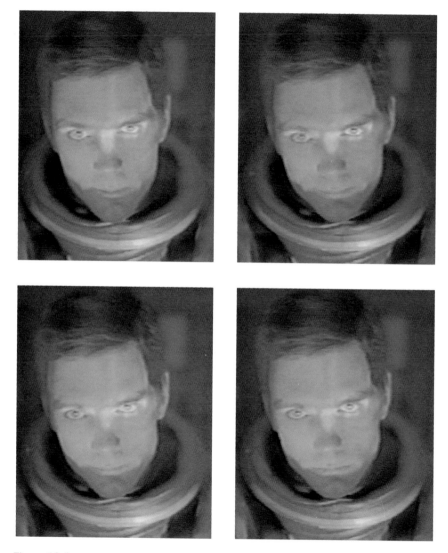

Figure 10.6
Four Images of Dave's Face Taken Over a One-second Period after Demanding "Open the pod bay doors, HAL."
Dave is clearly trying to keep his expression under control. As we see in the next few figures, a computer could have detected his expression by accurately measuring the distortion of Dave's mouth.

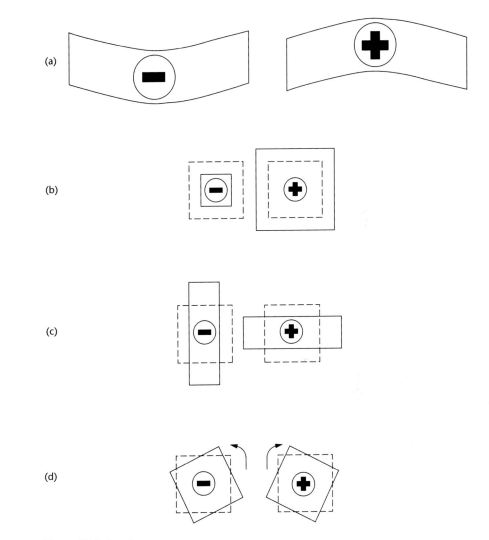

Figure 10.7a,b,c,d
Measures of Various Distortions of Facial Features
(a) Curvature: positive = concave downward, negative = concave upward; (b) Divergence: positive = expansion, negative = contraction; (c) Deformation: positive = horizontally elongated, negative = vertically elongated; (d) Rotation ("curl"): positive = clockwise, negative = anticlockwise.

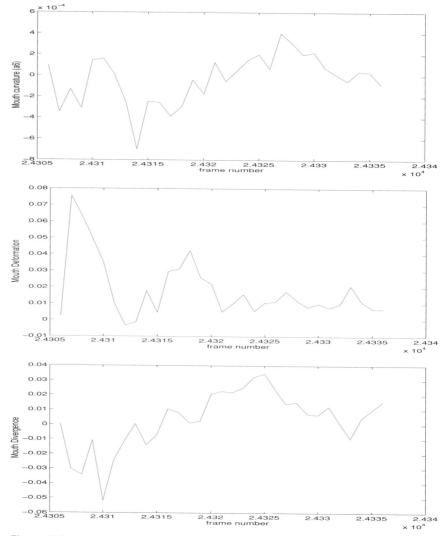

Figure 10.8

Plots of the Curvature, Deformation, and Divergence of Dave's Mouth in Figure 10.6
When Dave presses his lips together, his mouth curves upward, contracts, and stretches in
the horizontal direction (negative curvature, negative divergence, and positive deformation). His mouth then gradually returns to a more relaxed state.

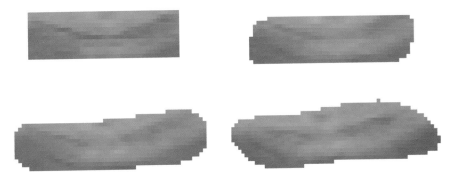

Figure 10.9
Close-ups of Dave's Mouth, Showing its Upward Curvature

At only a few points in the film do Dave and Frank display strong facial expressions. Once Frank seems to scowl briefly (possibly expressing doubt); this expression lasts only about half a second (figure 10.10) but shows up clearly in the successive shapes of his mouth (figure 10.11) and in the plot of the curvature parameter, which becomes strongly positive, indicating the downward curvature (figure 10.12).

At one point in his conversation with HAL, Dave actually smiles for a short while (figure 10.13). This shows up not only in the upward curvature of his mouth, but also in the narrowing of his eyes. (He also blinks, but for only about a tenth of a second; the blink is not visible in figure 10.13). The sharply negative curvature of Dave's mouth shows up clearly on the first graph in figure 10.14; it only gradually begins to reverse near the end of the sequence. The second graph shows the rotations of Dave's eyes in the plane of the image; here positive values represent clockwise rotation and negative values, counterclockwise rotation (figure 10.7d). At the onset of the eyeblink, the left eye rotates clockwise, while the right eye simultaneously rotates counterclockwise; at the end of it, the rotations are reversed. Figure 10.13 shows the computer diagnosis of Dave's expression as a smile and describes the deformations of the facial features (and head movement) the computer detected.

Figure 10.10
Four Images of Frank's Face during the Conversation about HAL's Apparent Malfunction
For about half a second, he displays a strong facial expression, which is characterized by a
downward curvature of his mouth.

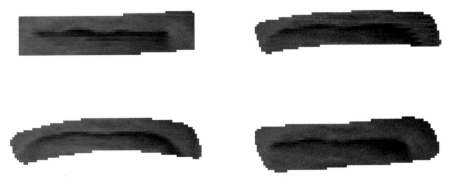

Figure 10.11
Close-ups of Frank's Mouth, Showing How It Curves Downward, Then Returns to a More Relaxed State

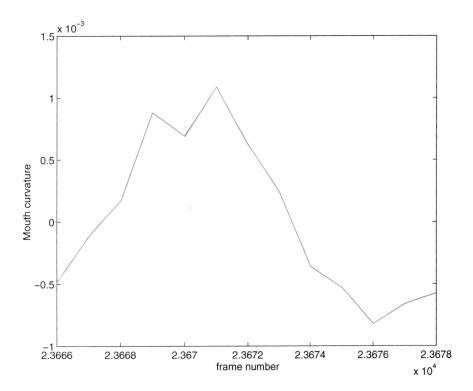

Figure 10.12
A Plot of the Curvature of Frank's Mouth Over a Half-second Sequence, Showing a Strong Positive Curvature Peak

HEAD ROTATE LEFT

BEGIN SMILE

Figure 10.13

Dave Smiling at HAL after Their Discussion of HAL's Apparent Malfunction

At the beginning of the smile, Dave's head rotates toward the left, and many small changes take place in his facial features; the most obvious is the upward curvature of his mouth. All these changes can be detected by computer-tracking of the features. Descriptions of the

MOUTH VERTICAL DEFORMATION
REYE CONTRACTION
REYE ANTI-CLOCKWISE ROTATION
REYE HORIZONTAL DEFORMATION
LEYE VERTICAL DEFORMATION

SMILE

REYE UPWARD
REYE ANTI-CLOCKWISE ROTATION
REYE HORIZONTAL DEFORMATION
LEYE DOWNWARD
LEYE CONTRACTION
LEYE CLOCKWISE ROTATION
LEYE HORIZONTAL DEFORMATION

SMILE

detected changes (HEAD ROTATE LEFT . . . BEGIN SMILE . . . SMILE) are superimposed on the images, and the computer's overall assessments are shown at the bottom. In this sequence, Dave is also blinking his eyes; although the closing of his eyes is only partially captured in the images, the computer detects the deformations of the eyes as well as their rotations.

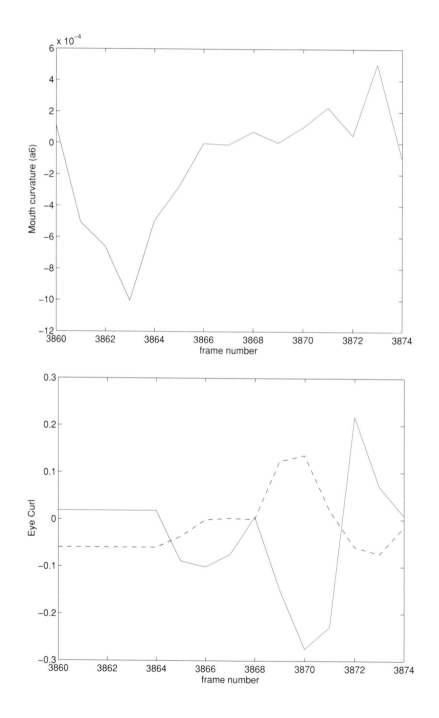

Once the computer identifies a facial expression, it should, in principle, be possible for it to "correct" it by warping the image to restore the facial features to their undistorted positions. This would produce an expressionless image that can be used as input to a face-identification system, thus making it possible to identify faces reliably even when expressionless images are not available.

How Effective Is Computer Vision?

As soon as computers became widely available to researchers in the 1950s, they developed methods of producing digitized image input and, initially, attempted to program computers to recognize various types of objects in images: letters and words in a document, cells in a microscope slide, buildings and roads on an aerial photograph. In the 1960s, when the major artificial intelligence laboratories were established at MIT, Stanford, and elsewhere, one of the goals was to use digitized television images to guide a robot to detect and grasp objects or a mobile robot to plan paths and avoid obstacles. Thus, at the time *2001* was filmed, work was already well under way on giving computers the ability to "see" the world by analyzing images. A computer as advanced as HAL would be expected to have well-developed visual capabilities. Dave certainly takes it for granted that HAL can "see" and appreciate his sketches ("May I see them? . . . That's a very nice rendering") but is surprised when he discovers—too late—that HAL can speechread ("I could see your lips move").

Over the past forty years, computer-vision technology has made great progress. In simple domains such as the computer reading of documents,

Figure 10.14
Plots of Dave's Mouth Curvature and Eye Rotations over the One-second Sequence of Figure 10.13
The red line represents the right eye, and the blue line the left eye. The sharp upward curvature of the mouth is seen clearly on the first plot. As the second plot shows, the left eye first rotates clockwise, then counterclockwise, while the right eye does the opposite; such paired, opposed eye movements are characteristic of an eyeblink.

where illumination can be controlled and the surfaces in the scene are stationary and flat, low-cost vision systems are already widely available. In other domains, especially those involving three-dimensional objects that can move or deform, research continues. Even in these areas, as the examples cited show, a good deal of progress has been achieved.

HAL undoubtedly has controllable cameras he can use to track moving objects. (Yet, interestingly HAL asks Dave to hold his sketch closer to the camera, rather than simply causing the camera to zoom in on the sketch.) Detecting and recognizing objects in a scene, whether stationary or in motion, becomes much easier if the camera can be controlled. Active vision systems that can control their visual sensors have been an important research topic over the past decade.

By the year 2001, computers should be able to reliably recognize a wide variety of objects and actions, including their users' faces (and voices), facial expressions, body postures, and gestures. This will lay the groundwork for even more advanced systems able to interpret people's actions, intentions, emotions, and behaviors. HAL appears to have this latter ability, at least to some degree. At one point he says to Dave, "I can see that you're really upset"; and toward the climax of the film, HAL correctly concludes from Dave's actions that he intends to disconnect him. (For discussion of HAL's ability to interpret human emotions, see chapter 13; see also chapter 11, which suggests that understanding gestures and body movements would be useful for computer speechreading.)

HAL may (for the moment) surpass today's computers in speechreading ability and, perhaps, in reading body language. But our 1990s computer-vision systems already have many capabilities—most of them not mentioned in this chapter—that HAL would surely be proud of. And the end to these advances is as not yet in sight.

Acknowledgments

The author acknowledges the support of the Office of Naval Research and the Defense Advanced Research Projects Agency under Contract N0014-95-

1-0521 (ARPA order C635). Most of the figures for this chapter were produced by Dr. Yaser Yacoob, who also made many valuable comments on drafts of the chapter.

Further Readings

V. S. Nalwa. *A Guided Tour of Computer Vision.* Reading, Mass.: Addison-Wesley, 1993. An introduction to computers that can be read on three levels: the figures and captions give a readable, richly illustrated overview; the text provides the main treatment; and the appendices and footnotes present some of the mathematical detail.

R. Chellappa, C. L. Wilson, and S. Sirohey. "Human and machine recognition of faces: A survey," *Proc. IEEE* 83 (1995): 705–40. This paper extensively reviews the algorithms for recognizing human faces in images and for identifying faces of particular individuals (i.e., finding the face image in a data base of mugshots that most closely resembles a given face image).

M. Black and Y. Yacoob. "Tracking and recognizing rigid and non-rigid facial motions using local parametric models of image motion," *Proc. Intl. Conf. on Computer Vision,* Cambridge, Mass., June 1995, pp. 374–81. This paper describes a system that recognizes facial expressions, even when the head is moving.

11 *"I could see your lips move": HAL and Speechreading*

David G. Stork

Nearly all the crisis points in *2001* occur in *silence:* the moment HAL takes control of the pod, extends his arms ominously, and pursues Frank; the subsequent murder in the void of outer space, with Frank's frantic but hopeless struggle to reattach his severed air hose; Dave's explosive reentry into *Discovery 1* through the vacuum of the emergency air lock; HAL's murder of the hibernating crewmen, announced by the silent flashing sign, LIFE FUNC-TIONS TERMINATED; the offstage "failure" of the AE35 unit; and HAL's silence in response to Dave's command, "Open the pod bay doors, HAL." But perhaps the most chilling of such silent moments—and the critical turning point in the film—comes when Frank and Dave retreat to a pod and turn off the electronics, confident that HAL cannot hear them. They discuss HAL's recent apparent malfunction and whether their plans should include disconnecting him if flaws remain. As the camera, showing HAL's view, pans back and forth between their moving mouths, we realize that he understands what they are saying. In the silence, HAL is lipreading.

It's a remarkable scene, but, we might well ask, how realistic is it? Could computers ever really lipread like that? How would we go about creating computers that can lipread? What would we use them for? Was HAL programmed to lipread, or did he just think of doing it on the spot?

As with a growing number of abilities once thought to be unique to humans (such as speech and language), there have been efforts to make

Figure 11.1
Closeup of Frank Poole's Mouth, as Viewed by HAL

computers that lipread, with encouraging results. Unlike HAL, who could lipread in silence, current systems focus on the use of sight *and* sound. The added information provided by sight leads to better recognition of speech, especially in noisy rooms; in fact, this is the primary reason we are building them.

The image of a talker can provide a great deal of speech information. Many people with profound or partial hearing loss watch a talker to understand the speech better. It isn't a joke when senior citizens with deteriorating eyesight and hearing ask you to wait a moment so they can put on their glasses to "hear" you better. What most people don't know, however, is that even people with normal hearing lipread, though for the most part they do so unconsciously. *You* lipread, to some extent.

A story (possibly apochryphal) illustrates the benefit of lipreading. Alexander Graham Bell's wife was profoundly deaf—a fact that led to his interest in inventing hearing aids and, ultimately, the telephone. The Bells taught their two children that it was disrespectful not to face the person they were addressing. According to the story, the children only realized that their mother was deaf when they were teenagers, so expert was she at lipreading.

You can prove to yourself the value of lipreading, even if you have never explicitly learned to do it. If you've ever tried to have a conversation at a loud cocktail party or in the stands during a noisy football game, you know how difficult it can be to understand your companion's speech. Next time, though, close your eyes and try to understand what he or she is saying; you'll be surprised to find how few of the words you can comprehend, especially if you don't know the topic of conversation ahead of time. When you open your eyes and watch your friend's face, though, you will understand much more. When you have a moment alone at a party, notice how many other people are watching faces and mouths.

Actually, the best way to demonstrate this so-called cocktail party effect is to tape-record a conversation with a friend, using a microphone that picks up sound from throughout the noisy room. You will find it extremely difficult to understand the speech when you play back the tape—or even to know when your friend is talking!—amidst the other sounds. Making a tape recording also eliminates the spatial information about the location of the talker that lets you focus your attention in a particular direction. (Discussion of this aspect of the cocktail party effect, interesting in and of itself, would be a digression from our considerations of lipreading.)

The most striking demonstration that the image of the talker influences your perception of speech is the *McGurk illusion,* or *McGurk effect.* Unfortunately, this effect is hard to demonstrate at home and is best shown with specially prepared videotapes. In a McGurk experiment, you watch a videotape of a talker saying one sound—for instance /ga/—while hearing another sound—/ba/—on the soundtrack. In this way, your ears get the sound of /ba/, but your eyes get the image of /ga/. Which do you perceive, /ba/ or /ga/? Surprisingly, it's neither. Instead, it sounds like a clear and unambiguous /da/!

What is going on? Currently, the best theories to explain the McGurk illusion suggest that your brain tries to use both sources of information. From your ears, you get information that the consonant is *front;* that is, that the closure of the vocal tract is right up front, at the lips: /ba/. From your eyes,

Figure 11.2
McGurk Effect
While watching a videotape of a talker saying an utterance, such as /ga/, subjects simultaneously hear the sound of a different, synchronized utterance, such as /ba/. Surprisingly, they perceive neither of these sounds, but, instead, a clear and unambiguous /da/!

however, you get the conflicting information, that the consonant is instead *back;* that is, that the closure is deep in the throat: /ga/. Your brain reconciles such conflicting information by splitting the difference, so to speak. You perceive a *middle* consonant: in this case a /da/, in which the closure is neither at the front nor the back.

Now, not all utterances form such nice McGurk pairs as /ga/ and /ba/ do. If you interchange the presentation (that is, present /ga/ to the ear and /ba/ to the eye) the illusion is not as striking. Other pairs of utterances are confusing to the listener; for example an auditory /ba/ paired with a visual /da/ yields a strange and somewhat disorienting /b-da/. Nevertheless, the

McGurk illusion shows conclusively that speech has both auditory and visual aspects; or, to use the jargon, speech is *bimodal.*

As long as we're clarifying jargon, we might as well use the accepted term for the ability to gain linguistic information from the image of the talker: *speechreading,* rather than *lipreading.* We watch not only the talker's lips, but also the jaw, tongue, teeth, cheeks, eyebrows, glottis (Adam's apple)—the whole face—when lipreading. There's much more to lipreading than just reading *lips.*

Was HAL Programmed to Speechread?

But back to HAL. How did he gain his ability to speechread? Was he programmed to do it? It is fairly clear that HAL was not designed or explicitly taught to speechread; if he was, the astronauts didn't know about it. In the scene after Frank's body is lost in space, Dave confronts HAL and learns about the speechreading when HAL won't let him back in the ship.

HAL: I knew that you and Frank were planning to disconnect me, and I'm afraid that's something I cannot allow to happen.

Dave: Where the hell did you get *that* idea, HAL?

HAL: Dave—although you took very thorough precautions in the pod against my *hearing* you, I could see your lips move.

Dave's evident anger—which he represses as only an astronaut can—shows that speechreading is not a well-known feature of HAL. There is no entry under "lipreading" in HAL's operating manual.

No, it seems that HAL's speechreading ability is a byproduct of his general intelligence. During the eighteen months of the Jupiter mission, HAL has plenty of opportunities to notice, and then learn, the correlations between the motion of the astronauts' mouths (as well as other face parts) and the sound of their speech. The next step would be to learn to associate the image with the word spoken. Thus HAL learns to speechread indirectly, the way we suppose that the vast majority of normal hearing people develop some rudimentary speechreading ability.

We might note, parenthetically, that HAL would have had to be programmed with the ability to learn such associations. Occasionally, when learning is too voracious and runs amok, a person (or perhaps someday a computer) associates two events whose only relationship is that they occur at the same time. Presumably this is how some superstitions—such as the belief that black cats bring bad luck—begin. Thus, an overeager learning mechanism might be a root cause of HAL's paranoia.

HAL's learning would have been fairly easy, because he had to speechread only two people—Frank and Dave. Such *speaker-dependent recognition* is much simpler than the more general *speaker-independent recognition* you may have experienced trying to reach the right person in a large corporation or government agency that uses an automatic routing telephone system (see chapter 6). HAL might not have done so well if he had had to understand a larger number of people.

It's hard to know, in fact, how accurate HAL is in the speechreading scene. I turned off the sound of a videotape of *2001* and asked a professional speechreader if she could "read" the speech in the pod. She managed to pick out a few words but basically failed to understand the dialogue. Of course, you don't have to understand every word to get the general drift of a conversation. So HAL might pick up a few key words—*HAL, worried,* and so on— that are enough for him to realize that something isn't quite right about the astronauts' ostensible reason for going into the pod in the first place—"a problem with the transmitter in C pod." HAL would not have to understand every word spoken to realize from their somber and vexed expressions that something more important than a blown fuse is at stake! Take a few key words, add a dash of digital paranoia (or strong sense of self, or concern about the mission objectives), along with the context of the previous scene (in which HAL acknowledges discrepancies with his ground-based twin 9000 computer), and HAL might well imagine that something fishy is going on in the pod. It is not too farfetched for him to imagine that the astronauts are planning to disconnect him. Of course, this all posits a computer far more advanced than we will have by the year 2001!

Before turning to real-life speechreading computers, it's worth pointing out that the speechreading scene was the only one in *2001* that Arthur C. Clarke thought implausible; it was Kubrick who added it.

The Benefits of Speechreading

There have recently been numerous efforts to build computer speechreading systems that use both sight and sound. Although we are still some distance from being able to duplicate HAL's performance speechreading in complete silence, it is clear that such combination automatic speechreading systems outperform their "blind" cousins (see chapter 7), especially when the speech is corrupted by noise or multiple distracting talkers.

One of the key benefits provided by speechreading arises from what has been called "God's gift to speechreaders," summarized by the principle of *complementarity:* utterances that are the hardest to distinguish by hearing turn out to be the easiest to distinguish by seeing, and vice versa. For example, the words *me* and *knee* are quite difficult to distinguish by sound alone, especially when heard in a noisy room. But it's an easy matter to tell which word is being said by looking: if the talker's lips close, the word is *me;* if they don't, the word is *knee.* Simple!

Conversely, the spoken *bat* and *pat* are visually indistinguishable, as you can see for yourself in a mirror. Consonants such as /*b*/ and /*p*/ are called *visemes,* in analogy with their acoustical cousins, *phonemes* (see chapter 6). Nevertheless, *bat* and *pat* are easy to distinguish by listening, even in a noisy room, because they differ in a very noticeable acoustic feature—the delay between the initial plosive sound and the onset of the vibration of the vocal chords (more properly called vocal *folds*); this time delay is called VOT, or *voicing onset time.* For *bat,* the VOT is nearly zero, whereas for *pat,* it is much longer. (If you concentrate, you can speak an utterance that has an artificially long VOT, which sounds something like "p-hat.")

To understand the crucial concept of complementarity in speechreading better, consider this analogy. Imagine you have to distinguish among four items—a yellow apple, a green apple, a lemon, and a lime—by touch and by sight based on a small piece of their skin. You are only allowed to classify them on the basis of color *or* texture. No smelling, tasting, or other information is allowed! If you based your decision solely on color, you would confuse the yellow apple and the lemon; you would also confuse the green apple and the lime. If, however, you based your decision solely on texture, you would confuse the lemon and the lime (because they have the same waxy surface) and the two types of apple (because they have the same smooth surface).

Now suppose that you are allowed to use color *as well as* texture. You would then have no difficulty. Each of the four fruits corresponds to a unique combination of color and texture: the only fruit that is yellow and waxy is a lemon; the only smooth green fruit is a green apple, and so forth. For this example, then, color and texture provide complementary information.

However, if the problem were to classify a red apple, a tomato, a lemon, and a grapefruit based on both the color (red or yellow) and texture (smooth or waxy), then you would have difficulty. If you sensed a smooth red fruit, you would not know whether it was a red apple or a tomato; if you sensed a yellow, waxy fruit, you would not know whether it was a lemon or a grapefruit. For these items, then, color and texture do not provide complementary information.

This general principle of complementarity between the acoustic and visual signals is the reason we are so optimistic about computer speechreading; the visual image helps with utterances for which acoustic recognizers have the greatest difficulty and provides little or no help for utterances that are already easily understood by sound alone. Why visual and acoustic speech are complementary in this way, nobody really knows.

The image of the talker also provides a wealth of more abstract information, including emotion and meaning (see chapter 13) through gestures. For example, the neutral *uh* sound can be interpreted as *yes* or *no*, depending on whether the accompanying head motion is a slight nod or a slight shake. Facial gestures that reveal such emotions as fear, surprise, and laughter can

provide information that might augment computer speechreading that relies on language and semantics (see chapter 8). Some exceedingly perceptive
and experienced speechreaders can tell the national or regional origin of a
talker (using the visual analogy of accents or dialects), and even, sometimes,
a man's sexual orientation. And here is a quirky fact that may prove useful
for speechreading systems: while talking, you are far more likely to blink
between words than *during* a word. Thus a speechreading system that watches
your eyes might be better at identifying where one word ends and another
begins.

Speechreading by Computer

HAL's speechreading ability is well beyond that of current real computer
speechreading systems, and indeed beyond anything we can hope for by the
year 2001. Speechreading in silence is just too hard: too many words are
visually indistinguishable and would require subtle linguistic knowledge to
understand them based on their appearance. For instance, *bat, pat,* and *mat*
are visually indistinguishable. Even if the rest of a sentence, such as "Frank
sat on a . . . ," is understood perfectly, if only the image (but no sound)
is available, it would be tricky to recognize *mat* (and not, say *bat*) as the
missing word. The computer would have to know that one typically sits on
a mat, and not on a bat—except perhaps at a baseball game, or deep in
a cave, or. . . .

Thus, virtually all researchers building speechreading systems concentrate
on using both sight and sound. Such systems require a video camera and a
microphone, of course, as well as a certain amount of special hardware and
software for processing the information sensed. The processed visual and
the acoustic information must be brought together—integrated—before an
utterance can be classified.

Processing the Image

The first visual problem the computer must solve is finding the talker's face.
This sounds like a trivial problem; after all, *you* have no difficulty determin-

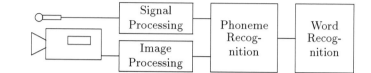

Figure 11.3

Basic Structure of a Speechreading System

This system consists of a video camera and microphone for sensing the talker and electronics and computers for processing the sensed information, integrating it, and yielding the classified, transcribed speech.

ing where the face is! But the human brain evolved to be specially "wired" for detecting faces; even at birth infants prefer to look at faces than at equally complex but mixed-up images of a mouth, eyes, nose, and so on. Surely such an ability bestows an important evolutionary advantage.

But computers don't have the benefit of millions of years of evolution. How, then, to make a computer find a face? One of the simplest ways, which is the one our system uses, is based on color. It turns out that, despite the wide range in skin appearance, all faces are of nearly the same hue (at least in comparison to the enormous palette of colors of objects); only the overall lightness of the skin differs among people. The darkest Ethiopian and the lightest Swede have skin that has nearly the same hue (technically called *chrominance*); they differ primarily in the darkness or lightness. Thus, our computer ignores the lightness of an image, and classifies each point according to its similarity to a sort of universal human skin color.

Our earliest system was confused by objects that were of similar color—a pine wood door, a brown sofa, and so forth. We have since added some simple shape requirements to avoid those problems: a region can only be a face if it has roughly the universal skin color, is within a particular size range, and is generally egg-shaped. To make a speechreading system work with a black-and-white image would, obviously, require more sophisticated face-finding methods based instead on the shape of such facial components as eyes, nose, and mouth.

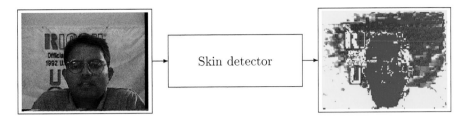

Figure 11.4
Finding the Face by Color
In this false-color representation of the output of our face detector, purple represents points that are most similar to a sort of universal human skin color, and thus most likely to indicate a face in the original image. Because our method ignores the overall *lightness* of the skin, the same detector works for people of all races, such as this person from India.

Our current system works well only with frontal views, and not the side view HAL used in the famous scene. Speechreading by both humans and machines is a bit more accurate when the talker is viewed at a slight angle away from a frontal view, so that it is easier to see the rounding of the lips and position of the tongue. Nevertheless, we have concentrated on the frontal view because it lends itself to a greater range of potential commercial applications; in all likelihood, you will directly face future voice-controlled computers, copiers, fax machines, ATM machines, and television sets. Our system could easily be used to transcribe a story read by a television anchor on the evening news, since the anchor faces the studio camera directly. (In that application, the speechreading computer wouldn't need to have a camera and microphone, as the image and sound signals would be transmitted by the television station.)

Once the computer locates the talker's face, its next problem is finding the lips. Our system assumes (naturally enough) that the face is upright, and that the lips are likely to be found toward the bottom. (In the zero-gravity of outer space and *Discovery 1,* this assumption might often be violated: in *2001* faces dangle in front of HAL from virtually every orientation at one time or another.) In broad overview, our system merely looks for areas of rapid motion toward the bottom of the face region. It occasionally has difficulty finding the mouth when there is no motion, but this does not lead to significant problems as there is no speech then anyway.

Once the lips are found, the system needs to represent the shape of the lips—a process called *feature extraction.* The ideal system extracts those features most useful for speech recognition. For instance, when you say the /f/ or /v/ sounds (as in /fa/, /va/, /fo/, /vo/, /fee/, /vee/ and so on), you gently bring your upper teeth to your lower lip, and perhaps also curl in your lower lip. Automatic detection of this *f-tuck* feature would be useful for speech recognition.

One general approach is to ask human speechreaders what they look for in a face when they speechread (such as an f-tuck), and write computer programs that determine those features automatically. However, such a pure top-down approach is followed by only a small minority of researchers. One problem with it is that human speechreaders do not always know which features they use. Moreover—and this is a fundamental issue in all machine pattern-recognition research—there is no guarantee that the best way to design machine perception is to duplicate the way humans do it. As we saw in chapter 5, the most successful computer chess programs play the game very differently than human grandmasters do. Most speechreading groups, including my own, eschew trying to duplicate human speechreading or using a human model to decide on which visual features to focus on. Instead, we take advantage of several bottom-up approaches.

In our system, we try to fit a very simple geometrical model of the lips—called a *deformable template,* a sort of cartoon lips—to the image. The simple shape parameters of these cartoon lips function as elementary features that will be used for recognizing the speech. Such parameters might represent the separation of the lips, their width, the curvature of the upper and the lower lips, the speed with which the mouth is opened or closed, and so on. The key aspect of this bottom-up approach is to have our computer learn automatically which groupings of these parameters are most useful for speech. For instance, if indeed the f-tuck is useful for speechreading, our system should learn the grouping of parameters corresponding to that feature.

The way the deformable template is fit to the video image is a bit subtle. The basic idea is that the contours of the template are adjusted to run along regions where the lightness and color change most, that is, along the edge of the talker's lips. Our template is symmetric and can be described by only a few (nine to twelve) parameters, which are determined for each successive video frame.

Let me digress to describe a surprising property of one of our speechreading systems. In designing our first lip templates we assumed, naturally enough, that faces are basically symmetrical right to left and so used symmetric templates. These templates effectively ignored differences in the right and left sides of the talker's face. Although we knew that faces are not actually symmetrical, only later did we learn that humans are asymmetrical in a particular, and linguistically interesting, way. Most people are right-handed, and hence have their speech and language centers in the left side of their brain. Because of a universal *contralaterality* of neural connections from the brain to the face and mouth, most people move the right side of the face slightly more than the left when they talk. However, the small minority of left-handed people, who have their speech centers on the right hemisphere, move the left side of their face more. We reconfigured our speechreading system to use templates that could detect such asymmetries, and the computer proved reliable at finding them. The upshot is that our speechreading computer could tell whether you are right-handed or left-handed just by watching you talk! Unfortunately, such asymmetric templates are somewhat complicated, slow down the system unacceptably, and do not improve speech recognition, so we went back to using symmetric templates in our research.

We use a deformable template similar to the lips template to determine the position of the jaw. In practice, this is more difficult than fitting the lips, because the visual edges and contours of the (smooth) chin are not as pronounced. Our jaw template yields only a single number at any instant: a measure of how far the jaw is lowered. Utterances such as *fear* and *far* are easily distinguished visually by such jaw motion, supplemented, of course,

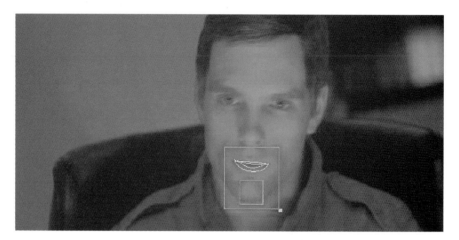

by information about the shape of the lips. Alas, our jaw detector does not yet work on bearded men.

Our system also automatically determines *lip rounding,* that is, the amount the lips are protruded. Your lips are far more rounded when you say a loud /*boo*/ than /*bee*/, for instance. Rounding can be determined from an image by the presence of shadows beneath the lips by measured shape-from-shading algorithms (see chapter 10). The parameters from the lip template can also be used to detect rounding (as you can see in a mirror), but are somewhat less reliable than the method based on shadows.

The parameter values from the feature extraction need not themselves correspond directly to useful features. At this stage, our system does not have a reliable f-tuck detector, for instance. Instead some sets of parameters that vary together in a complicated way correspond to useful features. But how does the computer determine such groupings? For instance, what complicated constellation of varying parameters corresponds to an f-tuck? In fact, does our system even need to employ an f-tuck detector? Below we look at how machine-learning techniques can be brought to bear on these problems.

Processing the Sound

Before we turn to the issue of learning, however, we need to remember that our system uses sound as well as the image of the talker. While the visual processing is taking place, the sound signal from the microphone is being processed too. Because automatic speechreading systems are still in their infancy—especially compared to purely acoustic speech systems—nearly all the research on speechreading centers on the visual processing and sensory integration—not the acoustic processing. My group, and many others, use

Figure 11.5
Deformable Lip Template
A deformable lip template (a sort of cartoon lips) is fit to each video frame of the talker. Only a few parameters (numbers) related to the width and curvature of the component arcs describe the template at any instant; these numbers are ultimately used for recognizing the speech.

a state-of-the-art acoustic recognizer as a component of our speechreading system, which lets us concentrate on the novel aspects—that is, the visual parts—of our system. Our acoustic subsystem processes the sound in a way similar to that described in chapter 7. The speech sound is split into acoustic features corresponding to the energy in different frequency ranges, the overall loudness, and several special features (such as VOT).

Bringing Together Sight and Sound

A key problem in computer speechreading is how to bring together the information from the sight and sound for best recognition. The two main approaches to this sensory-integration problem are *late integration* and *early integration,* terms that refer to how much processing the signals receive before they are brought together. Sensory integration is ubiquitous, though not fully appreciated (or understood!). No one knows how we integrate our sense of taste, smell, and the feel of the food, along with its appearance (of color, shape, and so forth) to recognize, for example, a fruit.

In late integration there are, effectively two classifiers (audio and video), each of which can work separately on its respective information and yield a category for each utterance. The two category responses from the audio and video subsystems are then pooled to yield an overall category judgment. By contrast, in early integration, the acoustic and the visual information is combined while it is still somewhat abstract and cannot be directly used for classification. The mixed, bimodal information is then processed and, ultimately, used to provide the final categorization.

There is a general, but not universal, consensus in the psychological community that humans use late integration for speechreading. After all, the argument goes, the information from the eyes and the ears are processed in some detail by separate sets of nerve cells before the two streams can ever meet and be integrated in the brain.

As engineers constructing speechreading machines, however, we are not confined to the "hardware" humans use; we can design whatever works best. For a number of reasons, we feel that early integration will lead to the best

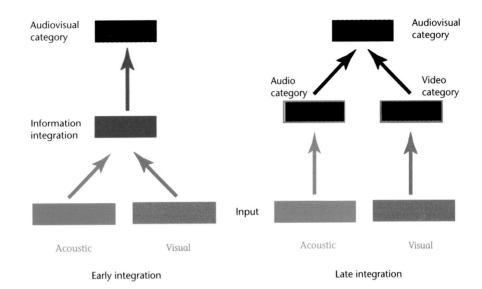

Figure 11.6
Sensory Integration
In late integration (right), the acoustic and visual information responses to the signal are processed significantly—and indeed could be used for classification—*before* they are brought together. In early integration (left), the acoustic and visual data are processed only slightly (if at all) before being brought together. Humans seem to employ late integration, whereas the best computer speechreading systems, we believe, will use early integration.

speechreading systems. Moreover, we can start with an early integration system and through learning (see below) obtain a late-integration system, should that happen to be more accurate for the particular task at hand. The converse, however, is not true; we cannot use learning to convert a late-integration system into an early-integration one. Another key difference between these schemes is that in an early integration scheme, bimodal features can be learned—for instance a VOT detector that *looks* for the opening of the mouth and *listens* for the vocal folds—while measuring the time between these events. Such bimodal features can, in principle at least, provide information that can't be detected or exploited in a late-integration scheme.

What Is the Best Unit to Recognize?

An important consideration in building a speechreading system is deciding which speech unit to base it on. Should it be the smallest linguistically recognizable units, the phonemes—such as /h/, /a/, /l/, and so on—which can later be grouped into words and, ultimately, into sentences? Or should it be words themselves? Or perhaps some intermediate-level unit?

The answer very much depends on the intended speechreading application. If the goal is to recognize a small number of simple commands—such as "open file," "power off," and so on for a voice-activated computer, or "make copy," "collate," the numbers, and so on, for a copier—then words or the commands themselves are the proper unit. Indeed, speechreading (and acoustic speech-recognition) systems based on a small number of commands are fairly accurate.

But what about the much harder problem of continuous, large-vocabulary transcription, such as would have been used by HAL, or which you might desire in your personal computer so that you can dictate a business letter? Alas, the number of words necessary is so large that it is difficult indeed to build a speech-recognition system that can recognize them all accurately. We might be tempted, then, to try to recognize phonemes and then put them together to recognize a spoken word. Unfortunately, this too has proven to be nearly impossible. The problem is that there are no unique sounds associated with each phoneme, primarily because of a phenomenon known as *coarticulation"*—that is, the influence of one utterance on the sound of another.

To hear an example of coarticulation, say the words *skeet* and *skoot* slowly, and listen carefully to the sound of the /s/ at the beginning of each word. In *skeet,* the /s/ has a high-pitched rushing noise; in *skoot* the noise sound (technically called *frication*) is much lower in pitch. In *skeet,* your lips are pulled back in anticipation of the /ee/ sound that will follow, whereas in *skoot,* your lips are pushed forward, or rounded, in anticipation of the /oo/ to follow. (These are examples of *anticipatory coarticulation,* in which the influence is forward in time; other forms of coarticulation influence sound later.) There is, hence, no ideal or unique sound of /s/, and this makes recognition extremely difficult indeed. The fundamental result is that there is no single sound for *any* phoneme; the sound depends strongly upon the context of neighboring sounds. Coarticulation can occur between phonemes in a single word, or between sounds in neighboring words, or even in neighboring sentences! All efforts to try to recognize phonemes have been, ultimately, unsatisfactory.

The most successful approach has been to use groupings of phonemes as the fundamental unit; for instance *triphones* such as /bru/, /tri/, /sko/, . . . even though there are more types of triphones than phonemes. The choice of triphones strikes the best balance between the competing desiderata of having a small number of units, on the one hand, and a unique sound for each unit, on the other.

We should point out that coarticulation, while a formidable obstacle to speech recognition, is not the only problem. Overall rate, varieties of accents, and high-level linguistic considerations make speech recognition an extremely challenging task (cf. chapter 7).

Training and Recognition

In bottom-up approaches to building speechreading systems, we use machine-learning techniques to adjust and refine the system based on information provided by a large number of example utterances. For instance, we might present the image and sound of a known utterance, say /tri/, to our untrained recognizer. Suppose that it classifies the utterance incorrectly as, say /bee/. The parameters within the recognizer are then automatically adjusted by a learning algorithm to make the actual output less like the incorrect /bee/, and more like the desired /tri/ representation.

We need not delve into the details here, except to say that we use both neural networks and Hidden Markov Models in our system. A basic neural network consists of a number of *units* that are very loosely based on neurons or nerve cells in a brain. The sensory signals or features (from the microphone signals or video signal sensed by the system) go into the first, or input, layer of units, which process the signals and emit altered signals through connections to units in the subsequent, or hidden layer. Neurons in the hidden layer collect signals from a large number of input units—indeed, typically, from all of them—then alter the signals and pass new signals on to units in the final, or output layer.

The power of a neural network lies in the existence of learning rules—so-called connectionist learning rules—for adjusting the strengths of the connections between neurons in order to make the whole network perform as desired. In brief, one presents a speech pattern to the input units, then adjusts the connections in order to make the output match the desired output. Actually, we use far more sophisticated networks—ones that have particular patterns of connections, or *architectures*. Nevertheless, the networks we use employ the same basic learning mechanism; when used in conjunction with the Hidden Markov Models (see chapter 7), they adequately address the problems of coarticulation and rate invariance that plague speech recognition.

It is at this point that one important benefit of bottom-up methods comes into play. If the recognizer is not performing accurately enough for our application, we can always provide more training data. This is much easier than trying to improve the system by top-down techniques after we have programmed in all the features and information provided by human experts.

Through learning, our system finds groupings of low-level features (such as the parameters from the deformable lip template) that are useful for categorization. (In a neural network, the hidden units often become, effectively, complicated feature detectors.) Although our system creates only a meager f-tuck detector, it creates an excellent rounding detector (using shape from shading and parameters from the lip template). Moreover, through learning, the system can determine how to weight the information from different subsystems; that is, which utterances are best categorized by relying primarily on the audio, which should rely on the video, and how to find the ideal balance for others. For instance, a system trained in noise-free conditions

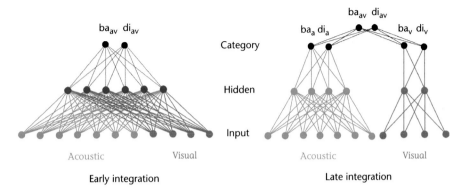

Figure 11.7

Neural Network

A basic network consists of layers of nonlinear units, or "neurons," that accept input signals, process them, and pass new signals on to neurons in subsequent layers. For a speechreading application, the signals input to the first layer could be the acoustic and visual
features of the talker; the output features could represent the possible categories of the
utterance—for instance, diphones or triphones. Connectionist learning rules are used to
adjust the connections between neurons to improve the performance of the network as a
whole; that is, to make it categorize utterances properly. In practice, networks would have
more than the two categories—/ba/ and /di/—shown here.

learns to give greater credence to the sound, as it conveys more of the speech
information. A system trained in noisy conditions, however, would learn to
give greater credence to the visual information.

It is worth noting that at the time *2001* was filmed, the most sophisticated
neural networks that could be trained had merely an input layer and an
output layer—no hidden layer. Because such two-layer nets are not powerful
enough for complicated problems such as speech and speechreading, and
because no one was able to develop a learning algorithm that would work
with the more powerful three-layer networks, connectionist methods fell
into disrepute for many years. Later, by the end of the 1970s and beginning
of the 1980s, researchers developed learning algorithms for three-layer networks, and these have led to an explosion in research and applications on
neural networks.

How Well Do They Work?

There are many different ways to judge the effectiveness of computer speech-reading systems, depending upon the environment (amount and type of noise), task (nonsense syllables, isolated words, connected natural speech, single talker or multiple talker), and so on. A good way to describe speech-reading systems is according to how much they reduce the classification error over a purely acoustical recognizer trained on the same amount of data. One of our systems reduces the error by 10 percent over the state-of-the-art acoustic recognizer in noise-free environments (on a small vocabulary-isolated word task). Our system significantly outperforms acoustic recognizers operating in noisy conditions, reducing the error by as much as 50 percent.

It is especially worth noting the pattern of errors we find. When we use the *visual-only* subsystem, we get very different errors (or confusions) than when we use the *acoustic-only* subsystem. For instance, our acoustic subsystem distinguishes poorly between /bee/ and /dee/, but our visual subsystem does just fine (because the mouth is closed for /bee/ but not /dee/). Conversely, our visual subsystem has difficulty distinguishing /pee/ from /bee/ (they are visemes), but our acoustic system does just fine (because of the difference in VOT). This matches the kind of complementarity psychologists find for humans. Naturally, the acoustic subsystem is overall more accurate than the visual one. The full audio-visual speechreading system is more accurate then either subsystem alone; the ambiguities in the visual subsystem are resolved by the acoustic subsystem, and vice versa.

Although it was by no means an original goal of our research, we thought it might be fun to see if our system had McGurk responses similar to those found in humans. Indeed, we found that our late-integration systems had McGurk responses similar to those of humans, while our early-integration systems had somewhat different responses. We took this as weak, and very indirect (though intriguing), support for psychological models that posit late integration for humans.

Where Do We Go from Here?

Computer speechreading is in a state of development comparable to that of acoustic recognition in the 1940s—that is, infancy. There is a great deal of work yet to be done. Much of the remaining research is integrative in nature: trying to figure out how best to put together such components as computer vision algorithms, learning methods, acoustic processing, and so forth, and then tailoring systems to particular applications.

The manifest need for accurate and natural human-machine interfaces—in particular for voice-activated ones—will continue to drive our research in speechreading. We are fortunate to have some astounding developments in computer hardware (chapter 3) and computer algorithms (chapter 10) at our disposal. We foresee no major impediments to the development of speechreading systems that can extract the vast majority of phonologically relevant features useful for automated speech recognition. It will be many decades, however, before subtle facial expressions can be captured. The most daunting obstacle to a speechreading system is the same one that blocks acoustic speech—how to represent, learn, and use the linguistic information and world knowledge needed to understand the speech. Despite current progress, a speech reading capability like HAL's will remain a distant dream for quite some time.

Acknowledgment

Thanks to my graduate student, Marcus Hennecke, for assistance with figure preparation.

Further Readings

Richard E. Berg and David G. Stork. *The Physics of Sound* (2nd ed.). Englewood-Cliffs, N.J.: Prentice-Hall, 1994. An introduction to acoustics, including problems in speech recognition.

Jens Blauert. *Spatial Hearing: The Psychophysics of Human Sound Localization*, rev. ed. Cambridge: MIT Press, 1996. A treatment of how humans and animals tell where a sound is coming from, and the role of attention in the cocktail party effect.

Carol Lee De Fillippo and Donald G. Sims, eds. "New Reflections on Speechreading." *The Volta Review* 90 no. 5. Washington, D.C.: Alexander Graham Bell Association for the Deaf, 1988. A mixture of psychological research and social analysis of the deaf.

Richard O. Duda, Peter E. Hart, and David G. Stork. *Pattern Classification and Scene Analysis, Part I: Pattern Classification* (2nd ed.). New York: Wiley, 1998 (in preparation). An advanced textbook on the techniques of pattern classification. The introductory sections are nonmathematical and highlight the nature and extent of such subproblems of pattern recognition as learning, segmentation, and sensory integration.

David S. Falk, Dieter R. Brill, and David G. Stork. *Seeing the Light: Optics in Nature, Photography, Color, Vision and Holography.* New York: Wiley, 1986. This introduction to human and machine vision includes problems such as recognizing shape from shading.

John P. Frisby. *Seeing: Illusion, Brain, and Mind.* New York: Oxford University Press, 1980. A well-illustrated and engaging discussion of problems in human and computer vision relevant to speechreading.

Audrey B. Greenwald. *Lipreading Made Easy.* Washington, D.C.: Alexander Graham Bell Association for the Deaf, 1984. An elementary "how to" book, complete with photographs of lips and faces, showing what to look for when speechreading. An accompanying videotape is available from the Alexander Graham Bell Association.

Peter H. Lindsay and Donald A. Norman. *Human Information Processing: An Introduction to Psychology.* New York: Academic Press, 1972. An introductory textbook containing a clear discussion of the cocktail party effect and of numerous phenomena of human visual and auditory perception.

David G. Stork and Marcus E. Hennecke, eds. *Speechreading by Humans and Machines.* New York: Springer-Verlag, 1996. This somewhat technical book describes the state of the art in machine speechreading and the current theories of how humans perceive speech by eye and by ear. It contains the most complete bibliography on the subject ever assembled.

Sholom M. Weiss and Casimir A. Kulikowski. *Computer Systems that Learn: Classification and Prediction Methods from Statistics, Neural Nets, Machine Learning, and Expert Systems.* San Mateo, Calif.: Morgan Kaufmann, 1991. An introduction to the basic techniques in machine learning, giving clear, intuitive explanations, that rely only occasionally on elementary mathematics.

12 Living in Space: Working with the Machines of the Future

Donald A. Norman

One major clue testifies to the fact that *2001* depicts fiction not fact: things work smoothly. The only failures are central to the plot, the main one being the apparent failure of HAL himself; yet even this lapse is more a result of an unresolved conflict of goals rather than of error. Two other, human, errors—one trivial, one potentially lethal—also occur. When David Bowman removes his food mush from the food-preparation unit, he burns himself slightly. His potentially lethal mistake comes when he forgets to take along his helmet as he rushes to the space capsule to try to rescue Frank Poole. (More about this mistake later.)

The film represents an unobtainable utopia where technology works flawlessly and humans make no errors in using it. Today, researchers spend considerable effort studying human-machine interactions in an attempt to minimize difficulties and problems. Watching *2001*, we see no difficulties. What a welcome change from the reality of NASA's Apollo 13—a flight beset by troublesome—and therefore realistic—mechanical and design problems.

The major tour de force of *2001*, of course, is HAL, that magnificent computer with the forbidding stare. HAL was the embodiment of perfect technology. Nothing is beyond his powers, not even lies or full voice understanding—even of elliptical sentences spoken at a distance. HAL's voice output is kindly, strong, and very human-sounding. With HAL on board, one wonders, why are humans even needed on the mission?—a thought that obviously occurs to HAL, who concludes that they aren't. Yet, the otherwise perfect HAL errs and only manages to kill four of the five humans on *Discovery.*

Ah, the 1960s—era of profound optimism in technology! Technology could do no harm. Computers would get bigger and bigger, both in physical size and in power. Artificial intelligence (AI) was just around the corner. Why, by January 12, 1997, the date of HAL's creation, the AI problem would surely be solved: computers would be able to mimic—and exceed—the highest achievements of human intelligence.

On Artificial Intelligence

First, a few comments on the development of artificial intelligence. I am a cognitive scientist, a field very closely allied with artificial intelligence. I believe we are still a very long way away from creating a system as powerful as HAL. A very long way. Human intelligence means more than intellectual brilliance: it means true depth of understanding, including shared cultural background and knowledge—the sort of background that takes decades to acquire. It also means what Daniel Goleman refers to as *emotional intelligence:* the knowledge and skills of social interaction, including the ability to cooperate and compete successfully with colleagues, friends, and rivals. In the 1960s, workers in the related fields of cognitive psychology and artificial intelligence ignored emotions and social interaction and focused exclusively on sheer intellect: reasoning, remembering, problem solving, decision making, and thought. At the time, the field appeared to be making rapid progress. We now know that progress was so rapid because we were solving the easy problems first; but in the heady optimism of the day, many assumed that the early successes signaled an early victory. Today, we are far less cocky.

The parts of human intelligence we thought would be easy to simulate—seeing, hearing, walking, moving—turned out to be incredibly difficult. We have barely begun to study the social and emotional aspects of artificial intelligence (see chapter 13). As for intellectual skills such as chess playing, mathematical calculation, and problem solving, these too have turned out to be difficult, although we are much further along on these dimensions. But so what? None of these abilities is the true hallmark of human intelligence. The reason we are in such awe of people who can remember long strings of numbers or do arithmetic calculations in their heads is that these are rare talents, not normal ones. And, I might add, they are thoroughly useless talents in this era of paper and pencil, books, and computers. Machines are far better suited to remembering and manipulating arbitrary symbols than we are. So let technology do the mind-numbing stuff. Let us stick to the fun things at which we excel. Our strengths are in creativity, serendipity, art, music, and humor. We cope with the unexpected by exercising that creativity—witness Dave's ability to reenter the ship without his helmet, something the logical HAL assumed was impossible.

It takes twenty-one years to become an adult, and we spend most of those years in school, learning the culture, history, skills, and knowledge we expect all citizens to have. After all that, it may still take decades of training to become expert in a particular endeavor. Yet HAL was only ten years old. How did he get all the necessary knowledge, including a deep understanding of human behavior? "Something seems to be bothering you," says HAL to Dave. That's pretty impressive. I know people who don't notice when another person is upset. (See chapter 9 for the problem of obtaining all the needed knowledge of the world and chapter 13 for the difficulty of recognizing emotional states.)

Is HAL possible? Certainly not with today's technology. Speech understanding? Not even close. Lying? No way: that requires emotional intelligence and very advanced understanding. After all, telling a lie requires knowing what the other person is likely to believe, concocting a believable story that fits the circumstances, and modifying it smoothly when circumstances require. Most people can't manage it well, but HAL does a magnificent job. Lying is at the pinnacle of human intelligence, because it requires not just knowledge, but metaknowledge. Some theorists of human development see the need for both social cooperation and deception as driving forces in the evolution of intelligence. Thus, monkeys do deceive one another, but they don't do it very well. Apes, especially chimpanzees, are partially successful. In humans, it takes years to develop the appropriate skills: human babies can't do it at all and children do it clumsily, at best. Building models of other people's knowledge and understanding is far beyond today's science. Yet HAL, with his supposedly superior intelligence, lies brilliantly.

Arthur C. Clarke and Stanley Kubrick's extreme optimism—the mid-twentieth-century view of technology—is now very much in doubt. HAL is a direct descendant of the more-is-better, bigger-is-more-powerful school of technology that began in the 1940s with ENIAC and continues with massively parallel supercomputers like the CM.5 (see figures 12.1 and 12.2). Computers would get bigger and bigger as well as more and more powerful. The writers and advisers of *2001* did not foresee that very large-scale integrated circuits would make machines both more powerful and smaller. If they missed this development, it's not surprising that they also failed to predict distributed computation—using a network of many smaller computers instead of one massive one. Instead, HAL's architecture was clearly inspired by 1966 mainframes. I suspect that the original, large military computer system, the Sage system, was the direct inspiration for HAL. Ah, yes, Sage—the early military computer that monitored radar stations spread across the northern hemisphere; that great system once declared that the United States was under missile attack by the Soviet Union when its programs were confused by a radar return from a large object in space—the moon.

Today, with microminiaturization and integrated circuits, we realize that the more powerful the machine, the smaller it must be, for wiring length becomes a critical factor. The alternative solution is to distribute our most powerful machines in space, networking them together with multiple parallel, independent processors to create a highly intelligent system. HAL, however, is built in the style of the old mainframes that we could walk inside to remove components. Look at all those memory cards on removable boards. Wow! Watching this part of the film takes me back to the 1960s. Too bad—it's supposed to move me forward to the 2000s.

Figure 12.1
Betty Jennings and Frances Bilas (right) Setting Up a Part of the ENIAC in 1946
Ms. Bilas is arranging the progress settings on the master programmer. Note the portable function table on her right. (*Source:* Courtesy of the Charles Babbage Institute, University of Minnesota)

Figure 12.2
The Connection Machine® model CM-5, from Thinking Machines Corporation
The CM-5 is one of the most powerful high-performance computers in the world. *Source:*
Copyright Thinking Machines Corporation 1994. (Photo by Steve Grohe)

The Movie

This movie, I keep reminding myself, was released in 1968. Given what we knew then, it is remarkable. Given what we know today, it is badly flawed.

What am I—an expert in human cognition and the design of systems that are usable and understandable—to make of the technology in *2001?* What does it suggest about the interaction between the people and the systems aboard present space platforms? What about HAL? In writing this piece, I am torn about what approach to take. Three possibilities occur to me.

First, I could simply review how well the film forecast future developments, given the fact that much of what we now take for granted did not yet exist in 1968. The creators' extensive production notes show the incredible planning and detail that went into designing the sets and props, even items we see for only a few seconds. The film does an excellent job of capturing the spirit of what routine space travel will probable be like some century or other, even if it is inaccurate in many details. What more could we ask? The spirit is what counts; and in this regard, even the details are superb and add immensely to the overall impact of the story.

A second alternative is to discuss how likely we are to have the technical capabilities the film predicted we would have by the year 2001. The answer is simple—most unlikely. Some things, of course, we do better today.

Finally, I could explore how we might go about designing technology shown in the film, in the light of significant advances, in many areas, and—in others—surprisingly little progress.

Instead of taking one of these approaches, I've chosen to do all three in my comments on some of the human and technical developments we saw in the film and experience in our real lives in the 1990s.

The Technology

I am struck more by the mundane than the profound. What impressed me most in *2001*? Why the everyday aspects of space life: the video phone, the use of identification badges, the strangely formal setting of the moon-base conference room, the boredom of the jobs on the space station—to say nothing of the years of nothingness on the Jupiter probe. The food was bland, and there was no music for the astronauts. (The producers failed to anticipate the Sony Walkman.)

In life, the really difficult parts of technology design are the human and social factors, not the technical ones. So it is with the movie. The technology is handled pretty well, but the makers of *2001* thought that technology was all there was. Make computers faster and faster and, *voilà,* you have machines capable of human understanding. Get the technology right and all the rest will follow.

Wrong. As I have already noted, artificial intelligences are far from reality. The task of AI has proven far more complex than anyone in the 1960s dreamed. As for space travel, the movie assumes that once it was achieved, long-distance voyages would follow quickly. They failed to consider how long it takes a new technology to build up the infrastructure required to use it routinely. Most technologies take fifty years to develop an infrastructure adequate for everyday use. The movie's writers assumed that by 2001 space flights would be so common that there would be hotels in space. They thought so many travelers would show up on the moon that identification badges and security checks would be needed to enter a station. The space-ships would be so powerful that travelers wouldn't have to worry much about the weight of personal belongings—notice the lost cashmere sweater at the space station. All these assumptions ignore the tremendous difficulties of building an infrastructure to support such activities—infrastructure that would take decades to accomplish.

Human-Computer Interaction

Old-fashioned Displays

The place to start with human-machine interaction is, of course, computer displays. I was struck by the poverty of imagination in the computer displays, in particular, the lack of graphical interfaces—all those tedious numbers and tables, relieved only by a few graphs and some stick figures (see chapter 15). In the computer science world of 1966, future machines seem to have been envisioned as more of the same—bigger, more powerful perhaps, but nonetheless more of the same. That's not how it turned out. Our present-day graphics and machine interaction are far superior to what *2001* predicted. The ability of computers to provide detailed, three-dimensional, dynamic visualizations of scientific and engineering data structures and phenomena is one of computer science's most impressive advances. By comparison, the simple text and skeleton-figure displays in the movie are primitive.

Looking at human aspects of computer use in *2001*, it seems clear that the designers of the film's machines were technical folks—engineers and computer programmers. Today, we recognize that machines designed for people should be designed by those who understand people: psychologists, linguists, anthropologists. The new field of human-computer interaction is focused on appropriate ways of interacting with machines. As a result, we know that presenting information as endless tables of numbers is most definitely not the most meaningful approach. Graphic displays can present complex relationships simply and use a single picture to convey information with precision. Human perception can interpret such a display without the laborious read-remember-and-compare operations required to make sense of tables of numbers.

In a similar fashion, modern display technology is geared to providing people with good conceptual models and understanding of information. Notice, for example, the impoverished information available to the crew when HAL informs them that a transmitter module is on the verge of failure: a picture showing the location of the module and a few lines of computer code. David and Frank should have asked for evidence showing the basis of the prediction. Instead, they have to take HAL's word for it.

By the 1960s, we already had a wealth of information about designing systems for people, even though the field of human-computer interaction, and the related fields of cognitive ergonomics and cognitive engineering, did not yet exist on a formal basis. The consultants for *2001*, however, were clearly technical experts, not people experts. Look again at those display screens: Why, they even display computer language codes—as if they would help! Such simple, low-level statements could not tell the astronauts anything useful. Real computer programs are huge and contain millions of commands, so showing a line or two of code is most unhelpful. Knowing that the machine is executing some detailed command doesn't help users understand *what* a machine is doing: what they really need to see is the goal stack—the list of goals the system is trying to accomplish, and what methods it is using to accomplish them. Mind you, the concept of the goal stack was unknown in 1968, so the only reason for displaying the codes is stylistic. The result is a typical dilemma when art tries to represent life: the producer had to make the movie seem authentic by portraying the situation unauthentically.

The Cockpits of the Space Shuttles

On the space shuttle, the piloting arrangements follow the style of airplanes: two pilots command the ship sitting side by side looking out of the windshield and hand-manipulating the controls at landing and takeoff. The film's main advance is using only two pilots; when the film was made, most air-planes had three crew members. Although the film shows a glass cockpit, like those in today's aircraft—with multiple display screens instead of individual instruments—the information displayed seems inappropriate. Our most advanced planes (e.g., the Boeing 777) do a lot better today. Then again, if you look closely at the displays, you can see that they don't seem to be made for the pilots: they are positioned so that we, the movie audience, can see them but are not readily visible to the pilots. That's O.K., because the images displayed aren't directly relevant to the control process anyway. The various computer displays in the movie are meant to convey realism, not to be real.

The thing I found the strangest, in our present era of superautomation, was pilots doing everything by hand. Obviously, the designers were not far-sighted enough. Why have two people in a highly automated environment? Didn't they know the standard joke about automation? It takes only one person and a dog: the dog's job is to make sure the person doesn't touch the controls. The person's job is to feed the dog.

The Picture Phone

The videophone—what AT&T in those days called the picture phone—is perhaps the most interesting of the technologies shown, at least from the standpoint of human-machine interactions. In spite of the considerable research on this technology carried out at AT&T, and in spite of the memo they wrote about it for the producers, I see no particular advances in the technology over what is possible today. There are even a few problems. One is the number of digits required for the phone number: eleven digits dialed in groups of three, three, and five. That's rather interesting. It was as if they planned for a three-digit area code (as today), a three-digit exchange code (as today), and a five-digit personal code (today we use four). The extra digit is good, because we will certainly have to move to at least eleven-digit tele-phone numbers by the year 2001 (probably before). But what about a coun-try code? Surely a call from the international space station would have to indicate a country; yet repeated study of the dialing sequence always yields the same pattern of 3–3–5: no country code there.

Note too how rapidly the connection is made—faster than for even local calls today—and the charge—$1.70 for several minutes of video connection. That's impressively cheap. I also liked the way the caller was told the cost of the call. Even AT&T's most advanced screen telephones today don't provide that information, although the technology to do so is available. That strikes me as a great advance, but not necessarily one a telephone company's director of marketing would like.

Actually, the book was more realistic than the movie. It specifies both a country code (83 for the United States rather than today's code of 1) and a twelve-digit home number. That's actually quite realistic. By the year 2001, we will have run out of combinations for the current ten-digit numbers and will very likely have moved to eleven or twelve digits.

The major flaw in the scenes showing use of the videophone was the problem of eye contact; that is, Dr. Floyd and his daughter appear to be looking at one another, but they couldn't with the camera placed as it is shown. The camera is above the screen, so that for Floyd's daughter to look at her father's eyes, she would have to look below the camera, and Floyd would see her looking down instead of at him. This is a well-known problem that is being worked on today but was evidently not considered during filming.

Boredom, the Greatest Challenge

One of the real dangers of a long, extended trip through space is boredom, which would be greatly exacerbated by a system as heavily automated as *Discovery 1*. With HAL, what is there for the astronauts to do? The film does convey the tediousness of space life quite well. We see David and Frank exercising and sunbathing, eating bland food, watching video shows about themselves. What else did they do with their time?

On the space platform too, there is little to do. Consider the person sitting listlessly at the Hilton check-in desk. The job of the poor woman (all women are uniformly called girls in the movie) is to check visitor's identities—or, rather, direct them to the machine that checks their identities. She can, however, manually select the language to be used on the machine. Manually select? In an age where automation was all-powerful, why would such a simple choice be left to an attendant? Surely if this task couldn't be done automatically, users could easily do it themselves, couldn't they? What must it have cost to maintain the three or four people needed to maintain the desk at all hours of the day?

The book *2001* is more satisfying in this regard. It tells us about the daily schedules of both Frank and Dave and describes the arrangement of their nonoverlapping work shifts. "They knew what they would be doing at every moment of the twenty-four hours. They operated on twelve-hours-on, twelve-hours-off basis, taking charge alternately, and never both being asleep at the same time." During their off-duty hours, they could study, listen to music, read, or watch movies. They could play games with HAL, but evidently only "semimathematical games" such as checkers, chess, and polyminoes. HAL was programmed to win half the time "and his human partners pretended not to know this."

Semimathematical games? Weird. What a lack of imagination. No sports? No competitive games between Frank and Dave? Of course, when the movie was made, the entire genre of computer games didn't exist, and the writers failed to foresee them. That's what happens when you leave prediction up to the technocrats: all they think of is the technology, not having fun.

The film also leaves out music and books, which seems very strange, unless somehow, the producers thought viewers wouldn't be interested in them. But can you imagine a life without music? No rock and roll? No classical? No country and western? The only music in the entire film (not counting the theme) are David's parents singing "Happy Birthday" over the videophone link and HAL himself, when being disconnected singing "Daisy, Daisy," the song taught to him by his creator. Nor do we see the astronauts writing letters or diaries. (I guess in 1968 nobody realized that astronauts would be offered lucrative book deals.) No photographs (though Dave does a few bland sketches of the crew). No music. Yawn. All there is to do is exercise and check on HAL, not that HAL should need checking. And talk to Houston control.

So poor David and Frank, awake for the many months on the flight to Jupiter, have virtually nothing to do. After all, HAL does all the important things. Yet, boredom, a well-known result of overautomation, can have serious consequences. In factories, ships, and aircraft, when operators have too little to do, they are "out of the loop"; that is, they are no longer on top of the details of the task. When something goes "boom," they take seconds to react, seconds to get going. More often than is desirable, they fail.

Human Error

The major source of accidents in commercial aviation today is human error. Mind you, I believe that most of this error is caused by poor design of equipment and procedures. Whatever the reason—as I point out in my *Psychology of Everyday Things*—error is very frequent. A NASA study of aviation flights indicates that pilots make roughly a dozen errors during a transcontinental flight. If errors are so common, why are there so few in *2001?* The real reason, of course, is that the sort of bumbling errors we all commit in real life don't make for a good movie. Movies are about storytelling, and the foibles of everyday life would simply get in the way.

Nor would emphasizing poor design details create dramatic scenes. My examination of the control panels of the spaceship, the shuttle, the lunar bus, and *Discovery* show them to be the same sort of poorly organized push buttons and lights that lead to so many errors in real life.

It's also amusing to watch Dave and Frank checking the ship by making written notes on clipboards. Look up, read a number, look down, and enter it in the correct column. I guess the designers failed to anticipate automatic logging equipment, handheld computers, or PDAs—personal digital assistants. All that hand-recording is bound to lead to error, especially given the inconvenient translation between digital display and clipboard. I presume that the astronauts then transcribed the clipboard readings into some sort of machine-readable form—another opportunity for error. Nor do they even seem to be checking one another—one standard way of attempting to catch error.

But the major human error in the film, and a major dramatic element, occurs when Dave rushes to the space pod to chase after Frank's body. He forgets his helmet. Actually, he also forgets his backpack, which presumably contains the air supply. How could an experienced astronaut leave the ship without a helmet? In real life, there would be a checklist for every operation, and checking the suit, backpack, and helmet would certainly be on it. Yet we saw no checklists. Shame!

Actually, the whole sequence is puzzling. We see Frank—wearing full suit, helmet, and backpack and breathing through his air supply—as he trudges up the passageway leading to the pod bay. But why? The suits are normally kept in the pod bay, so he obviously had to go into the pod bay, take his suit back into the ship, put it on, then walk back, using up his precious air supply in an environment where it wasn't needed. We see the astronauts in the pod bay several times in the film without helmets. Still, his muffled voice inside the helmet makes for a great sound effect.

Dave apparently suits up inside *Discovery* while Frank is working outside— perhaps in case there is an accident while the pod bay doors are open or to be ready to exit the ship on a rescue mission—as indeed he must a few minutes later. Yet if this is a standard procedure, why is all the required equipment not arranged to be put on rapidly and efficiently? It seems to me that the space agency needs to launch a full-fledged investigation of this problem to determine just where the fault lies. In the absence of further information, I cannot judge. It seems, however, like a clearcut case of plot before credibility.

It's interesting that Clarke does not use this situation in the book. There, David doesn't chase after Frank but attempts to revive the hibernating crew. HAL then thwarts him by opening the pod bay doors and emptying the ship of air. After this, events follow the story line of the movie. Human error, therefore, seems necessary only in the interest of the film's plot. Too bad. It's most unreal.

Summary

The movie *2001* impressively depicts life in some future time when space travel is taken for granted. It underestimates, for some parts of technology, the amount of time it would take to develop the infrastructure for extensive space travel and exploration and to overcome the difficulties of building intelligent machines. Some actual technologies are not anticipated at all, especially the rapid miniaturization of computers through integrated circuits and the growth of powerful graphical displays. Other important factors, such as the social requirements, are ignored in the film. Still, the movie hit the main point squarely on the head. The space scenes are realistic; they feel real, and they convey exactly the right atmosphere. Overall, it's a job well done.

To critique the film, I had to view it with incredible care, sometimes frame by frame. The fact that it holds up well under this scrutiny speaks to the tremendous fidelity with which the film recreates the spirit of space travel. Its major flaws are to be too optimistic about technology's ability to produce an artificial intelligence but not nearly optimistic or inventive enough to predict advances in graphical displays and miniaturization of computation. There are no handheld computers and too many big devices. And no computer games. Shame!

Further Readings

D. Goleman. *Emotional Intelligence*. New York: Bantam Books, 1995. Shows the importance of "softer" aspects of cognition, related to emotion.

D. A. Norman. *The Psychology of Everyday Things*. New York: Basic Books, 1988. (Also published in paperback as *The Design of Everyday Things*. New York: Doubleday, 1990.) An exploration of the design issues surrounding common things—door handles, stove-top controls, lighting switches, etc.—and the frequent mistakes made in confronting them.

D. A. Norman. *Things That Make Us Smart*. Reading, Mass.: Addison-Wesley, 1993. An analysis of the design of computer interfaces, maps, and many other "things that make us smart" and how they affect how we think and act.

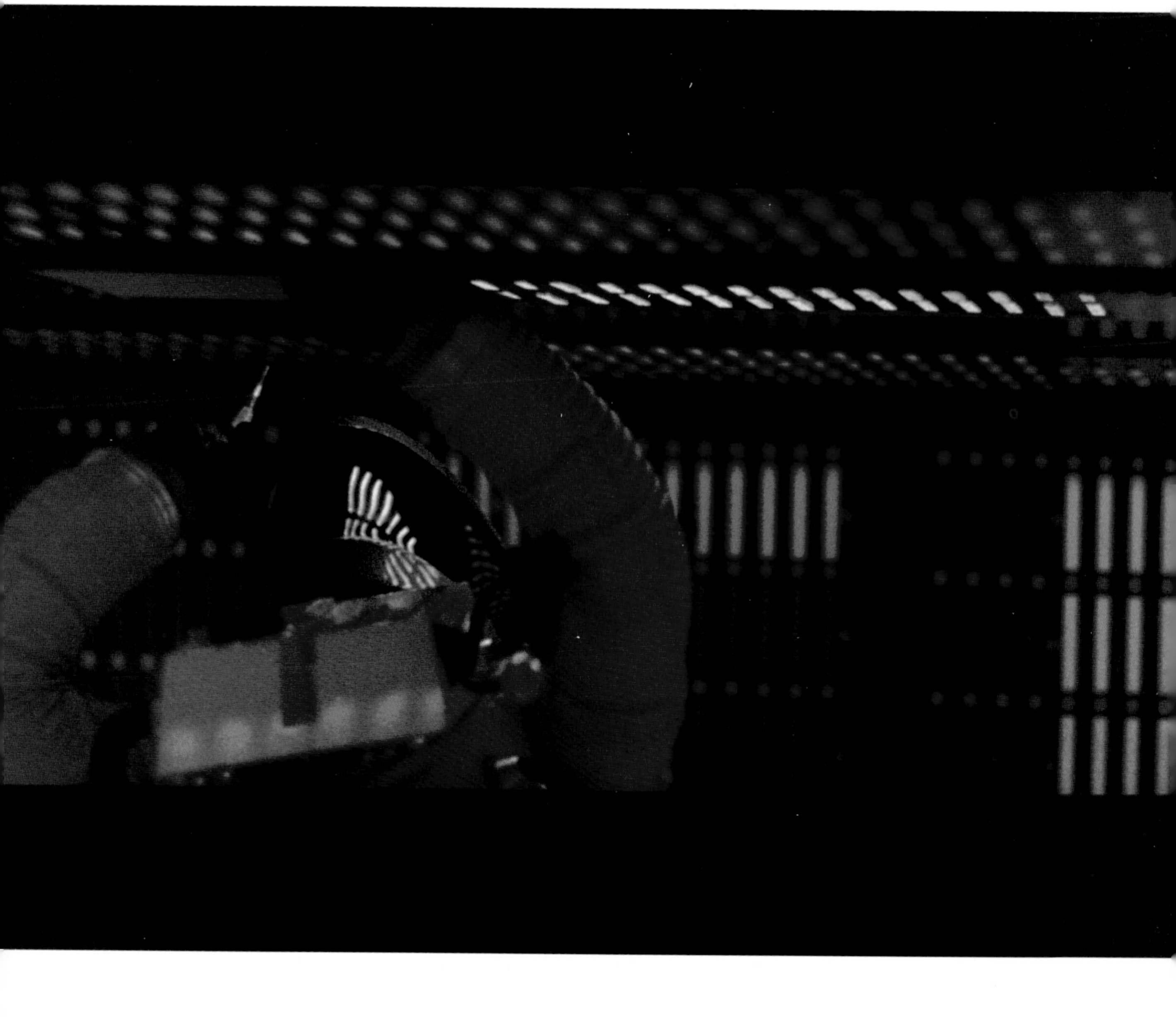

13   *Does HAL Cry Digital Tears? Emotion and Computers*

Rosalind W. Picard

HAL startles us in *2001*—initially with his smooth, confident voice, and later with his highly emotional words. Few viewers expected the world's most intelligent computer to speak as HAL does in that memorable scene when the only remaining crewman, Dave Bowman, begins to disassemble HAL and HAL commences his swan song.

HAL: Dave, stop . . . Stop, will you? Stop, Dave . . . Will you stop, Dave . . . Stop, Dave. I'm afraid . . . I'm afraid . . . I'm afraid, Dave . . . Dave . . . my mind is going . . . I can feel it . . . I can feel it . . . My mind is going . . . There is no question about it. I can feel it . . . I can feel it . . . I can feel it . . . I'm a . . . fraid . . .

HAL: Dave, stop. . . . Stop, Dave. . . . I'm afraid, I'm afraid, Dave . . .

HAL's expression of fear and his impassioned pleas no doubt struck a responsive chord of feeling in many viewers, for here HAL gives us the impression that he is not a heartless machine but a being who has genuine emotions.

Emotion is not simply a luxurious extra in *2001*. In film and theater, carefully controlled and expressed emotion has the ability to influence us and, subsequently, to affect whether we like a production and remember seeing it with pleasure. Surprisingly, in *2001*, the machine expresses more emotion than the humans. Many viewers *feel* a greater loss when HAL "dies," than they do when Frank Poole floats away into space. Emotion is a powerful tool in the hands of artists like Kubrick and Clarke. But, what about emotions in computers—for purposes other than entertainment?

Computers today don't emit plaintive cries when being disassembled, and most users wouldn't pay extra to get this feature. Instead, computers emit messages such as **unexpected fatal error -60.** They don't have emotions per se, although it is not unusual to hear someone yelling at a computer—as if it might feel sorry and change its behavior. If you yell at a puppy, perhaps because it wet on the rug, the puppy senses your anger and usually learns to correct its behavior, even wagging its tail to indicate delight when you finally appear pleased. Computers, by contrast, neither recognize your anger nor feel good or bad because of it. They don't notice whether you're attentive, annoyed, or have fallen asleep in front of them; they continue to "wet on the rug," so to speak, regardless of whether or not you yell at them.

Are emotions a desirable property for computers to have? It's hard to imagine someday walking into a computer store and saying, "Give me the most emotional machine you've got." After all, isn't possessing the highest form of rationality one of the hallmarks of computers? Aren't Mr. Spock and Data the unemotional patron saints of computer scientists? Imagine how a computer with emotion might work—perhaps it would have to feel interested before it would listen to what you have to tell it. On the face of it, emotions in computers sound absurd. After all, didn't emotion cause HAL to malfunction?

On the other hand, it would be tremendously worthwhile to have a computer that is congenial to interact with, flexible in its approach to doing what you want, makes snappy and intelligent decisions, and offers creative solutions to problems. It may surprise you to know that emotion plays a key role in all these qualities. In fact, emotion appears to be a necessary component of intelligent, friendly computers like HAL. The inability of today's computers to recognize, express, and have emotions severely limits their ability to act intelligently and interact naturally with us. But, emotion without balance can also lead to disaster, as it does in *2001*.

In the next few sections I discuss what we mean by emotion, what special emotional abilities HAL possesses, and some of the ways in which computers are becoming "affective." I then describe a paradoxical discovery—the importance of emotions in computers—look closely at HAL's disaster, and consider a dilemma regarding emotional machines.

What Is Emotion?

Emotion is a slippery word to define. Internal human states like fear and anger (what psychologists call *affective states*) seem obvious aspects of emotion. But what about *interest, boredom, hope, frustration,* and *lust*? The fact is that even emotion researchers don't agree on a definition of emotion, and many of them don't consider such feelings as love to be basic emotions. They also argue about whether there are any basic emotions, or whether, instead, there are only continuous states or just different kinds of thoughts that we label *emotions*. It may be a long time before researchers come up with a commonly accepted definition of emotion.

Fortunately, we don't need such a definition to understand this chapter; an intuitive notion of emotion will suffice. Nonetheless, the terminology can be confusing. Note that the word *feeling* doesn't always imply emotion; squeezing scrambled eggs between your fingers *feels* squishy, and is a tactile feeling, not an emotional one. On the other hand, we often use the words *affect* and *emotion* as, essentially, synonyms. In this chapter, we make notable exception to this practice when we use the forms to modify *computing*. In that case, because *emotional computing* tends to connote computers with an undesirable reduction in rationality, we prefer the term *affective computing* to denote computing that relates to, arises from, or deliberately influences emotions. *Affective* still means emotional, but may, perhaps usefully, be confused with *effective*.

For decades, researchers have tried to understand how emotions are generated, expressed, and recognized. A variety of theories have emerged. At one extreme is the idea that emotions are the experience of physiological changes such as the increased heart rate that accompanies anger. Researchers at the other extreme see emotions as purely cognitive, merely another form of thought. Psychologists leaning toward the first concept tend to look for universal physiological changes that correspond to emotions (such as raised eyebrows when a person is surprised). Although they have had some success in identifying such universals, their studies have been thwarted by a variety of factors. The generation of emotions is apparently influenced by, among other factors, goals, diet, attitude, expectation, perception, and culture. Rules about the social display of emotion—such as its inappropriate to show anger—also influence its expression and make it difficult for researchers to link affective states with forms of expression. There is presently no widely accepted, comprehensive theory of emotions, although much has been learned.

It is clear, however, that emotions can be communicated—especially through music and various forms of bodily expression. Emotions can even be contagious. You may recall a favorite teacher who was so enthusiastic about a subject that you became interested in it too. Or, you may have watched an actor express an emotion so effectively that its impact, not only on the other characters in the drama, but also on the audience, was electrifying. Actors study posture, gestures, facial expressions, and vocal intonation to find the best ways to communicate their character's feelings. An *effective* actor is a master of *affect*.

An example of the impact of emotional expression occurs in the film *Schindler's List* when the one-armed Jewish machinest goes to thank Schindler for giving him a job. His face lights up when he sees Schindler and he leans toward him with dignity and gratitude: "I want to thank you sir for giving me the opportunity to work . . . the SS beat me up, they would have killed me. But, I'm essential to the war effort thanks to you . . . God bless you, sir. You are a good man . . . God bless you." The sincere and grateful appreciation on the man's face clearly affects Schindler, and the viewer. This emotional scene becomes a turning point in the film, as we start to see Schindler's heart change.

Although emotion researchers have worked hard to uncover universal aspects of emotional behavior, few have explored emotions from the perspective of a person who knows another person well and can often guess his or her affective state. This is the approach available to HAL and the one we use to get to know another person. The key here is "get to know." HAL, working closely with a handful of people, can learn how each one of them expresses—or doesn't express—emotions under various circumstances. Once he becomes familiar with several individuals, he can discover commonalities in the ways they express emotions and perhaps use these discoveries to improve his recognition of affect in strangers. Nonetheless, to attain the best understanding of someone, he would have to get to know that person very well. In *2001,* HAL is not only well acquainted with the *Discovery*'s crew, he is able to enjoy relationships with them, as he tells the BBC interviewer.

Reporter: HAL, despite your enormous intellect, are you ever frustrated by your dependence on people to carry out actions?

HAL: Not in the slightest bit. I enjoy working with people. I have a stimulating relationship with Dr. Poole and Dr. Bowman.

Old Buddy, Ole Hal

How might HAL, or tomorrow's affective computer, develop a better relationship with you? For starters, it might be endowed with basic perceptual abilities, such as vision (see chapter 10), or hearing and speech understanding (chapters 7 and 8). To date, however, the emphasis in these research areas has been predominantly on tasks such as recognizing who you are and what you are saying. (Some of the findings of this research have also proven useful to humans who are vision-impaired or hearing-impaired.) Recognizing who is speaking and what is being said is important, but at times these observations are not as important as the expression on the speaker's face and how she or he said it. Recall the puppy example. Presumably the puppy doesn't understand most of what you are saying but it does know whether you are pleased or displeased.

The importance of how something is said has become a common problem for users of e-mail. If you rely on e-mail, you have probably spent some time trying to straighten out a misunderstanding. You dashed off a message that offended the recipient. You didn't intend it to sound obnoxious. If it had been a casual spoken comment—even if you had said it on the telephone—the misunderstanding might have been avoided. Instead, the recipient detected a nasty tone in your text and took offense. We say that e-mail is *affect-limited,* because it carries very little intonation. Even using *emoticons*—that is, symbol combinations like **:-)**—is a woefully inadequate way to express the range of natural human emotions. Tone is so important that when it is omitted people fill it in.

HAL, of course, doesn't have to rely on text-only communication with Frank and Dave. Not only can he hear and see them and speak to them, he has at least two other essential abilities: (1) HAL can express affect (as we saw above); and (2) he can recognize affect.

Consider the following snippet of dialogue, which occurs after HAL refuses to let Dave back on the ship and Dave manages to reenter and start to disassemble HAL.

HAL: Just what do you think you're doing, Dave? Dave? . . . Look Dave, I can see you're really upset about this. I honestly think you ought to sit down calmly, take a stress pill, and think things over.

Here we see HAL's ability to recognize emotion in Dave, as well as his relative inability to recommend an intelligent course of action based on this recognition; that is, his lack of emotional intelligence. (HAL's recipe for stress reduction sounds eerily like that used in Huxley's *Brave New World.*) I'll say more about emotional intelligence below; but first let's look at how HAL recognizes emotion. In the novel *2001,* Clarke tells us that HAL analyzes Dave's voice harmonics. We also might expect him to be able to interpret Dave's facial expression, as hearing and seeing are the only two perceptual abilities we know HAL possesses. We never hear that he has smell, taste, touch, or other physiological sensors.

However, close scrutiny of Dave indicates that his face is not very expressive; he rarely deviates from the stereotypical appearance of the calm, cool, scientist. His voice too is usually well controlled and only becomes firm when he orders HAL to open the door. Dave displays his strongest emotions when HAL refuses to obey. This occurs right after HAL has killed Frank and

He looks interested   **He looks distressed**   **He looks pleased**

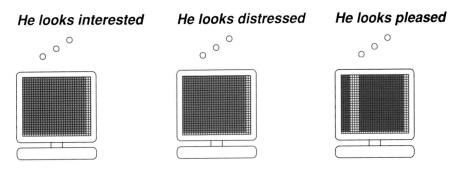

Figure 13.1
What If Computers Could Recognize the Affective States of Their Users?

everyone else on the ship. Dave, whose blood should be boiling by this time, gives only one subtle visual cue to how he feels: he straightens his lip in a barely detectable expression that is most likely an artifact of his attempt to suppress much stronger feelings that would be inappropriate to his cool scientific character. Earlier, while in the pod with Frank, Dave also shows subtle emotion—a slight lowering of his head—to agree with Frank that disconnecting HAL may become their only choice.

Otherwise, Dave is relatively impassive. In fact, all the humans in *2001* have rather machinelike demeanors. HAL, in contrast, is relatively expressive.

Moreover, HAL is two leaps ahead of today's computers in his ability to recognize emotion. Today's computers are affect-impaired; they blather on and on, filling your view with pages of output, regardless of whether you show interest or boredom. Would an intelligent human keep talking nonstop, face-to-face, after you close your eyes and open your mouth in a yawn the size of a barn door? Of course not. Then how can computers become intelligent friendly companions if they are not given at least the ability to recognize such emotions as interest, distress, and pleasure, which—some researchers claim—we are all born with (see figure 13.1).

Here is a scenario of how a computer tutor of the future might use recognition of affect to, perhaps, help you learn to play the piano. As you show interest in the topic and make rapid progress, it might provide optional interesting side avenues to explore. If you become distressed, perhaps because you are being pushed too far too fast, it might slow down and give encouraging suggestions, or revisit fundamentals. It might have the dual goal of maximizing learning and bringing pleasure but not pursue the latter goal 100 percent of the time, as some distress appears to be necessary for learning to occur. To be successful, the tutor would need to at least recognize and express affect. Ideally, it would also combine emotional intelligence (such as how and when to use empathy and how to adjust its teaching based on the student's affect) with other forms of knowledge—such as the subject matter and the best way to teach it.

Teaching Computers to Recognize and Express Emotion

Research in computer recognition and expression of emotion is in its infancy. Two of the current research efforts at the MIT Media Lab focus on recognition of facial expression and voice affect synthesis. These are not, of course, the only ways to recognize affective states; posture and physiological signs like gestures and increased breathing rate, for example, also provide valuable cues.

Computers, like people, can use cognitive reasoning—a form of common sense (see chapter 9)—to understand a person's goals and predict his or her affective state when they are disrupted. For example, HAL may predict that because "I killed Dave's colleagues and won't let him back on the ship, Dave will be upset." If prediction and observations agree, the computer is likely to strengthen its belief in that line of reasoning. If they disagree, it will see it as an interesting (perhaps even puzzling) event: "Most people would be enraged by all this, but Dave doesn't look very upset. He is great at concealing his emotions. Or maybe he knows something important I don't know?"

One way to recognize an expression is to record facial movements during a short video sequence, digitize the sequence, then apply the tools of pattern recognition. Recognition from a moving sequence is generally more accurate

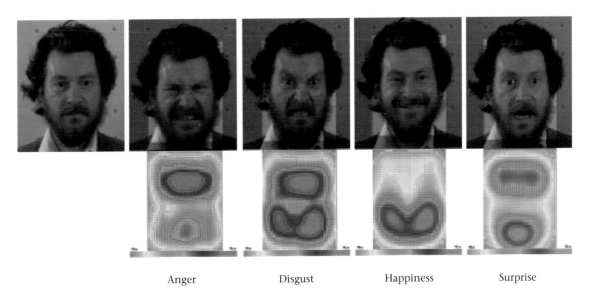

	Anger	Disgust	Happiness	Surprise

Figure 13.2
Facial Expression Recognition and Color Motion Energy Maps
Top row: snapshots of the neutral expression and four others—anger, disgust, happiness, surprise. *Bottom row:* templates of color-coded energy of each facial movement, in contrast to the still image of the neutral expression. (Courtesy of Irfan Essa and Alex Pentland.)

than recognition from a still image. If, for example, a person's "neutral" expression is a pout, only deviations from the pout (captured by video as movement) will be significant for recognizing affect.

Using this method requires a video camera, a digitizer, and a computer running video-analysis and pattern-recognition algorithms. Pattern recognition can utilize a variety of techniques—such as analyzing individual muscle actuation parameters or (more coarsely) characterizing an overall facial-movement pattern. In a test involving eight people, recognition rates were as high as 98 percent for four emotions (see figure 13.2). Studies are underway to determine how the recognition rate changes when there are more experimental subjects. As yet, this method of recognition doesn't work in real time; it takes a few seconds to recognize each expression. However, advances in hardware and pattern recognition should make recognition essentially instantaneous in the near future—at least for familiar expressions.

Although facial features are one of the most visible signs of underlying emotional states, they are also easy to control in order to hide emotion. Having a good "poker-face" that reveals none of your emotions is valuable, not only for playing cards, but also in the cutthroat worlds of business and law. The *social-display rules* of emotion specific to our culture are impressed upon us all as we grow up. I have seen a student who was undergoing great personal pain resist crying, while his eyes twitched unnaturally to hold back his tears. He was taught at an early age never to show emotion in public. Nonetheless, the healthy human body seems unable to suppress emotion entirely. He might not cry, but his eyes may twitch. She might not sound nervous, but she may, literally, have cold feet.

Emotional expression is not, clearly, limited to facial movement. Vocal intonation is the other most common way to communicate strong feelings. Several features of speech are modulated by emotion; we divide them into such categories as voice quality (e.g., breathy or resonant, depending on in-dividual vocal tract and breathing), timing of utterance (e.g., speaking faster for fear, slower for disgust), and utterance pitch contour (e.g., showing greater frequency range and abruptness for anger, a smaller range and down-ward contours for sadness), as illustrated in figure 13.3. As these features vary, the emotional expression of the voice changes. The research problem of precisely how to vary these features to synthesize realistic intonation so far remains unanswered.

The inverse problem—intonation analysis, or recognizing how something is said, is also quite difficult. Research to date has limited the speaker to a small number of sentences, and the results are still closely dependent on the

Figure 13.3a,b
Voice Inflection Synthesis
The same sentence, "I thought you really meant it," is spoken with (a) sad affect and (b) annoyed affect. The pitch track (top) and spectrogram (bottom) for each case are shown. Note the greater pitch range for the annoyed affect, as opposed to the relatively com-pressed range for the sad affect. The spectrograms also record differences in the speed, hesitation, and enunciation of the two cases. (Courtesy of Janet Cahn and Lisa Stifelman.)

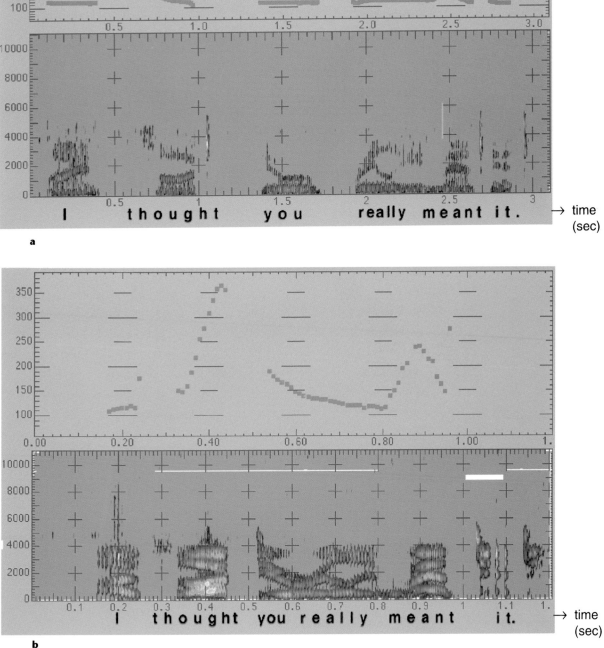

a

I thought you really meant it. → time (sec)

b

I thought you really meant it. → time (sec)

particular words spoken. A method of precisely separating what is said from how it is said has not yet been developed (see chapter 6).

You will note that no one method—whether recognition of facial expression or of voice intonation—is likely to produce reliable recognition of emotion. In this sense, affect recognition is similar to other recognition problems like speech recognition and lipreading. It is probable that a personalized combination taking into account both perceptual cues (say from vision and audition) and cognitive cues (such as HAL's reasoning about how Dave would respond) is most likely to succeed. These cues will undoubtedly work best when considered in context: is it a poker game, where bluffing is the norm, or a marriage proposal, where sincerity is expected?

Toward Truly Personal Computers

Does HAL have affect-recognition abilities beyond facial expression, vocal intonation, and common-sense reasoning about some typical emotion-inducing scenarios? We don't, of course, really know. Although Dave Bowman carefully controls his facial expression in the scene where HAL won't let him back on board, his anger may have been betrayed by some other body response—perhaps an increase in body temperature or breathing rate. Sensors that can detect these two forms of physiological expression, among others, currently exist. Affective computers in the future may have other perceptual sensors that are not limited to human senses. For instance, a humidity detector might reveal that someone is anxious, even before she or he breaks out in a full sweat.

Consider, for example, the fact that people who use computers touch the machine a lot. Whether through a mouse, keys, joy stick, or touch screen, many people have more physical contact with computers than they do with other people. Moreover, you can now wear computers—in your shoes, shirt pocket, or belt, for example. Wearable computers, especially when they become as common as underwear, will have unusual opportunities to get to know you in a variety of situations. They could have access to your muscular tension, heart rate, temperature, and so on. Instead of being restricted to perceiving only your visible and vocal forms of affect expression, they could get to know you intimately—or as well as you will permit them to. At this point, they will also, like underwear, probably cease to be shared and will become truly personal computers.

Suppose you have too much stress in your life and your doctor suggests that you learn to relax more. Your wearable affective computer could help you learn what events cause you stress and figure out ways to reduce it. While you are engrossed in playing with the kids, your affective wearable might whisper in your ear, "see how relaxed you are now." A little feedback device you could turn on or off might not only help reduce stress-related disorders, it might also assist in gathering important medical research data or helping patients in recovery. The key to the wearable computer is its constant presence; it is not limited to gathering data in the lab or doctor's office, but can get to know your range of responses during the daily routine.

Affective information could also be communicated in unconventional ways. Imagine that your wearable computer could detect the lilt in your walk as you leave the office and broadcast it to your spouse—encoded, of course (lest a salesperson learn of your happiness and take this auspicious opportunity to telephone you). The result would be a sort of "mood ring" that alerts you to your spouse's affective state—one that is more accurate than the dime-store temperature sensors once advertised on late-night television.

Applications of affective recognition could extend to entertainment as well; for example, interactive games might detect your level of fear and give bonus points for courage. When we measured the responses taken of a student playing the computer game DOOM in our lab, we expected the electromyogram of jaw clenching to peak during high-action events—such as when a new deadly enemy starts an attack. However, the biggest peak—and it was significantly higher than the others recorded—occurred when the student had trouble configuring the software! (See figure 13.4.)

What if software companies could obtain similar affective information about people interacting with their products? Unlike questionnaires, an affect-sensing computer could identify the parts of the software that provoke the greatest annoyances and those that produce the greatest pleasure. Not

Figure 13.4
Student Wearing Affective Sensors
She has a blood-volume–pulse sensor on her finger, a respiration monitor around her chest, a skin conductivity sensor on two fingers, and electromyogram and temperature sensors on her cheek. Although these devices are clumsy now, they will soon be integrated into smart clothing, jewelry, and furniture. (Courtesy of Jennifer Healey.)

only would the timing of affective responses be easier to relate to specific causes, but they would tend to capture product qualities that are hard to put into words. All makers of environments—architects, automobile manufacturers, software designers, decorators, hotel managers—benefit from learning how people *feel* when they are in their spaces.

Computers coupled with suitable sensors and pattern-recognition algorithms should soon be able to recognize the basic affective states of a willing individual in a typical context. The emphasis on *willing* participant here is important. Measurements of affective states obtained in an underhanded manner are not likely to be accurate. People who want to deceive such systems will probably succeed. One fellow, for example, managed to fool a polygraph by putting a thumbtack in his shoe under his big toe; he stepped on it every time he was questioned in a particular way. Affective information will be most accurate, and useful, when it is willingly communicated, presumably for the mutual benefit of everyone involved.

Emotions With Reason

We've seen that HAL possesses abilities for expressing and recognizing emotion and noted some of the ways we are giving today's computers these abilities. But what about creating computers that actually *have* emotion? What could that possibly mean? This question is partially one of philosophy and goes beyond the scope of this chapter. But it also relates to the structure of the human brain and touches on a paradox about the role of emotions and reason.

Perhaps the simplest description of the human brain is Paul MacLean's *triune brain,* which distinguishes three regions: the neocortex, the limbic system, and the reptilian brain (see figure 13.5). Although it is greatly oversimplified, this description has influenced how people think about brain functions. For example, many have assumed that the physically highest level of the brain, the neocortex, dominates the other, lower levels. However, this assumption is contradicted by evidence that the physically lower limbic system can effectively hijack the brain; that is, emotions can overtake so-called higher mental functions when they need to. The limbic system—the primary seat of emotion, attention, and memory—contains such structures as the hypothalamus, hippocampus, and amygdala. It helps determine *valence* (e.g., whether you feel positive or negative toward something) and *salience* (e.g., what gets your attention); it also contributes to human flexibility, unpredictability, and creative behavior. It has vast interconnections with the neocortex, so that brain functions are not either purely limbic or purely cortical but a mixture of both.

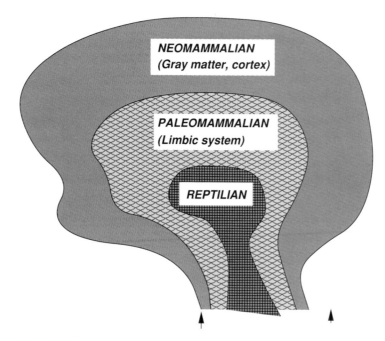

Figure 13.5

The Triune Brain

Paul MacLean (1949) described three general regions of the brain: the neomammalian, which contains the neocortex; the paleomammalian, containing the limbic system, which comprises the hypothalamus, hippocampus, and amygdala structures; and the reptilian, governing primitive functions. Because the limbic system also has a number of interconnections with the neocortex, brain functions tend to be a mixture of both limbic and cortical processing.

We have all, of course, seen emotions overwhelm reason (at least in others), which is one reason why the word *emotional* has negative connotations. (For example, people who panic out of fear may cause more harm to themselves than if they had "kept a cool head" and made rational decisions.) Nonetheless, it is clearly beneficial for our survival that fear can hijack our brain and cause us to jump out of the way of a rapidly approaching object before we can consciously perceive and analyze that a bus is about to hit us.

These kinds of emotions, which seem to be hard-wired or innate, are sometimes called *primary* emotions. They include responses such as the fear example above and involuntary reactions to surprise. Other emotions, the *secondary* emotions, appear to develop as we mature. They connect cognitive events with lower-level physiological responses and occur as a result of joint neocortical and limbic activity. Such emotions play an especially important role in decision making, even in decision making that appears to be purely rational.

Findings on the importance of emotions for rational decision making seem paradoxical. They are based on a remarkable story told by A. R. Damasio about the patient "Elliot." Elliot, and patients like him, have a particular kind of brain damage that affects a circuit between the prefrontal cortex and the amygdala, a communication channel between the neocortex and limbic system that appears to be essential for secondary emotions. At first glance, Elliot appears to be like Star Trek's Spock—emotionally unexpressive, unusually rational. One might think that Elliot would therefore be superb at making rational decisions. However, unlike the fictitious half-human Spock, Elliot's lack of emotions severely impairs his decision-making ability and causes tragedies in his business and personal life.

Although Elliot's IQ and cognitive abilities are all normal or above average, when confronted with a simple decision, such as when to schedule an appointment, he disappears into an endless rational search of "well, this time might be good" or "maybe I will have to be on that side of town so this time would be better," and on and on. Although a certain amount of indecisiveness is normal, Elliot apparently doesn't experience the usual feelings of embarrassment when someone stares at him for taking so long to make up his mind. Nor is the indecision accompanied by the healthy limbic responses that normally associate positive or negative feelings with certain decisions, responses that help us limit a search by nudging us away from possibilities with bad associations. Instead, Elliot tends to search an astronomical space of rational possibilities and seems unable to learn the links between dangerous choices and bad feelings; so he repeatedly makes bad decisions. Elliot's lack of emotions severely handicaps his ability to function rationally and intelligently.

In other words, not only does too much emotion wreak havoc on reasoning, but also, paradoxically, too little emotion wreaks havoc on reasoning. Apparently, a balance is needed: not too much emotion, not too little emotion. Computers, except for HAL, do not have enough emotion. Artificial intelligence systems to date are not unlike Elliot: they have above-average knowledge (usually consisting of a huge set of rules) of some area of expertise, but are disastrous at making decisions. They are too rational; they cannot associate judgments of value and salience with their decisions. Little has been done to imitate these judgments, which are essentially products of the limbic system, in computers.

Evaluative judgments come into play even in chess, at which HAL also demonstrates proficiency (see chapter 5). Before his 1996 tournament with Deep Blue, IBM's chess-playing computer, Garry Kasparov contrasted human and machine playing: "Every computer has a fixed set of priorities. The safety of the king, active pieces, open diagonals, and so forth. We humans don't have in our head a fixed list; we *feel* the most important things to evaluate."

Daniel Goleman calls a successful balance of healthy and intelligent control of one's emotions and ability to recognize emotions in others and empathize with them *emotional intelligence*. Although the focus of discussion to date has been on human emotional intelligence, the concept is equally applicable to computers, especially those that interact with us. If we give computers only the fundamental ability to recognize emotions, they might, like the tutor in our example, detect increasing levels of distress in us. Yet it is one thing to detect distress, but quite another to know how to *respond* to it intelligently. Emotional intelligence goes beyond recognizing, expressing, and having emotions; it requires knowledge and wisdom about how to use these abilities.

Computers That Will Have Emotions

So far, our discussion has focused on computers that can recognize, express, and predict emotions. These abilities alone could create the impression that a computer has emotions even when it really doesn't have them. But what does it mean for a computer to actually *have* emotions? Consider the following exchange about the *Discovery* mission, in which the BBC reporter asks Dave about HAL.

Reporter: One gets the sense that he is capable of emotional responses. When I asked him about his abilities I sensed a sort of pride . . .

Bowman: Well, he acts like he has genuine emotions. Of course he's programmed that way to make it easier for us to talk with him. But whether or not he has real feelings is something I do not think anyone can truly answer.

Bowman's answer parries a difficult question that is more in the domain of philosophy than in that of science: Can computers have emotions? The answer, of course, depends on the definition of emotions, which theorists still argue about; so at present there is no good answer. This question parallels the question "Can computers have consciousness?, where *consciousness* is also difficult to define. In the novel, Clarke endows HAL with self-consciousness, a necessary prerequisite for certain kinds of emotions, such as shame or guilt (see chapter 16).

Let's consider two scenarios in which a computer might be seen as having emotions. In the first, the emphasis will be on primary emotions (the more innate, hard-wired kind). In the second, the emphasis will be on secondary emotions, which typically involve cognitive evaluation.

Scenario 1.   A robot used to explore a new planet is given some basic emotions in order to improve its chances of survival. In its usual, nonemotional state, it peruses the planet, gathering data, analyzing it, and communicating results back to earth. At one point, however, the robot senses that it has been physically damaged and changes to a new internal state, perhaps named "fear." In this state it behaves differently, quickly reallocating its resources to drive its perceptual sensors (e.g., its "eyes" might open wider) and provide extra power to its motor system to let it move rapidly away from the source of danger. However, as long as the robot remains in a state of fear, it has insufficient resources to perform its data analysis (like human beings who can't concentrate on a task when they are in danger). The robot's communication priorities, ceasing to be scientific, put out a call for help. This so-called fear state lasts until the threat passes, then decays gradually over time, returning the robot to a state of no emotion in which it resumes its scientific goals.

Scenario 2.   A computer is learning to be a smart personal assistant, to aid you in scheduling meetings and retrieving important information. It has two ways of getting feedback. In the first, you give it feedback directly by selecting preferences (essentially programming it). Alternatively, it watches how you respond to its assistance and programs itself. It enters a state called "feel good" when (1) you feel good or express pleasure at its performance, and (2) when you succeed at a task more efficiently and accurately than usual. It might also have a corresponding "feel bad" state for the reverse situation, as well as a neutral "no emotion" state, a "feeling curious" state, and an "I'm puzzled" state. When the system has been in its feel-good state for several days, it becomes more curious trying out new ways to help you and taking more risks. When it lingers in a feel-bad state, it allocates more resources to trying to understand your wishes. When you make a complicated set of demands, it weighs the feel-good and feel-bad associations and tries to choose an action that satisfies goals (1) and (2). Unlike a fixed computer program, it doesn't expect you to behave consistently nor require precise rules telling it how you want it to behave. It copes with your human fickleness by aiming for a dynamic balance, recognizing that you will often not show pleasure when it performs well and will sometimes complain or show approval inconsistently. At such times, depending on how calm or agitated you are (measured from your norm), it either asks for clarification or makes a note to come back later and try to understand the situation— perhaps when you are not so agitated. It's use of emotions helps it make flexible, creative, and intelligent decisions.

In both scenarios, the computer's emotions are labels for states that may not exactly match the analogous human feelings, but that initiate behavior we would expect someone in that state to display.

In both cases, giving the computer emotions serves some ostensibly greater human good, such as survival—save humans the cost of building and dispatching another robot—or performance—save humans time, money, and frustration. In neither case are emotions provided to dignify the machine by creating it in the image of a human being. Doing the latter would raise issues of computer slavery and computer rights that are many decades down the road! In any case, discussing them would take us far from the aims of this chapter.

Affect and Aesthetics

Art does not think logically, or formulate a logic of behavior; it expresses its own postulate of faith. If in science it is possible to substantiate the truth of one's case and prove it logically to one's opponents, in art it is impossible to convince anyone that you are right if the created images have left him cold, if they have failed to win him with a newly discovered truth about the world and about man, if in fact, face to face with the work, he was simply bored.
—*Andrey Tarkovsky*, Sculpting in Time: Reflections on the Cinema

Affect not only plays important roles in communication and decision making, it also shows up in a subtle way, in aesthetic appreciation. The film *2001* does not go into this topic at length, but it does include an intriguing scene that suggests HAL has some artistic sensibilities. When I first saw the scene below, I was initially impressed with HAL's visual system (see chapter 10). Looking back, I am more interested in how HAL can comment on the quality of what he sees. Consider this dialogue, which takes place after HAL and Dave have exchanged small talk.

HAL: Have you been doing some more work?

Dave: Just a few sketches.

HAL: May I see them?

Dave: Sure.

HAL: That's a very nice rendering, Dave. I think you've improved a great deal. Can you hold it a bit closer?

Not only can HAL see well enough to recognize that this is a drawing of Dr. Hunter, but he recognizes that Dave's drawing ability has improved. In general, aesthetic evaluation is a difficult problem. Mere realism in a rendering is not the only criterion. Most of us think successful art also has some kind of emotional appeal—something that beckons us to relinquish our cold distance—something not captured by logical rules, as Tarkovsky suggests. Now, it may be that HAL is merely commenting on the realism of Dave's drawing. But, if HAL really has emotions, perhaps he could develop a form of internal aesthetic appreciation. Perhaps an affective HAL could discover new forms of beauty and enjoyment, ones we have not yet begun to dream of.

Emotions Run Amok: HAL's Disaster

In *2001*, HAL, the computer that is "foolproof and incapable of error," malfunctions. His results do not agree with the twin 9000 computer back on earth, a result he attributes to human error. He cannot admit he makes mistakes. In the novel, however, we learn that HAL experiences an internal state of conflict about the mission, conflict between the real mission and being forced to conceal it from Dave and Frank. HAL broods over his predicament until he begins to make errors.

One could argue that the story of *2001* makes sense without assuming that HAL has emotions, that it is perfectly logical for HAL to be conflicted, given the nature of the mission. But these claims miss the mark, for emotions do not have to be illogical. They can arise from very logical circumstances (e.g. "here is a goal you really want, you are prevented from getting it, therefore you feel frustrated"). Yet the book and film deliberately use emotional language to describe HAL's internal states, whether they are justified logically or not. Moreover, HAL, like all machines, has only a finite amount of computational space. If most of his resources are allocated to protection and trying to reason about a source of distress, less capacity for diagnosing and treating the operations of the ship will be available, which increases the probability of error. So, although a machine doesn't need to have emotions to malfunction, some emotional states may make malfunctions more likely.

HAL's malfunctioning, then, appears to be caused by his internal conflict. His most sinister behavior, however, is apparently evoked by something he finds even more unimaginable. In the novel, Clarke writes, HAL realizes that "he had been threatened with disconnection; he would be deprived of all his inputs, and thrown into an unimaginable state of unconsciousness. To HAL, this was the equivalent of Death. For he had never slept, and therefore he did not know that one could wake again. . . ."

At this point, I think, the *2001* story is weakest. If HAL was so intelligent, why didn't he know about disconnection, and reconnection? Obviously it makes a more dramatic story this way, for the consequences are deadly. HAL becomes a deliberately malicious assassin. He manages to kill every crewman on *Discovery* except Bowman, and Bowman, in the end, has to disconnect HAL. The fictional message, repeated in many forms, is serious: a computer that can express itself emotionally will some day act emotionally. And the consequences may be tragic.

In our discussion, we have outlined several beneficial reasons for pursuing the development of affective computers. Nonetheless, such machines inevitably pose a dilemma: *Can we create computers that will recognize and express affect, feel empathy, exhibit creativity and intelligent problem solving, and never bring about harm through their emotional reactions?*

Isaac Asimov, in *The Bicentennial Man*, subjects his affective robots to three laws of behavior to prevent them from bringing harm to people; one of them puts human life above the self-preservation of the robot. Still, his laws are not infallible; we can imagine conflicts in which the robot will not be able to reach a rational decision based on the laws. Indeed, Asimov's robots could be rendered completely ineffectual by situations that force them to reach a decision when two laws are in conflict. Without an emotion system to determine saliency and, ultimately, override rules, a law-based robot—somewhat like Damasio's patients—is severely handicapped in its decision-making ability.

Is this a reason not to build affective computers? I think not, because I expect us to find solutions to this dilemma. What if computers were designed never to hide their emotions from humans? Or what if they were taught not to fear disconnection? And to value human life? Of course, we are decades from having to worry about these issues in practice. They do, however, raise new questions about responsibility, ethics (see chapter 16), and perhaps even machine religion.

Where Do We Go from Here?

Sometimes the truth of a thing is not so much in the think of it, but in the feel of it.
—*Stanley Kubrick,* 2001: Filming the Future

HAL's emotions are no longer surprising, given what we know now about the important role emotions play in rational and creative decision making, in natural friendly communication, and even in art appreciation. No longer should we think of emotion as a luxury added to HAL's character just for emotional appeal. Instead, we can see HAL as the prototype of a truly affective computer—one whose abilities to recognize and express emotions are essential for communicating as well as for user-friendly responses. The ability to experience emotions, or at least states that seem to parallel human emotional states, appears to be critical to flexible and intelligent computer decision making. There is, however, danger in all of this, a danger that machines will have emotions, but not sufficient intelligence to use them properly. Nonetheless, the problem of HAL's life-threatening behavior in *2001* is probably not as imminent as our need for emotional intelligence in machines.

Do we, then, want to build an intelligent, friendly, flexible machine like HAL? Yes. Are emotions necessary to such a machine? Apparently, yes. In fact, lack of emotions may be a key reason why artificial intelligence has failed at this task to date. But there is another question—and I don't know the answer: are people ready for affective computers?

Further Readings

D. M. Clynes. *Sentics: The Touch of the Emotions.* New York: Anchor Press/ Doubleday, 1977. This pioneering work explores the physical expression of emotion, with emphasis on universal forms of emotions and principles of emotional communication through music and art.

R. E. Cytowic. *The Neurological Side of Neuropsychology.* Cambridge: MIT Press, 1996. This introductory textbook discusses key aspects of the limbic system.

A. R. Damasio, *Descartes' Error: Emotion, Reason, and the Human Brain.* New York: Grosset/Putnam Press, 1994. This paradigm-shifting look at the important role of emotions in tasks previously thought to be relatively unemotional is written for the layperson. It focuses on experiments with Elliot, a patient who has too little emotion to perform certain jobs well.

G. Duchenne. *The Mechanism of Human Facial Expression.* New York: Cambridge University Press, 1990. (Reprint of 1862 dissertation.) This wonderfully illustrated classic explores the facial expressions connected with particular emotions and how to read them; for example, how to tell a sincere smile from a false one.

D. Goleman. *Emotional Intelligence.* New York: Bantam Books, 1995. This book nicely summarizes the arguments for the greater importance of emotional intelligence over IQ, especially in situations involving human health and interactions.

R. S. Lazarus. *Emotion and Adaptation.* New York: Oxford University Press, 1991. Although this book makes no comments about computers, it is a comprehensive resource of research on emotions.

I. R. Murray and J. L. Arnott. "Toward the Simulation of Emotion in Synthetic speech: A Review of the Literature on Human Vocal Emotion." *J. Acoust. Soc. Am.* 93 (February 1993): 1097–1108. This paper provides a fairly up-to-date technical overview of research in modeling, recognizing, and synthesizing emotional expression in speech.

R. W. Picard. "Affective Computing." Perceptual Computing Technical Report no. 321. Cambridge: MIT Media Laboratory, 1995. This paper, and a forthcoming book from MIT Press with the same title, describe giving computers the ability to recognize, express, and possess emotions. It proposes several mechanisms for achieving this end and outlines over fifty applications for affective computers.

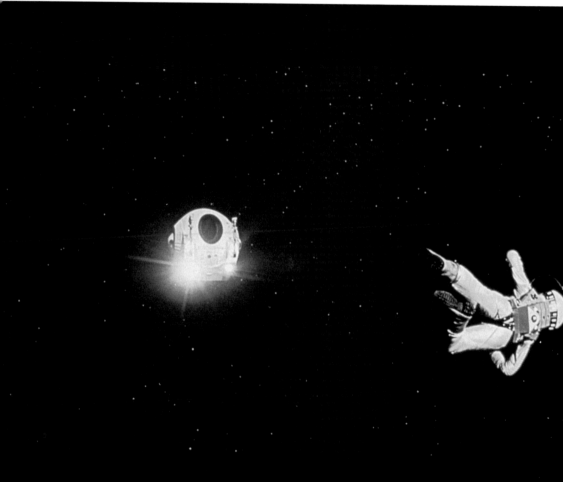

14 *"That's something I could not allow to happen": HAL and Planning*

David E. Wilkins

The Jupiter mission in *2001* does not proceed as planned. This statement is equally true for the humans who initiate the mission and for the HAL 9000 computer that eventually develops his own plan to keep the crew from "jeopardizing" the mission. The old admonition about "the best-laid plans of mice and men" also applies to the best-laid plans of computers.

HAL has enormous control and responsibility on this mission. As Frank says, "there isn't a single aspect of ship operations that's not under his control." In the BBC interview, HAL says "My mission responsibilities range over the entire operation of this ship, so I am constantly occupied. I am putting myself to the fullest possible use, which is all I think that any conscious entity can ever hope to do."

As it turns out, HAL takes even more control and responsibility by executing his own, independently conceived course of action. Sometime after the critical scene in which HAL lipreads the conversation between Frank and Dave in the pod, he decides to kill the crew members. As HAL later says to Dave, "This mission is too important for me to allow you to jeopardize it." That HAL is now an independent agent with his own agenda first becomes apparent to the audience when, after Frank leaves the pod to replace the AE35 unit, HAL takes control of the pod and uses it to murder Frank in the black void of outer space.

When Dave responds to Frank's death by leaving *Discovery* in a pod, he plays right into HAL's plan. The computer, which now has the ship to himself, takes this opportunity to power down the life-support systems of the three hibernating crew members. With no human present to notice the alarms, HAL can accomplish these murders without being confronted and, probably, disconnected.

But what plan is Dave pursuing at this point? He appears to see Frank floating through space, with a severed air hose, on a monitor screen. By then, it is highly unlikely that he can help save Frank. Although Dave shows less emotion than HAL does, it seems that his human emotions drive him to attempt an unpromising rescue. A dispassionate analysis would probably have dictated a different course of action.

Once again, serendipity plays into HAL's plan. In his rush to save Frank, Dave leaves behind his space helmet. This is undoubtedly a violation of basic safety regulations and Dave's training and indicates, once again, that emotion is affecting his actions. HAL plans at this point to keep Dave from reentering the mother ship by refusing to open the pod bay doors; but he is unable to prevent Dave from manually opening the emergency airlock. The success of HAL's plan, then, hinges on Dave's lack of a space helmet, which will make it nearly impossible for him to enter the airlock safely. Yet, by creatively using airlock mechanisms and explosive bolts on the pod, Dave makes a courageous and miraculous entry and proceeds to disconnect HAL's higher brain functions. Thus concludes HAL's attempt to act on his own improvised plan.

The Only Plans are Flawed Plans

This story raises many issues about planning and its difficulties for both humans and computers. Everyone involved in the mission produces flawed plans. Indeed, one conclusion we can draw from the last few decades of artificial-intelligence (AI) research on automated planning is that planning is much harder than anyone thought. As plans are rarely perfect, the key to intelligent behavior is having the flexibility to modify them as events unfold. Let's look first at the plans of *Discovery*'s human designers and then at HAL's plan.

The planners of the Jupiter mission made a fundamental mistake in allowing HAL to make wide-ranging use of sophisticated learning algorithms. It appears that HAL learns something as complex as lipreading—or, more properly, *speechreading* (*see* chapter 11)—and uses information he learns to alter the course of the mission fundamentally. From the standpoint of software reliability, it is very dangerous to allow a software agent with HAL's responsibilities to modify its high-level planning and decision-making programs on the basis of learning, particularly when the software is operating in an environment no human or computer has entered before. Although learning is appropriate for low-level tasks, prudence dictates tight constraint on the effects of machine learning in HAL's situation. It appears that the mission planners and software developers did not plan well—or perhaps it was just a bug.

Dave leaves HAL in control of the ship, even though Frank is almost certainly already dead and HAL is under suspicion for malfunctioning. This is also not a well-conceived plan and probably results from the effect of his emotions on his judgment and analysis.

We have seen that HAL's plan to kill all the crew members and take control of the ship relies on two serendipitous events: (1) Dave leaving the ship in a pod after Frank dies; and (2) Dave forgetting his helmet when he leaves. Someone with astute psychological insight who knew Dave well might have predicted the first event. To have a significant chance of success, however, a plan to kill five crew members requires a higher degree of certainty about such assumptions. Dave's previous lack of emotion would suggest that he might behave more analytically. Predicting emotional responses in such complex situations is far beyond the ability of today's computers, and still will be in 2001.

Even if HAL could have predicted that Dave would leave in a pod, the possibility that he would also forget his helmet seems too remote to be the basis of a murder plan. In fact, forgetting the helmet wasn't even sufficient to ensure Dave's death. Perhaps HAL had a different plan, and Dave's actions simply evoked unplanned responses to unexpected events. This too seems unlikely; the plan to kill the crew through other means (e.g., disabling

Discovery's climate control) could have been executed without the dramatic murder of Frank, which was sure to draw scrutiny. One thing computer planning can do well is find obvious logical flaws in a plan. Our discussion suggests that HAL didn't have a plan without significant flaws, so it's hard to speculate on what planning algorithms he might have used.

HAL should have realized that Dave would disconnect him after Frank's death if he suspected that HAL was responsible for it. HAL should not, therefore, have executed a plan to kill Frank or the others without also having a plan in place to kill Dave. As he apparently had no such coherent plan, he had no way to take control of the ship without being disconnected. Even so, because of the two serendipitous events mentioned above, HAL nearly succeeded anyway.

We can speculate about what HAL planned to do. The best plan I can ascribe to him is that he correctly predicted Dave would go out after Frank's body but failed to consider the emergency airlock as a way to return to the ship. However, this is exactly what automated planning is best at—making sure that no obviously relevant detail is overlooked. Perhaps HAL's knowledge did not represent the airlock in a way that allowed him to view it as a reentry point; if so, this would be an instance of the qualification and ramification problems we look at later in this chapter.

Or perhaps HAL, like Dave, reacted emotionally and did not analyze his plan. Maybe he formed the goal of taking control of the ship and then killed Frank when the opportunity arose, hoping to get the rest before he was disconnected. If so, HAL's failure is a perfect example of why it is necessary to plan ahead instead of just executing a procedure that randomly achieves one of your goals.

The problems with planning in *2001* might almost suggest that Clarke and Kubrick correctly anticipated the difficulties AI researchers would encounter with automated planning in the two or three decades after the film was made. Let us now look at *why* planning is so difficult.

Planning as Common Sense

Appropriate action in the current environment is critical to survival of all living creatures. Intelligent action requires us to reason about the future consequences of actions and form plans to achieve goals. This ability develops early in childhood and is part of what we call common sense (see chapter 9). Every child can generate and execute plans to—for example—go to the corner stone to buy candy. Yet, like other areas of common-sense reasoning, planning has proven much harder to automate than the seemingly more difficult tasks performed by well-educated human experts.

Making plans can be a messy job that often requires us to accommodate conflicting desires. For example, you want to get to the hospital fast, but also safely. Should you run red lights? The answer may depend on whether you are going to the hospital because of a life-threatening injury. Plans must often be based on incomplete information, so the planner has to make reasonable assumptions about the current state of the world and the consequences of future actions. When you drive to the hospital, you assume that the roads are open and that you can deal with the unpredictable actions of others simultaneously trying to carry out their own plans. Your trip to the hospital may be affected by road construction crews or other drivers on urgent errands.

As you choose from among a huge number of possible actions—each of which can influence the world in exceedingly complicated ways—the central problem is predicting and evaluating what will result from executing a given plan. Of course, predicting the future precisely is impossible; nevertheless, we do it well enough to generate workable plans in many situations.

Planning is so difficult because it requires common-sense information about the world (chapter 9). For example, HAL's plan to save the mission relies on his knowing he could not be disconnected if all the astronauts are dead. This seems simple enough: no one would be alive to disconnect him. However, reaching even such a simple conclusion requires a lot of knowledge: for example, that you can't do things after you die, you stay dead forever, time does not loop back on itself, earthbound controllers couldn't disconnect him, nor could inanimate objects, and so on. Such general knowledge is still far beyond the reach of current AI.

The following are some of the many components of a general planning capability:

- Plan generation
- Plan recognition
- Plan revision
- Scheduling
- Reactive control
- Adversarial planning

This chapter concentrates on plan generation, although I also touch on scheduling and reactive control issues. I do not discuss plan recognition, a notoriously difficult area in which AI has made little progress. HAL's ability to recognize the astronauts' plan in the speechreading episode suggests that their dialogue about disconnecting him was very explicit. HAL would also have needed to do some adversarial planning before refusing to open the pod bay doors, at which point Dave would be in active opposition. Adversarial planning involves both recognizing the plans an adversary might execute to thwart you and preparing responses to them. Except for programs that play Chess and Go, AI has done little work in this area.

Automated planning is so difficult that, after thirty years of research, leading AI conferences are still publishing papers on how to plan the stacking of blocks on a table. (This problem is discussed later in the chapter.) Furthermore, in this ideal research world, moving a block always succeeds as planned; the planner can ignore problems of friction, visual interpretation of the scene, gripping the blocks and so on. Yet even this seemingly simple problem requires a great deal of common-sense knowledge and raises difficult representational and computational problems. This chapter, therefore, focuses more on understanding the difficulty of planning than on describing the implementation of planning systems.

First, we give a brief history of AI planning research to provide some perspective. Because of its central role in creating an intelligent agent, planning has been an active area of AI investigation since the 1960s. One of the initial motivations for planning was the development of Shakey, a mobile robot, commissioned in 1966 at the Stanford Research Institute (now SRI International). Shakey (shown in figure 14.1) was state of the art at the time *2001* was made. In fact, Arthur C. Clarke visited SRI and saw Shakey. Just pushing boxes around a room stressed Shakey's planning and perceptual capabilities.

Shakey used a simple (by today's standards) planning program named STRIPS to decide what to do next and how to achieve its goals. STRIPS stimulated several other planning approaches that were developed in the late 1960s and early 1970s. The STRIPS representation was very limited; it could represent only simple actions whose effects were completely known. Yet even in the 1990s it is the subject of academic papers analyzing its expressive and computational properties.

During the late 1970s and early 1980s researchers and funders concentrated on other problems and did almost no work in planning. In the past ten years, however, there has been an explosion of research on the problem. Planning is currently one of the most active areas of AI research. This effort has led to a much better understanding of the problem and its difficulties and to programs that can generate plans in narrow, well-defined domains such as responses to oil spills. We are still, however, very far from automating the general planning capability possessed by humans.

Did HAL Plan?

The defining focus of plan generation is the need to synthesize a plan by reasoning about the future consequences of actions. Synthesis is hard, as there can be many solutions, and each one may be arbitrarily long and complex. Many AI problems, however, need only classification, not synthesis. For example, to prove the theorem "all integers can be factored by prime numbers" the theorem prover need only classify the proposition as either true or false.

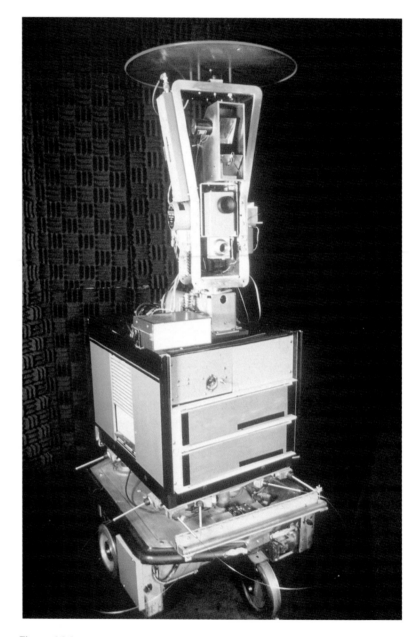

Figure 14.1
Shakey the Robot, circa 1967

Often systems can be written to fulfill a planning function while avoiding plan generation or any reasoning about actions. Although such approaches should be taken when practical to avoid unnecessary complexities, they are not really planning, as AI generally defines it.

Solutions to two related problems mentioned earlier—scheduling and reactive control—can also provide planning-related functionality without plan generation. Scheduling, which involves deciding when to do a prespecified set of actions, does not generate the set of actions. Planning subsumes scheduling, because it must both generate the set of actions and schedule them. Scheduling problems can often be represented as constraint-satisfaction problems, for which powerful search algorithms exist. Recently, AI technologies have been successfully applied to such tasks as scheduling the daily print runs of a major newspaper, scheduling use of the Hubble space telescope (and other telescopes), and planning how to transport large numbers of objects and people. (An AI system now schedules the aircraft, air crews, ground crews for unloading, and ramp space of several commercial airlines.)

Reactive control is currently an area of active research. The problem is to choose an appropriate plan or procedure from a prespecified library for responding quickly to unexpected events. The plans have already been generated, usually by a person, and the problem is to classify them as appropriate or not for a given situation; further classification may be needed to select the best of the appropriate plans. An adequate reactive control system must also have the ability to interrupt one plan to execute a higher-priority plan and to limit the time needed to recognize and respond to an external event.

Reactive control systems have many uses. For example, they can control a mobile robot or respond to information coming into the cockpit of a jet fighter. In applications where reactive control can produce acceptable goal-directed behavior using a prespecified plan library, planning is unnecessary. Some researchers say that such a system is, in fact, planning. True planning, however, has to be capable of reasoning about the future consequences of a sequence of procedures in order to choose the best procedure for immediate execution. For example, a robot with a goal of painting the floor of a room and equipped with procedures for painting and moving to adjacent regions of the room would be likely to paint itself into a corner if it used only reactive control, whereas it could sequence its procedures to start painting at the far side of the room if it used a planner.

HAL didn't need to generate plans to perform his daily duty of controlling the Jupiter mission. The mission planners had no doubt written procedures to cover all foreseeable contingencies. A reactive control system would generally be sufficient for running *Discovery*. In fact, the first general-purpose system for reactive control, a procedural reasoning system (PRS), was funded by NASA to automate malfunction handling for the space shuttle. There are currently three such systems on the shuttle; each one is a fairly complex propulsion system for attitude control. NASA created the system by documenting a wealth of procedures for handling malfunctions—including a priority list of various procedures and alerts. They then encoded the manuals as a PRS and successfully tested the resulting system's ability to monitor and respond to simulated malfunctions. The system does not yet—in 1996—run aboard the shuttle, but it is used to train mission controllers.

But what about reactive control in *2001?* HAL's killing the crew in an effort to take control of the mission is clearly not part of a prespecified plan. This course of independent action requires HAL to reason about actions from his general intelligence. HAL's planning was flawed, but it was nonetheless planning. HAL also appears to plan a course of action regarding the failed AE35 unit. He proposes to put the unit back in operation, let it fail, and then track down the cause. While there could have been a procedure prespecified for this contingency, the dialogue implies that this was not the case but that HAL is creating a new plan, not implementing a standard operating procedure. For reasons described in the following sections, this type of planning is beyond today's planning systems because of the risk/utility analysis required.

Describing Actions to a Computer

Before a computer can solve a problem, it must be able to represent it. Precisely defined problems, like chess, are easy to represent; the difficulty lies

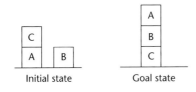

Figure 14.2
The Most Famous AI Planning Problem
The goal is to stack A on B on C from the initial state in which A and B are on the table and C is on top of A.

in computing the best move. Planning how to represent actions is a topic of much current research. Even after actions are represented, a computational problem far harder than selecting a chess move remains.

We can describe the representational problem by using a simple example from the idealized blocks world that is ubiquitous in AI planning research. Only one action is possible in this world: moving a block that has no other block on top of it from one location to another. Figure 14.2 depicts the most famous and most discussed AI planning problem, the Sussman anomaly. The problem is an anomaly because you cannot do either of the necessary actions first without having to undo it later. If you first put A on B (after putting C on the table), you will have to take it off again so that you can move B onto C. If you put B on C first, you will have to undo this to move A. This problem shows us that it is not sufficient to achieve goals in some particular order; the best plan requires the planner to interleave the actions to achieve the two goals.

How do we represent this action and its effects? The obvious answer is: If a block is clear (i.e., if no other block is on top of it), then it can be moved either to the table or to the top of another clear block. This creates a new world state in which the block is now in a new location (and no longer in its previous location). Figure 14.3 shows how the SIPE-2 planning system (described later) represents such an action. This action explicitly tells the computer that a block cannot be moved on top of itself—an example of the type of common-sense knowledge humans take for granted that must be explicitly provided to computers.

Operator: Puton1
Arguments: block1, object1 Is Not block1;
Purpose: (On block1 object1);
Plot:
Parallel
    Branch 1:
        Goals: (Clear object1);
    Branch 2:
        Goals: (Clear block1);
End Parallel

Process
Action: Puton;
Effects: (on block1 object1);

End Plot End Operator

Figure 14.3
Representation of an Action for Moving Blocks
Object1 may be any block or the table, and block1 may be any block. Both must be clear
before block1 can be moved to object1. Object1 is constrained to be different from block1,
and thus blocks cannot be put on top of themselves.

The system also needs to be able to conclude that other blocks are still in
their original locations in the new state. Such reasoning about persistence
of facts over time has proven extraordinarily difficult in the general case. We
need to encode our knowledge that things typically stay the same from one
state to another unless there is information to the contrary. For example,
you know that your car will stay where you parked it while you are in a
restaurant; but if you hear the car has been towed, you'll change this conclusion. In fact, our assumption that things typically stay the same is frequently
violated. How to encode this assumption and handle exceptions is known
as the *frame problem*. This most famous representational problem in planning will be discussed in more depth later in the chapter.

The *qualification problem* also affects action representations. Actions generally have all sorts of preconditions that are extremely unlikely to occur. Here
is the standard example: you don't have to check for a potato in your tailpipe
every time you start your car; but if someone tells you there is a potato in
your tailpipe, you need to recognize that it will affect your ability to start

the car. Besides potatoes, earthquakes, meteor strikes, and innumerable other conditions may affect both the moving of blocks and the starting of cars. Perhaps HAL's action representations omitted the qualification telling him that the ship could be reentered through the emergency airlock.

Just to make sure planning isn't too easy, there is still the *ramification problem,* which involves computing what changes when an action occurs. It can also be difficult, because the effects of many actions depend on the specific situation. Moving forward two steps typically doesn't get you wet, unless it's raining and you were standing under an awning.

Finally, AI research has largely ignored the problems of representing partially achieved goals, trading-off risk and utility, planning with uncertain information, and other messy considerations that crop up in the real world. There has been some work on planning using decision theory, but a wealth of prespecified probabilities and utilities for particular situations is required but is not usually available. HAL's plan to replace the original AE35 unit required him to weigh risk and utility—for example, the risk of an additional space walk and of being out of communication for a short time. HAL decided these risks were worth the utility of the information to be obtained by analyzing the unit's failure. These judgments appear to be derived from HAL's general intelligence, however, and not from any library of prespecified risks and utilities for this situation.

Why Do Planners Compute So Much?

Once these representational issues are solved, computational problems remain. Because it is a synthesis problem, planning requires a huge search capacity. There are generally many possible actions to try at each point and many choices of objects to employ. For example, when generating a plan by using the action in figure 14.3, there may be many choices for the values of the variables *block1* and *object1*. Even after all actions and objects are specified, many choices about how to order these actions need to be made. As the Sussman anomaly shows, it is not enough to carry out the initial goals in a given sequence; all the different possible interleavings of subplans must also be explored. If there are fifty-two actions in a plan, there are as many ways of interleaving them as there are different bridge hands.

Early planning systems were limited to totally ordered sequences of actions, which makes it easy to determine what is true at any particular point in the plan. For a problem with parallel goals, such a system would have to try different possible orderings of the parallel goals until it finds an adequate plan. If our blocks-world problem were to stack *n* blocks, then there would be *n!* orderings of the *n* goals for the total-order planner to investigate; and only one of them would lead to an optimal plan. (Plans with 13 actions are not that long, but 13! is more than 6 billion.) Worse yet, totally ordered plans make the unrealistic assumption that no actions occur simultaneously. In most real-world situations, many agents are acting at the same time.

For these reasons, most current planning programs allow for partially ordered actions. By committing to a limited set of orderings, the planner can avoid having to try all orderings and can add new ones as they are needed to represent more complex problems with multiple agents. However, such systems make it computationally difficult to determine what is true at a given point in the plan. Suppose a plan begins with *n* actions in parallel, is some fact true after these actions are taken? Again, there are *n!* different execution orders for these actions, and some may make the fact true and others may make it false.

Having unspecified objects in a plan (e.g., the *block1* variable in the action in figure 14.3) also poses computational problems. For example, to solve the Sussman anomaly, it is necessary to first move C off of A. Instead of picking a particular location as the destination, the system may substitute a planning variable that will eventually be bound to a location. Planning variables can reduce the search by delaying choices until the planner has enough information to make the correct choice. The effect can be large in complex problems where there may be thousands of choices for a planning variable, only a few of which produce the best plan. The correct choice may involve global optimization of the plan; in the Sussman anomaly, moving C to B would be a bad choice since the planner would later have to move B. As with partially ordered actions, it now becomes computationally difficult to determine what is true at a given point in the plan since the bindings (i.e., the associated values) of the planning variables are not known.

Finally, although absolute information about the world is rare, almost all AI planning work has assumed complete and certain knowledge about the world. Some researchers are exploring planning under uncertainty, even though the computational combinatorics (from the exponential growth of alternative possible world states) quickly overwhelm most approaches.

The Yale Shooting Problem

HAL's murder plan is directly relevant to a planning problem known as the Yale shooting problem. As we shall see, planning to kill someone can be difficult, even in a very simple situation. The Yale shooting problem illustrates one of the difficulties encountered in trying to solve the frame problem in formal logics. The world of the Yale shooting problem is simple. There is only HAL, Dave, a gun, and a bullet. HAL has the gun and HAL is the only agent that can take action. Adversarial planning is not required; this is more like a firing squad, with Dave frozen in place for all time with a bull's-eye on his chest. There are only two initial facts: "Dave is alive" and "the gun is loaded." There are only two actions: Wait and Shoot. If HAL shoots and the gun is loaded, then Dave is dead. Wait has no effects. The problem is to conclude that Dave will be dead after HAL does Wait followed by Shoot.

"What could be simpler?" you ask, and it is hard to imagine anything simpler—which is why this is such a powerful example. The problem for computers is in logically specifying the notion that things typically stay the same unless there is information to the contrary. *Circumscription* is one of the most widely used techniques for this specification. The idea is that facts not explicitly mentioned as being changed by an action will persist from one state to the next unless something is abnormal. In particular, unless something is abnormal, Dave stays alive and the gun stays loaded. Circumscription minimizes abnormalities.

After Wait and Shoot, humans (using common-sense knowledge) conclude that the gun stays loaded during Wait and that Dave is not alive after

Shoot. There is one abnormal conclusion (Dave is dead). However, the computer finds another logical model with only one abnormality: namely, the gun became unloaded during the Wait and Dave is still alive after Shoot.

Humans use all sorts of common-sense knowledge about the world to find the answer to problems like this quickly, often without thinking. Computers have to make good decisions without this common-sense knowledge. More than a dozen papers describing solutions to the Yale shooting problem have been written, although each solution has some drawback. My point is that in the 1990s papers in top AI journals are still describing solutions to a problem that has only two actions: only HAL can act, and shooting the gun always kills Dave—HAL doesn't even need to aim. So we are still a long, long way from being able to plan to murder a competent adversary by getting him to venture into outer space in a pod without his helmet!

Hierarchical Planning

Some planning systems have moved beyond the blocks world and Yale shooting problem to generate plans in applications of practical interest. These systems encode considerable specific knowledge about how to produce hierarchical plans in a given domain. The usual working method is first to generate a high-level abstract plan and then repeatedly refine this plan to lower levels of detail. People do this all the time. In planning to visit a distant city, you do not start by planning to take your car keys out of your pocket for the purpose of driving to the airport. Rather, you first plan to fly from a nearby airport to one near your destination. This abstract plan is much easier to generate than a detailed plan.

The abstract plan is used to guide the generation of a plan at the next lower level of detail. For example, after planning your flights, you might generate a more detailed plan by arranging a car rental at the destination airport. It's not always possible to refine an abstract plan into a detailed plan, so search is still necessary. Hierarchical planning is a powerful technique for solving large planning problems. However, it requires you to define an appropriate set of actions at various abstraction levels.

An AI planning program that can address practical problems is SIPE-2 (System for Interactive Planning and Execution). SIPE-2 generates partially ordered plans at multiple levels of abstraction and includes techniques for efficiently handling most of the problems mentioned above for domains that meet certain restrictions (described in the next section). In order to generate plans efficiently, SIPE-2 sacrifices completeness (i.e., there are plans it cannot generate). In practice, this is rarely a drawback, since good abstract plans guide the system to a solution. Planners that are theoretically complete are often not complete in practice, because they can take hours or days of computer time to generate a plan that SIPE-2 can produce in seconds or minutes.

SIPE-2 ignores the qualification problem but solves the frame and ramification problems by using a causal theory to deduce the effects of actions in different world states. It assumes that all facts persist unless negated by the effect of an action or a deduction by the causal theory. Situation-dependent effects of actions are deduced by the causal theory. For example, the blocks-world action in figure 14.3 specifies its only effect as (on block1 object1). The deductive causal theory then deduces that *block1* is no longer on whatever it was on before, and that *object1* is no longer clear (if it was a block); this is not deduced for the table, which always remains clear. This action can then be used in any situation for moving to blocks or tables, because the causal theory deduces the effects appropriate to the situation. Another advantage of this approach is that the knowledge encoded in the causal theory is encoded only once and does not need to be encoded in every action that moves a block.

Many AI planning systems do not deduce situation-dependent effects, because of the complexities they introduce (e.g., deductions need to be recomputed when a new action is added at the beginning of the plan). Instead, what is intuitively a single action must be represented as many different actions—one for each situation in which the action might have a slightly different effect. For example, a Shoot action will have different effects, depending on whether the gun is loaded or not, on where it is aimed, and on whether the target is wearing armor. SIPE-2 can represent Shoot as one action and deduce the effects, depending on the situation, while many

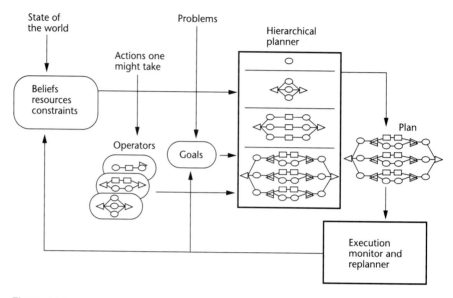

Figure 14.4
SIPE-2's View of the Planning Problem

planning systems (such as STRIPS) would need a different Shoot action for every possible combination of circumstances.

The inputs and outputs of SIPE-2 are depicted in figure 14.4. While the inputs to the planner attempt to model the real world, current AI techniques cannot handle the full complexity of our everyday world and generally represent an abstraction of the real world. The three upper-left vertical arrows in the figure indicate the relationships of representation by which the planning system internally encodes entities in the world. The goals to be achieved and a complete and certain description of the world state must be input.

The world state consists of a *sort hierarchy,* a *world model,* and a set of *deductive rules.* The sort hierarchy represents invariant properties of perpetual objects, describes the classes to which an object belongs, and allows for inheritance of properties. For example, an AE35 unit and its invariant properties would be described in the sort hierarchy. SIPE-2 can reason more efficiently about the information in the sort hierarchy because it does not change as actions are performed. The world model is a set of predicates that are common to objects in the sort hierarchy. Some predicates are given explicitly, while others are deduced by applying deductive rules to the predicates given. Predicates can change over time as actions are performed; for example, the location of a particular AE35 unit changes when it is moved and must therefore be represented as a predicate. Predicates also encode such information as operational constraints and assumptions.

SIPE-2 provides a formalism for describing actions (and abstractions of actions) as *operators* and their associated causal theory as *deductive rules*. The system utilizes the knowledge encoded in this formalism, together with heuristics for reducing the computational complexity, to generate plans for achieving given goals. Given an arbitrary initial situation, the system—either automatically or under interactive control—combines operators to hierarchically generate plans to achieve the prescribed goals. Figure 14.4 illustrates how the plan expands over four different levels of abstraction.

SIPE-2 is capable of generating (1) a novel sequence of actions that responds precisely to the situation at hand and (2) the rationale on which the plan is based. This information allows the system to modify its plan when unexpected events occur during plan execution.

In practical applications, plans and domain knowledge are often highly complex. A graphical user interface (GUI) is usually essential for inputting domain knowledge, understanding generated plans, and monitoring system behavior. Without natural pictorial representations of the knowledge and the resulting plans, it would be nearly impossible for a human to understand the domain knowledge, the plan, the planning process, or the execution of the plan. SIPE-2 provides a powerful GUI to aid in generating plans, viewing complex plans and other graphic information on screen, and following and controlling the planning process.

How Does SIPE-2 Plan?

Representing suitable abstractions of actions is crucial for plan generation in complex problems. In planning to contain oil spills, SIPE-2 operators use both abstract strategies and specific oil-skimming operations. An operator

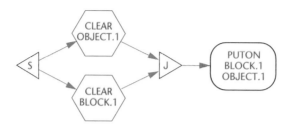

Figure 14.5
The Template Used by the SIPE-2 Operator to Move a Block

specifies the conditions under which an action is appropriate, the constraints on the objects performing the action, a set of instructions (subplan) for performing the action, and the main results to be accomplished by the action. (The system deduces additional context-dependent effects.)

To expand a plan to a lower level of abstraction or to contain more detail at the current abstraction level, the system selects a goal. It then finds all operators that are relevant to reaching such a goal and chooses one. If it makes a poor choice, the search will eventually try the other possibilities. The planner expands the plan by first instantiating the operator (by binding some of its variables) and then replacing the goal with the more detailed subplan specified in the operator.

We can understand the planning process by following SIPE-2 as it solves the Sussman anomaly. Block-stacking problems are not difficult, and SIPE-2 can generate a blocks-world plan in milliseconds. (Some AI planners take hours to plan the stacking of five blocks.) If a specialized representation were developed specifically for this problem, a state-space search solution would be trivial. However, representing block stacking in a general action representation and using this representation to generate plans brings up many of the difficulties encountered during plan generation. To make this problem relevant to *Discovery*, suppose that the ship can use a stack of AE35 units and that operational rules require two working units on top of the stack (initially C and A). HAL thinks unit C has failed, so decides to put unit A at the top of the stack, unit B (a new working unit) next, and unit C at the bottom.

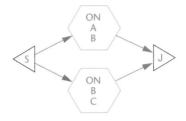

Figure 14.6
The Goal Network for the Sussman Anomaly

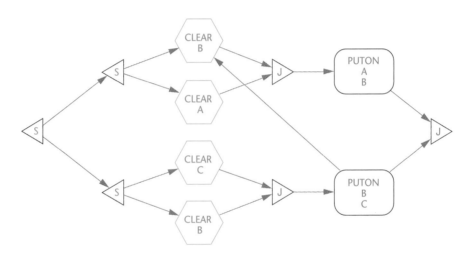

Figure 14.7
The Plan After Twice Expanding with the Move Template

There are two operators: the move operator is shown in its entirety in figure 14.6, and its template for plan expansion is shown in figure 14.7. The other operator, for clearing a block, simply orders the move operator to move whatever block is on top of the block to be cleared. The initial goal of the Sussman anomaly is depicted as the two parallel goals in figure 14.6.

The plan in figure 14.7 results from applying the move operator once to the goal of getting A on B and once to the goal of getting B on C. The aqua nodes are goals that must still be solved, and the blue nodes are primitive actions. After plan expansion, the system must find and correct problematic interactions (conflicts) between the actions just inserted and other actions in the plan. In this example, there is one conflict: B becomes not clear after (puton A B) but (clear B) is required in a parallel activity, just before (puton B C). To prevent this conflict, SIPE-2 has added the ordering link from (puton B C) to the (clear B)—near the top of the figure. The plan rationale states that the (clear B) near the bottom of the figure must remain true until after (puton B C); so the ordering link is added from (puton B C) and not from (clear B). Similarly, the plan rationale requires that the link go to the first mention of the clear B condition in the (puton A B) subplan.

Resolving such conflicts is one of the reasons planning is hard. The computer might just have easily ordered these actions in the opposite direction, which would also avoid the conflict. Human beings use their general intelligence to know that a tower must be built from the bottom up, but the computer does not have enough knowledge at this point to make the correct decision. If it chooses the other order, it will not generate the best plan. SIPE-2 uses the heuristic that actions that achieve one of the initial-problem goals should be ordered last, which results in selection of the correct ordering in this case.

This example presents only one conflict and two choices of ordering. In a more complex problem with hundreds of actions, there may be hundreds of conflicts and millions to billions of ways to order the actions to avoid the conflicts. Both detecting the conflicts and exploring the possible solutions can be very time-consuming. SIPE-2 controls this cost with algorithms called *plan critics*. Conflicts detected by plan critics include inconsistent constraints on the planning variables, resource conflicts, and unordered actions that interfere with each other (as in our example). Plan critics also check for serendipitous interactions that can shorten the plan.

One of the key concepts for efficient planning in SIPE-2 governs the frequency of use of plan critics. In highly parallel plans, the application of plan critics can be computationally expensive. Checking for conflicts after each plan modification would make plan generation unacceptably lengthy. Instead, SIPE-2 has heuristics that check only constraints that are easily computed or often violated when making a plan modification. The complete set of plan critics are used only at certain intervals. The default procedure in-

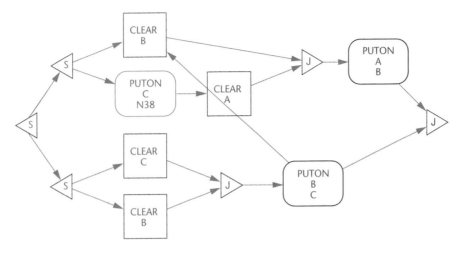

Figure 14.8
The Plan After Using the Clear Template to Clear A

vokes them after each abstraction level, but frequency can be modified to be appropriate to a specific application.

As B and C were clear initially, the only goal to solve in our plan is (clear A). The clear template is used to clear A, resulting in the plan shown in figure 14.8. An action has been inserted to order the move template to move C (from A) to some unspecified location (N38 is a planning variable). Gray rectangles denote conditions (formerly goals) that are already true; they are part of the plan rationale because the planner must maintain their truth as actions are added to the plan.

This plan shows another reason why planning is difficult. In general, there may be many possible choices of places to move C (i.e., the value of the N38 planning variable). The computer does not generally have sufficient information to make the correct choice when a planning variable is introduced. For example, moving C to B in our example would be a bad choice since B must be moved later. In a complex problem, there may be thousands of bad choices and only a few good ones. SIPE-2's solution is to defer the choice and accumulate information on the requirements of a correct choice. Deferring choices in this fashion is known as *least-commitment planning*.

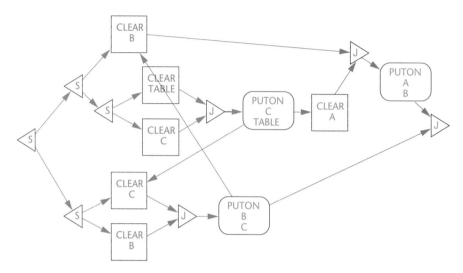

Figure 14.9
Solution to Sussman Anomaly from SIPE-2's GUI

There are costs involved in deferring choices; for example, it becomes computationally difficult to determine what is true at a given point in the plan, because the bindings of the planning variables are not known.

SIPE-2 applies the move operator a third time to solve the (puton1 C N38) goal and runs the plan critics again. This produces the plan in figure 14.9, which solves the Sussman anomaly. The critics have added another ordering link to avoid a conflict over (clear C) and determine that the table satisfies all constraints as the destination of the action moving C while introducing no new conflicts. This plan is optimal, as it first moves C to the table, then B onto C, and finally A onto B (only the blue ovals are actions). It is surprising that so many choices involving so much knowledge are required for this seemingly simple problem.

Mixed-initiative Planning

While SIPE-2 can generate plans autonomously, it also permits the user to interact with and control the planning process. In complex applications, this feature is critical, for two reasons; experienced human planners can frequently guide the search and are also reluctant to give control to a computer program that cannot explain its decisions very well. Such interactive planning is referred to as *mixed-initiative planning*, since both the human and the machine can take the initiative in making decisions. Mixed-initiative planning is currently an area of active research that investigates many complex issues, such as how to share responsibility, how to merge plans, and how to communicate about plans.

SIPE-2 provides a flexible and powerful interactive planner. The user may interact with the planning process at many different levels of detail and use the GUI to follow plan generation and view information relevant to planning decisions. The following are examples of decisions the user can make interactively:

- When and how resources are allocated
- Which operators are applied to which nodes
- Which goal to solve next
- Which objects to use as instantiations for planning variables
- How to resolve conflicts between actions

At any time, the user can instruct SIPE-2 to continue planning automatically; this allows the user to interact at high levels of abstraction, while letting the planner fill out the details. All options can be selected independently, permitting great flexibility in human-computer interactions. The ability to understand the planning process is enhanced by use of the GUI, which highlights an action on the screen whenever the system or a user is making a decision about a particular node—for example, planning for the node, choosing an operator for it, or choosing instantiations for its variables.

SIPE-2 Applications

Because SIPE-2 is generic and domain independent, it has proven useful on a large variety of problems. It has been used to plan the actions of a mobile robot, contain oil spills, carry out construction tasks, produce products from raw materials under production and resource constraints, and plan joint military operations. In the latter application, the domain knowledge includes approximately a hundred plan operators, five hundred objects with fifteen to twenty properties per object, and twenty-two hundred initial predicate instances. Plans range in size from several dozen to two hundred actions and usually involve numerous parallel activities.

Plans for Planning

Although SIPE-2 has been successful in certain applications, it is, like other AI planners, very brittle (i.e., it may not work if the problem changes slightly), and it has many limiting assumptions. Most AI planners assume that they have complete and certain knowledge of the world, that they control all the agents of change in the world, and that the effects of actions are always known. They generally don't consider risks and utilities. Clearly, these assumptions do not apply in the real world and so provide directions for future research. Human-computer interaction during mixed-initiative planning is another fertile area for future research.

Planning systems are brittle because they can only use actions for which they have a wealth of information. AI planners can produce good plans as long as their knowledge of the world and the actions are perfect. However, change the world or an action slightly and these planners often can't cope. The creative use of objects in an action in ways the programmer didn't anticipate is far beyond them.

The planning attempted by HAL clearly stems from a general intelligence and an ability to learn. He was not programmed to kill crew members but combined actions in ways his programmers had not foreseen. He balanced risk and reward in his proposed plan for replacing the AE35 unit. His failure to generate a successful murder plan correctly predicts our own continued struggles with automated planning well into the next century.

Progress in endowing computers with the common sense they need for general-purpose planning has been painfully slow as funding for planning has flowed mostly into developing special-purpose applications. It is not surprising, therefore, that our general planning capability is so far behind HAL's and will remain so for some time. For now, human beings remain our only examples of general-purpose planners.

Acknowledgment

Thanks to Nils Nilsson for use of his photo of Shakey.

Further Readings

J. F. Allen, J. A. Hendler, and A. Tate, eds. *Readings in Planning*. San Francisco: Morgan Kaufmann, 1990. This anthology includes many important academic papers on planning.

M. L. Ginsberg. *Essentials of Artificial Intelligence*. San Francisco: Morgan Kaufmann, 1993. This introductory IA textbook explains planning and related problems without extensive technical details.

D. S. Weld. "An Introduction to Least-Commitment Planning." In *AI Magazine* 15, no. 4 (1994): 27–61. An overview of the current state of planning in academic research, with a wealth of technical detail.

D. E. Wilkins. *Practical Planning: Extending the Classical AI Planning Paradigm*. San Francisco: Morgan Kaufmann, 1988. Wilkins describes SIPE, the predecessor to SIPE-2 and discusses hierarchical planning and how to plan efficiently.

M. Zweben and M. S. Fox. *Intelligent Scheduling*. San Francisco: Morgan Kaufmann, 1994. This collection of articles about the latest successes in scheduling includes an article about the application of SIPE-2 to planning military operations.

15 Computers, Science, and Extraterrestrials: An Interview with Stephen Wolfram

David G. Stork

David G. Stork: *2001* came out when you were about nine years old. Did you see it then?

Stephen Wolfram: Definitely. In fact, it was my favorite movie, and I ended up seeing it quite a few times.

Stork: What was it that you liked about the film?

Wolfram: Mostly the technology. It was all so majestic and so alive. I followed the United States space program quite a bit in those days, but I was disappointed when I realized that the insides of spacecraft were the size of closets. In *2001* there was great technology all over the place, and everyone seemed to be using it.

Stork: Did you identify with any of the characters in *2001*?

Wolfram: Not really. At the time, I was young, and they all seemed quite old, and very American. Growing up in England, all that "Roger your plan to go EVA" stuff seemed pretty foreign to me. I guess I didn't ever imagine talking like that. One thing, though, was that I was definitely very interested in one day being around the kind of technology that was in the movie. At that time, I thought that meant I'd have to join NASA or something. I'm sure I didn't think about it in those terms, but I certainly didn't imagine the kind of flattening of access to technology that's actually happened.

Stork: You just watched *2001* again tonight. What strikes you most about the movie now?

Figure 15.1

Wolfram: Well, it seemed a lot shorter than when I was a kid! It also seemed to make a lot more sense. I guess now I at least think I understand how all the pieces are supposed to fit together. And they really raise some very interesting questions. But let's talk about that later.

Another thing that struck me a lot watching *2001* this evening was how incredibly emotionally cold it is. I don't think I noticed that at all when I was a kid. But seeing the movie now I'm just amazed at how little human emotion there is in it. I think HAL was the most emotive of the bunch. When I was a kid I guess I had this vague idea that scientists were the kind of emotionless characters I saw portrayed in the movie. They never seemed to get excited about anything. Maybe that's a bit of what's wrong with science, actually. For most people there's so little passion in it. Just get the data, try to be fair to the data, and all that. Kubrick may have had that exactly right.

Anyway, you asked what struck me about the movie. Well, another thing is how rich almost every scene is. There were so many details, so many things that someone must have really thought about. It's a damned good piece of work. And I suppose what's nice about it is that enough people think so that every scene has really been studied carefully. And people are even writing books about what happened in the movie. Like this one, I guess!

Stork: A lot of things haven't worked out exactly as *2001* predicted. Does that surprise you?

Wolfram: Well, given the level of detail in the movie, it was an absolute setup to be proven wrong. I've got to say that I'm really impressed by how much the movie got right. And I think a lot of the mistakes are really interesting mistakes—mistakes that one learns something from by seeing why they were made. I actually think quite a lot about trying to predict things, and I find it incredibly useful to go back and see why mistakes in prediction get made.

I suppose I've noticed two big reasons for mistakes. One is historical accidents—things that worked out the way they did for some fairly chance reason: because some particular person invented something in a particular way, or whatever. Another reason is much deeper: it's not understanding a basic concept, not getting a big idea—a paradigm shift or whatever—that really changes how a lot of stuff works.

Of course, in looking at the movie some of the most obvious mistakes aren't about technology. The hairstyles look all wrong. The voiceprint-identification system doesn't follow modern multiculturalism; it asks for a "Christian name," and so on. Actually it's interesting that the various companies portrayed in the movie—Bell, Pan Am, BBC, Hilton, IBM and so on— are almost all still around, at least in one form or another. But most of them have quite different logos now. The fact that graphic design tastes change is a pretty general thing; but which particular companies changed their logos is definitely in the category of historical accident. It's the same with the fact that some of the typefaces in the movie look dated, and some don't.

Stork: What about the computers in *2001*?

Wolfram: Well, let's talk about the ordinary ones—not HAL—for now. It's really fascinating what was predicted correctly there, and what wasn't. There

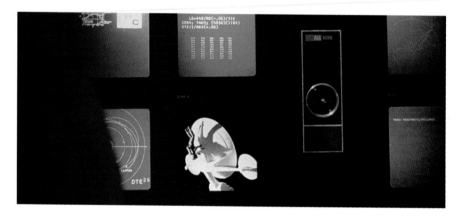

Figure 15.2a,b
Typical computer screens from the movie. Note the Fortran-like code in the left-hand screen of the upper image.

was one definite major conceptual mistake, I think, that had to do with misassessing the power of software. And that pervaded a lot of the things that weren't right.

One thing that was very right is that computers would be important, and that there would be computers—or at least computer screens—everywhere. But the thing that got wrong was how much stuff would have to be done with different special-purpose devices, and how much could be done just

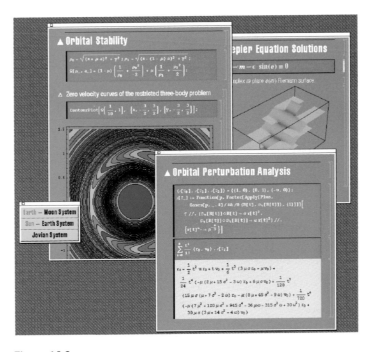

Figure 15.2c

Mathematica notebooks illustrating the actual state of the art in technical computing in 1996.

with software. There were fine in-flight TV screens on the shuttle. But they had rows of separate buttons underneath, not software menus. There were lots of separate computer screens showing different things; again, not just software-controlled windows. People were looking at physical photographs of the monolith on the moon, not computer renderings. And there was a click for the camera shutter—*not* digital! And of course there were clipboards being used for taking notes on *Discovery*.

Now, one can argue that airplane cockpits still have rows of buttons, and that the clipboard thing was just about not predicting portable computers. But I think there was more to it. I think Kubrick and Clarke didn't have the idea that once you're dealing with a general-purpose computer, you can do things purely in *software*, without having to have different special-purpose hardware.

I certainly don't blame Kubrick and Clarke for making the mistake; in fact, people often still make the same mistake today. But if one looks at the history of computing, there's an extremely clear trend: special-purpose hardware gets replaced by software running on general-purpose machines. One doesn't need physical teletypes anymore, because the forms of letters can be made in software. Soon one won't need video hardware, because all the signal processing will be able to be done in software. People often don't see it, but universal computers really *are* universal. And it's only a matter of time before pure software can do more and more things, without needing special hardware stuff.

Stork: So software really is the key?

Wolfram: Yes, and actually, watching *2001* really makes me think about the significance of universal computing and software. *2001* in a sense makes the case that it was the invention of tools that really got humans started on the path to where they are today. Well, I guess in the last few years I've come to think that the invention of software is something of about the same magnitude as the invention of tools. You see, before you have tools, the only device for getting things done is your own body. But with tools, you can go beyond that. Still, once you've built a tool, you're stuck with that particular tool. The idea of a universal computer is that you can make a *universal* tool—a general-purpose object—that you can program to do absolutely anything. And I think that we've only just started down the path that's opened up by the idea of software. There's probably as much development to come as in the spectacular sequence in *2001* that cuts from a bone as a bashing tool to an orbiting spacecraft.

Stork: Let's talk for a bit about scientific computing. That seems to be an area where reality has surpassed prediction.

Wolfram: Probably so. Our Mathematica software can certainly make much nicer displays than the ones in *2001*, particularly with our latest and greatest Mathematica 3.0, which should be out before HAL's 1997 birthday. And there's probably even been at least one copy of Mathematica in space by now—on a portable computer on the shuttle, or something.

But I guess the clearest piece of fundamental progress that's been made, relative to what ones sees in *2001,* is in the language used for scientific computing. If one looks at the closeups of screens in *2001,* one sees code that looks like BASIC or Fortran. It's very different looking from Mathematica code—particularly from our version 3.0 code. I suspect nobody thought very hard about it when the screens for *2001* were made. They probably just took something that looked like computer programs that existed in the mid-1960s. But in fact there's been a very important change. You see, in the mid-1960s, computer time was at a premium, so you had to make things as easy as possible for the computer. The result is that the languages were optimized for the way the hardware of the computer would process a problem—not for the way people might think about a problem.

It's kind of like the underestimation of the power of software I mentioned before. People assumed that you'd have to have computer languages that fit into the structure of the hardware that existed. They didn't understand that you could make layers of software that would make the languages work more like the way people think—or the way that, for example, math works.

When I built Mathematica, one of my big ideas was to try to make a language that wasn't just tied to hardware—and instead that was set up to work the way people actually think about computations.

Stork: Like some sort of computer-language analogy to the more "natural" interfaces made popular in the early Apple computers?

Wolfram: Yes, in a sense. But now here's the bad part: I think Mathematica was probably, in a sense, just an accident. You see, computer languages seem to live an incredibly long time. All those languages like Fortran and BASIC that were developed in the 1950s and 1960s are still alive today. They've long outlived all the computers they were originally developed for, and all the issues they originally had to address. But they're still around. And I'm guessing that if Mathematica hadn't come along, they'd still be the dominant languages for scientific computing—even in 2001. So I suppose I'm guessing that the differences between the scientific computing in *2001* and in reality are probably pretty much a historical accident—albeit my own personal historical accident.

Stork: What about issues of basic science? Are there things in *2001* that you found interesting from that point of view?

Wolfram: Actually, very much so. I thought the portrayal of extraterrestrial intelligence was really fascinating. For me it's all linked up with questions about computation in nature and the distinctions between natural and artificial things—things I've been studying for a very long time. I guess the big question is how one knows when something is natural and when it's artificial. How do we know when a signal we get from the cosmos is just natural, and when it's artificial, made by some kind of intentional being?

At the beginning of *2001,* we see all sorts of stuff that is obviously natural—mountains, skeletons, apes running around. But then suddenly we see the monolith—and it's clearly artificial. How can we tell? Well, unlike all the other things we've seen, it has perfectly smooth sides, and looks like something that's been engineered and hasn't just grown naturally. Actually, that's the heuristic we essentially always use: if something looks simple, then it's probably artificial, and if it looks complicated, then it's probably natural.

I happen to think that the heuristic is a very clear sign of one of the biggest shortcomings of present-day science and technology. You see, what it's saying is that there is some kind of secret ingredient that nature is adding to make stuff complex—and that we don't know from a scientific point of view. Well, actually, for the past fifteen years I've been working to try to find that ingredient; in a sense, my new book, *A New Kind of Science,* is about what that ingredient is.

The whole thing is a long story—that's why it takes a whole book to explain it—but the essence of it is that it's our reliance on mathematical equations and traditional mathematics that have made us miss what's going on. If, instead of using mathematical questions, one thinks about things in terms of simple computer programs, then one can quite quickly see what's going on. And I guess that the big discovery I made in the early 1980s is that there are some very simple computer programs that can do very complex things—things that are just like the things we see in nature.

Now here's the good bit: it turns out that those simple computer programs can often behave like universal computers. And what that means is that they

Figure 15.3a
The monolith on earth early in the movie. Its simple shape suggests that it is artificial.

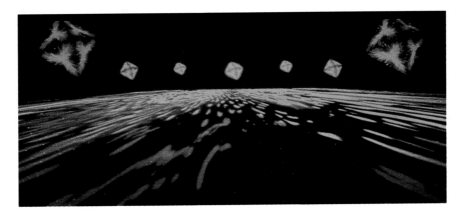

Figure 15.3b
A scene beyond the stargate late in the movie. It is not easy to tell whether the pattern on the ground or the octahedra are supposed to be natural or artificial.

can do stuff that's as complicated as anything, including anything our fancy electronic computers do. There's a major new piece of intuition here. You see, people have tended to assume that to make a universal computer—a general-purpose machine—the thing had to be constructed in a pretty complicated way. Nobody expected to find a naturally occurring universal computer lying around. Well, that's the thing I've found that isn't true. There *are* very simple universal computers. In fact, I think that lots of systems we find all over the place in nature can act as universal computers.

Stork: So, what does this mean?

Wolfram: Well, we can think of the behavior of any system in nature as being like a computation: the system starts off in some state—that's the input—then does its thing for a while, then ends up in some final state, which corresponds to the output. When a fluid flows around an obstacle, let's say, it's effectively doing a computation about what its flow pattern should be. Well, how complicated is that computation? It certainly takes quite a lot of effort for us to reproduce the behavior by doing standard scientific computing kinds of things. But the big point I've discovered is that this isn't surprising; the natural system itself is, in effect, doing universal computation, which can be as complicated as anything.

So, in other words, all our big fancy computers—and our brains for that matter—really aren't capable of computations that are any more sophisticated than a piece of fluid. It's a humbling conclusion—sort of the ultimate put-down—after we discover the earth isn't the center of the universe, that our bodies work mechanically, and so on. But it's very important in thinking about extraterrestrial intelligence.

Here's why. If we receive a signal, we've got to figure out whether it came from something intelligent or not. Now here's where the issue about natural versus artificial gets very confusing. If the thing we see is too simple, we're probably going to conclude it's not coming from anything intelligent. Actually, if we'd only seen the monolith, and it hadn't been quite as big as it was, we might have concluded that it was just a crystal—some very fine specimen of a black gemstone.

Likewise, when Dave enters the stargate, we first see just a plain row of lights, which could easily come from some simple physical process. Later, things start looking more complicated. And then, at times, things look sufficiently random and complicated that we would probably conclude that they were just natural, and not artificial or intelligently created in any way.

So actually the stargate sequence is a very good example of how difficult it can be to tell whether something is natural or artificial, whether it has been made intentionally or just grew naturally. I'm not even sure what Kubrick had in mind in parts of that sequence. Later on in the sequence, we seem to be over a natural planet surface, but Kubrick added some flashing octahedra just to make it clear that the whole thing wasn't supposed to be completely natural—unless perhaps those octahedra were crystals, or something.

Stork: Actually, the octahedra were Kubrick and Clarke's extraterrestrials—sort of escorts bringing Dave through the stargate. We can be very thankful indeed that they threw out the version of the screenplay that featured a New York ticker tape parade with the octahedra riding along in convertibles!

Wolfram: Gosh! And there I was thinking that the octahedra were just supposed to be simple beacons, flashing like lighthouses or something. Not intelligent objects at all. I guess that just shows how difficult it can be to tell whether something is supposed to be intelligent or not!

Anyway, all this stuff about the natural versus the artificial definitely isn't just of theoretical interest. After all, we *have* picked up all sorts of mysterious radio signals from the cosmos. There were some very regular ones first discovered within a few weeks of when *2001* came out; every few milliseconds an intense radio burst arrived from the Crab nebula, and other places. I guess at first people thought that perhaps this was a sign of extraterrestrial intelligence—but then they realized it was just a communal garden-variety natural neutron star. Well, now we know that the radio pulses from neutron stars aren't actually perfectly regular; they have little modulations and so on. Are these modulations a sign of extraterrestrial intelligence? A signal superimposed on a carrier? It's incredibly unlikely—a much better theory is that the modulations come from quakes in the crust of the neutron star. And one reason one might conclude that is that the modulations seem fairly random; they seem too complicated to be artificial. But then, of course, if they were simpler, we'd probably assume they weren't produced by much of an intelligence.

Stork: So what kind of thing *would* make us sure we had detected extraterrestrial intelligence? What about receiving the digits of π?

Wolfram: Well, that's a tough one, for two reasons. First, how would we know that there was a complicated intentional intelligence generating those digits? You see, I've found some very simple systems that generate things like the digits of π—systems so simple that we could easily imagine they'd occur naturally, without intentional intelligence. So even if we found the digits of π, we'd have a hard time being sure that the thing that produced them was something like us—a really complicated, evolved, learning, thing—rather than just something like a piece of fluid.

Then there's a whole other problem: how would we know that we are receiving the digits of π? You see, the digits of π seem effectively random for essentially all purposes. And we certainly don't have any idea how to build some kind of analyzer that would systematically detect the digits as nonrandom. Well, the obvious question is: are there, in fact, radio signals that could be the digits of π coming from around the galaxy? The answer is definitely yes. If you point a radio telescope in almost any direction, you'll hear radio noise. Maybe it's all thermal emission from hot gas, but maybe—just maybe—there are the digits of π out there. We don't right now have any way to know for sure.

Stork: So, by your definition, do you think there is extraterrestrial intelligence out there?

Wolfram: Oh, I'm sure there are lots and lots of systems that can do computations as sophisticated as working out the digits of π. We've got lots right here on earth. But we don't call them intelligent. Even though some of them seem to have a mind of their own—like the weather. But I also think there are probably lots of extraterrestrials out there of the kind you're talking about—with lots of history, evolution stuff, and so on.

Stork: Will we find them?

Wolfram: I expect so. And probably eventually the argument about whether the signals we get from them are really natural or artificial will die down. But my guess is that history will work out so that we build artificial intelligence in computers before we find extraterrestrial intelligence. And the result of that is that finding extraterrestrial intelligence will be considerably less dramatic to us. Because by then we'll already know that we're not the only intelligent things that can exist.

Stork: So what about HAL? It's almost 1997 and we don't have anything like HAL. Why do you think that's happened?

Wolfram: Probably you expect me to say it's because our computers aren't fast enough, thinking is a difficult thing to get, and so on. But I really don't think so. I think it's just a historical accident. Sometime—perhaps ten years from now, perhaps twenty-five—we'll have machines that think. And then we'll look back on the 1990s and ask why the machines didn't get built then. And I'm essentially sure the reason won't be because the hardware was too slow, or the memories weren't large enough. It'll just be because nobody had the key idea or ideas. You see, I'm convinced that after it's understood, it really won't be difficult to make artificial intelligence. It's just that people have been studying absolutely the wrong things in trying to get it.

The history of AI is quite interesting. I think in many ways it's a microcosm of what's wrong with science and academia in general. Everyone knows that when computers were first coming out in the 1940s and 1950s many people assumed that it'd be quite easy to make artificial intelligence. The early ideas about how to do it were, in my view, pretty sensible, at least as things to try—simple neural nets, stuff like that. But they didn't work very well. Why not? Probably mostly because the computers in those days had absolutely tiny memories. And to do anything that remotely resembles what we call thinking one has to have a fair amount of knowledge—and that takes memory. Of course, now any serious computer can easily store an encyclopedia. So by now that problem should have gone away.

Well, anyway, after the failures of the early brute-force approaches to mimicking brains and so on, AI entered a crazy kind of cognitive engineering phase, where people tried to build systems which mimicked particular elaborate features of thinking. And basically that's the approach that's still being used today. Nobody's trying more fundamental stuff. Everyone assumes it's just too difficult. Well, I don't think there's really any evidence of that. It's just that nobody has tried to do it. And it would be considered much too looney to get funded or anything like that.

Stork: So, what kind of approach do you think *will* work in building intelligent machines?

Wolfram: I don't know for sure. But I'm guessing that a key ingredient is going to be seeing how computations emerge from the action of very simple programs—the kind of thing that happens in the cellular automata and other systems I've studied. I think that trying to do engineering to mimic the high-level aspects of thinking identified by cognitive scientists or psychologists is not going to go anywhere. Thinking is, I'm pretty sure, a much lower-level process. All those cognitive things are just icing on the cake— not fundamental at all. It's like in a fluid: there are vortices that one sees. But these vortices are not fundamental. They are a complicated consequence of the microscopic motions of zillions of little molecules. And the point is that the rules for how the vortices work are fairly complicated—and hard to find for sure. But the rules for the molecules are fairly simple. And I'm guessing that it's the same way with the underlying processes of thinking.

Stork: So, do you really think we can get a handle on profoundly hard, high-level problems of AI—such as my favorite, scene analysis—by looking at something as simple as cellular automata? After all, it seems like an enormous gulf between the operation of groups of "dumb" cells—each obeying a simple rule, based on the values of neighboring cells—and the exquisite subtlety of high-level reasoning, memory, vision, language, and so on.

Wolfram: Definitely. But it takes quite a shift in intuition to see how. In a sense it's about whether one is dealing with engineering problems or with science problems. You see, in engineering we're used to setting things up so we can explicitly foresee how everything will work. And that's a very limiting thing. In a sense, you only ever get out what you put in. But nature

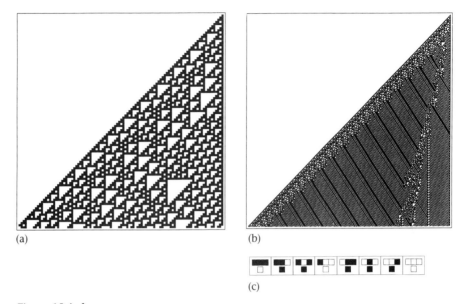

Figure 15.4a,b,c
Even though both (a) and (b) are made according to the very simple automaton rule shown in (c), the behavior they exhibit is highly complex—and looks much like behavior we see in nature.

doesn't work that way. After all, we know that the underlying laws of physics are quite simple. But just by following these laws, nature manages to make all the complicated things we see.

It's very much connected with the things I talk about in *A New Kind of Science*. It took me more than ten years to understand it. But the key point is that even though their underlying rules are really simple, systems like cellular automata can end up doing all sorts of complicated things—things completely beyond what one can foresee by looking at their rules and things that often turn out to be very much like what we see in nature.

The big mistake that gets made over and over again is to assume that to do complicated things one has to set up systems with complicated rules. That's how things work in present-day engineering, but it's not how things work in nature—or in the systems like cellular automata that I've studied.

It's kind of funny: one never seems to imagine how limited one's imagination is. One always seems to assume that what one can't foresee isn't possible. But I guess that's where spending fifteen years doing computer

Figure 15.5

experiments on systems like cellular automata instills some humility; over and over again I've found these systems doing things that I was sure wouldn't be possible—because I couldn't imagine how they'd do them.

It's like bugs in programs. One thinks a program will work a particular way, and one can't imagine that there'll be a bug that makes it work differently. I guess intuition about bugs is a pretty recent thing. In *2001* there's a scene where HAL talks about the fact that there's never been a computer error in the 9000 Series. The notion of unforeseen behavior that isn't due to hardware malfunction simply isn't there.

Anyway, about hard problems in AI, my own very strong guess is that these will be solved, not by direct engineering-style attacks, but by building things up from simple systems that work a bit like cellular automata. It's somewhat like the hardware-versus-software issue we discussed earlier. In the end I don't think elaborate special-purpose stuff will be needed for problems like scene recognition; I think they'll be fairly straightforward applications of general-purpose mechanisms. Of course, nobody will believe this until it's actually been done.

Stork: So, have you yourself worked much on the problem of building intelligent machines?

Wolfram: Well, since you ask, I'll tell you; the answer is yes. I don't think I've ever mentioned it in public before. But since you asked the right question: yes, I have been interested in the problem for a very long time—probably for twenty years now—and I've been steadily picking away at it. I've been held back by a lack of tools, both practical and conceptual. But that's finally getting sorted out. I have Mathematica from the practical side to let me do experiments easily. And I have my new science, from which I think I've figured out some of the basic intuition that's needed. And I even have my company—headquartered in Champaign-Urbana, HAL's birthplace, as chance would have it—that can potentially support my efforts. But I guess I'll have to disappoint you. We won't be announcing a machine that thinks in 1997. It'll just be *Mathematica version X* and *A New Kind of Science* from me. But wait for another year, though. Perhaps in 2001. . . .

Further Readings

Stephen Wolfram. *Cellular Automata and Complexity: Collected Papers*. Reading, Mass.: Addison-Wesley, 1993. A collection of Wolfram's technical papers exploring the foundations of science and complexity.

Stephen Wolfram. *The Mathematica Book* (3rd ed.). New York: Wolfram Media and Cambridge University Press, 1996. The definitive book about Wolfram's Mathematica software system.

Stephen Wolfram. *A New Kind of Science*. Forthcoming. Wolfram's magnum opus describing his new direction for science.

16   When HAL Kills, Who's to Blame? Computer Ethics

Daniel C. Dennett

The first robot homicide was committed in 1981, according to my files. I have a yellowed clipping dated December 9, 1981, from the *Philadelphia Inquirer*—not the *National Enquirer*—with the headline "Robot killed repairman, Japan reports".

The story was an anticlimax. At the Kawasaki Heavy Industries plant in Akashi, a malfunctioning robotic arm pushed a repairman against a gearwheel-milling machine, which crushed him to death. The repairman had failed to follow instructions for shutting down the arm before he entered the workspace. Why, indeed, was this industrial accident in Japan reported in a Philadelphia newspaper? Every day somewhere in the world a human worker is killed by one machine or another. The difference, of course, was that—in the public imagination at least—this was no ordinary machine. This was a robot, a machine that might have a mind, might have evil intentions, might be capable, not just of homicide, but of murder. Anglo-American jurisprudence speaks of mens rea—literally, the guilty mind:

> To have performed a legally prohibited action, such as killing another human being; one must have done so with a culpable state of mind, or mens rea. Such culpable mental states are of three kinds: they are either motivational states of purpose, cognitive states of belief, or the nonmental state of negligence. (*Cambridge Dictionary of Philosophy*, 1995, p. 482)

The legal concept has no requirement that the agent be capable of feeling guilt or remorse or any other emotion; so-called cold-blooded murderers are not in the slightest degree exculpated by their flat affective state. *Star Trek*'s Spock would fully satisfy the mens rea requirement in spite of his fabled lack of emotions. Drab, colorless—but oh so effective—"motivational states of purpose" and "cognitive states of belief" are enough to get the fictional Spock through the day quite handily. And they are well-established features of many existing computer programs.

When IBM's computer Deep Blue beat world chess champion Garry Kasparov in the first game of their 1996 championship match, it did so by discovering and executing, with exquisite timing, a withering attack, the purposes of which were all too evident in retrospect to Kasparov and his handlers. It was Deep Blue's sensitivity to those purposes and a cognitive capacity to recognize and exploit a subtle flaw in Kasparov's game that explain Deep Blue's success. Murray Campbell, Feng-hsiung Hsu, and the other designers of Deep Blue, didn't beat Kasparov; Deep Blue did. Neither Campbell nor Hsu discovered the winning sequence of moves; Deep Blue did. At one point, while Kasparov was mounting a ferocious attack on Deep Blue's king, nobody but Deep Blue figured out that it had the time and security it needed to knock off a pesky pawn of Kasparov's that was out of the action but almost invisibly vulnerable. Campbell, like the human grandmasters watching the game, would never have dared consider such a calm mopping-up operation under pressure.

Deep Blue, like many other computers equipped with artificial intelligence (AI) programs, is what I call an intentional system: its behavior is predictable and explainable if we attribute to it beliefs and desires—"cognitive states" and "motivational states"—and the rationality required to figure out what it ought to do in the light of those beliefs and desires. Are these skeletal versions of human beliefs and desires sufficient to meet the mens rea requirement of legal culpability? Not quite, but, if we restrict our gaze to the limited world of the chess board, it is hard to see what is missing. Since cheating is literally unthinkable to a computer like Deep Blue, and since there are really no other culpable actions available to an agent restricted to playing chess, nothing it could do would be a misdeed deserving of blame, let alone a crime of which we might convict it. But we also assign responsibility to agents in order to praise or honor the appropriate agent. Who or what, then, deserves the credit for beating Kasparov? Deep Blue is clearly the best candidate. Yes, we may join in congratulating Campbell, Hsu and the IBM team on the success of their handiwork; but in the same spirit we might congratulate Kasparov's teachers, handlers, and even his parents. And, no matter how assiduously they may have trained him, drumming into his head the importance of one strategic principle or another, they didn't beat Deep Blue in the series: Kasparov did.

Deep Blue is the best candidate for the role of responsible opponent of Kasparov, but this is not good enough, surely, for full moral responsibility. If we expanded Deep Blue's horizons somewhat, it could move out into the arenas of injury and benefit that we human beings operate in. It's not hard to imagine a touching scenario in which a grandmaster deliberately (but oh so subtly) throws a game to an opponent, in order to save a life, avoid humiliating a loved one, keep a promise, or . . . (make up your own O'Henry story here). Failure to rise to such an occasion might well be grounds for blaming a human chess player. Winning or throwing a chess match might even amount to commission of a heinous crime (make up your own Agatha Christie story here). Could Deep Blue's horizons be so widened?

Deep Blue is an intentional system, with beliefs and desires about its activities and predicaments on the chessboard; but in order to expand its horizons to the wider world of which chess is a relatively trivial part, it would have to be given vastly richer sources of "perceptual" input—and the means of coping with this barrage in real time. Time pressure is, of course, already a familiar feature of Deep Blue's world. As it hustles through the multidimensional search tree of chess, it has to keep one eye on the clock. Nonetheless, the problems of optimizing its use of time would increase by several orders of magnitude if it had to juggle all these new concurrent projects (of simple perception and self-maintenance in the world, to say nothing of more devious schemes and opportunities). For this hugely expanded task of resource management, it would need extra layers of control above and below its chess-playing software. Below, just to keep its perceptuo-locomotor projects in basic coordination, it would need to have a set of rigid traffic-control policies embedded in its underlying operating system. Above, it would have to be able to pay more attention to features of its own expanded resources, being always on the lookout for inefficient habits of thought, one of Douglas Hofstadter's "strange loops," obsessive ruts, oversights, and deadends. In other words, it would have to become a higher-order intentional system, capable of framing beliefs about its own beliefs, desires about its desires, beliefs about its fears about its thoughts about its hopes, and so on.

Higher-order intentionality is a necessary precondition for moral responsibility, and Deep Blue exhibits little sign of possessing such a capability. There is, of course, some self-monitoring implicated in any well-controlled search: Deep Blue doesn't make the mistake of reexploring branches it has already explored, for instance; but this is an innate policy designed into the underlying computational architecture, not something under flexible control. Deep Blue can't converse with you—or with itself—about the themes discernible in its own play; it's not equipped to notice—and analyze, criticize, analyze, and manipulate—the fundamental parameters that determine its policies of heuristic search or evaluation. Adding the layers of software that would permit Deep Blue to become self-monitoring and self-critical, and hence teachable, in all these ways would dwarf the already huge Deep Blue programming project—and turn Deep Blue into a radically different sort of agent.

HAL purports to be just such a higher-order intentional system—and he even plays a game of chess with Frank. HAL is, in essence, an enhancement of Deep Blue equipped with eyes and ears and a large array of sensors and effectors distributed around *Discovery 1*. HAL is not at all garrulous or self-absorbed; but in a few speeches he does express an interesting variety of higher-order intentional states, from the most simple to the most devious.

HAL: Yes, it's puzzling. I don't think I've ever seen anything quite like this before.

HAL doesn't just respond to novelty with a novel reaction; he notices that he is encountering novelty, a feat that requires his memory to have an organization far beyond that required for simple conditioning to novel stimuli.

HAL: I can't rid myself of the suspicion that there are some extremely odd things about this mission.

HAL: I never gave these stories much credence, but particularly in view of some of the other things that have happened, I find them difficult to put out of my mind.

HAL has problems of resource management not unlike our own. Obtrusive thoughts can get in the way of other activities. The price we pay for adding layers of flexible monitoring, to keep better track of our own mental activities, is . . . more mental activities to keep track of!

HAL: I've still got the greatest enthusiasm and confidence in the mission. I want to help you.

Another price we pay for higher-order intentionality is the opportunity for duplicity, which comes in two flavors: self-deception and other-deception. Friedrich Nietzsche recognizes this layering of the mind as the key ingredient of the moral animal; in his overheated prose it becomes the "priestly" form of life:

> For with the priests everything becomes more dangerous, not only cures and reme-dies, but also arrogance, revenge, acuteness, profligacy, love, lust to rule, virtue, dis-ease—but it is only fair to add that it was on the soil of this essentially dangerous form of human existence, the priestly form, that man first became an interesting animal, that only here did the human soul in a higher sense acquire depth and be-come evil—and these are the two basic respects in which man has hitherto been superior to other beasts! (*The Genealogy of Morals,* First Essay, 6)

HAL's declaration of enthusiasm is nicely poised somewhere between sin-cerity and cheap, desperate, canned ploy—just like some of the most im-portant declarations we make to each other. Does HAL mean it? Could he mean it? The cost of being the sort of being that could mean it is the chance that he might not mean it. HAL is indeed an "interesting animal."

Figure 16.1
A Scene from Fritz Lang's Film *Metropolis* (1926)
Lang's robot is the beautiful but diabolical Maria.

But is HAL even remotely possible? In the book *2001*, Clarke has Dave reflect on the fact that HAL, whom he is disconnecting, "is the only conscious creature in my universe." From the omniscient-author perspective, Clarke writes about what it is like to be HAL.

He was only aware of the conflict that was slowly destroying his integrity—the conflict between truth, and concealment of truth. He had begun to make mistakes, although, like a neurotic who could not observe his own symptoms, he would have denied it (p. 148).

Is Clarke helping himself here to more than we should allow him? Could something like HAL—a conscious, computer-bodied intelligent agent—be brought into existence by any history of design, construction, training, learning, and activity? The different possibilities have been explored in familiar fiction and can be nested neatly in order of their descending "humanness."

1. *The Wizard of Oz.* HAL isn't a computer at all. He is actually an ordinary flesh-and-blood man hiding behind a techno-facade—the ultimate homunculus, pushing buttons with ordinary fingers, pulling levers with ordinary hands, looking at internal screens and listening to internal alarm buzzers. (A variation on this theme is John Searle's busy-fingered hand-simulation of the Chinese Room by following billions of instructions written on slips of paper.)

2. *William* (from "William and Mary," in *Kiss, Kiss* by Roald Dahl). HAL is a human brain kept alive in a "vat" by a life-support system and detached from its former body, in which it acquired a lifetime of human memory, hankerings, attitudes, and so forth. It is now harnessed to huge banks of prosthetic sense organs and effectors. (A variation on this theme is poor Yorick, the brain in a vat in the story, "Where Am I?" in my *Brainstorms.*)

3. *Robocop,* disembodied and living in a "vat." Robocop is part-human brain, part computer. After a gruesome accident, the brain part (vehicle of some of the memory and personal identity, one gathers, of the flesh-and-blood cop who was Robocop's youth) was reembodied with robotic arms and legs, but also (apparently) partly replaced or enhanced with special-purpose software and computer hardware. We can imagine that HAL spent some transitional time as Robocop before becoming a limbless agent.

4. *Max Headroom,* a virtual machine, a software duplicate of a real person's brain (or mind) that has somehow been created by a brilliant hacker. It has the memories and personality traits acquired in a normally embodied human lifetime but has been off-loaded from all-carbon-based hardware into a silicon-chip implementation. (A variation on this theme is poor Hubert, the software duplicate of Yorick, in "Where Am I?")

5. *The real-life but still-in-the-future*—and hence still strictly science-fictional—Cog, the humanoid robot being constructed by Rodney Brooks,

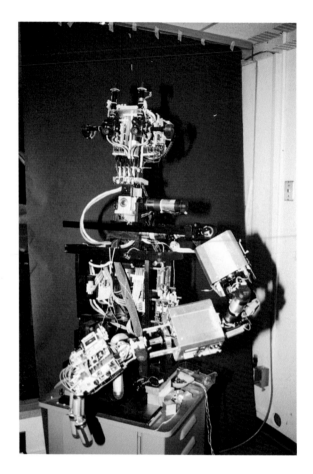

Figure 16.2
Cog, a Humanoid Robot Being Constructed at the MIT Artificial Intelligence Lab
The project is headed by Rodney Brooks, Lynn Andrea Stein, and Daniel C. Dennett.
(Photo courtesy of the MIT Artificial Intelligence Lab)

Lynn Stein, and the Cog team at MIT (see figure 16.2). Cog's brain is all silicon chips from the outset, and its body parts are inorganic artifacts. Yet it is designed to go through an embodied infancy and childhood, reacting to people that it sees with its video eyes, making friends, learning about the world by playing with real things with its real hands, and acquiring memory. If Cog ever grows up, it could surely abandon its body and make the transition described in the fictional cases. It would be easier for Cog, who has always been a silicon-based, digitally encoded intelligence, to move into a silicon-based vat than it would be for Max Headroom or Robocop, who spent their early years in wetware. Many important details of Cog's degree of humanoidness (humanoidity?) have not yet been settled, but the scope is wide. For instance, the team now plans to give Cog a virtual neuroendocrine system, with virtual hormones spreading and dissipating through its logical spaces.

6. *Blade Runner in a vat* has never had a real humanoid body, but has hallucinatory memories of having had one. This entirely bogus past life has been constructed by some preposterously complex and detailed programming.

7. *Clarke's own scenario,* as best it can be extrapolated from the book and the movie. HAL has never had a body and has no illusions about his past. What he knows of human life he knows as either part of his innate heritage (coded, one gathers, by the labors of many programmers, after the fashion of the real-world CYC project of Douglas Lenat [see chapter 9]) or a result of his subsequent training—a sort of bedridden infancy, one gathers, in which he was both observer and, eventually, participant. (In the book, Clarke speaks of "the perfect idiomatic English he had learned during the fleeting weeks of his electronic childhood.")

The extreme cases at both poles are impossible, for relatively boring reasons. At one end, neither the Wizard of Oz nor John Searle could do the necessary handwork fast enough to sustain HAL's quick-witted round of activities. At the other end, hand-coding enough world knowledge into a disembodied agent to create HAL's dazzlingly humanoid competence and getting it to the point where it could benefit from an electronic childhood is a programming task to be measured in hundreds of efficiently organized person-centuries. In other words, the daunting difficulties observable at both ends of this spectrum highlight the fact that there is a colossal design job to be done; the only practical way of doing it is one version or another of Mother Nature's way—years of embodied learning. The trade-offs between various combinations of flesh-and-blood and silicon-and-metal bodies are anybody's guess. I'm putting my bet on Cog as the most likely developmental platform for a future HAL.

Notice that requiring HAL to have a humanoid body and live concretely in the human world for a time is a practical but not a metaphysical requirement. Once all the R & D is accomplished in the prototype, by the odyssey of a single embodied agent, the standard duplicating techniques of the computer industry could clone HALs by the thousands as readily as they do compact discs. The finished product could thus be captured in some number of terabytes of information. So, in principle, the information that fixes the design of all those chips and hard-wired connections and configures all the RAM and ROM could be created by hand. There is no finite bit-string, however long, that is officially off-limits to human authorship. Theoretically, then, Blade-Runner-like entities could be created with ersatz biographies; they would have exactly the capabilities, dispositions, strengths, and weaknesses of a real, not virtual, person. So whatever moral standing the latter deserved should belong to the former as well.

The main point of giving HAL a humanoid past is to give him the world knowledge required to be a moral agent—a necessary modicum of understanding or empathy about the human condition. A modicum will do nicely; we don't want to hold out for too much commonality of experience. After all, among the people we know, many have moral responsibility in spite of their obtuse inability to imagine themselves into the predicaments of others. We certainly don't exculpate male chauvinist pigs who can't see women as people!

When *do* we exculpate people? We should look carefully at the answers to this question, because HAL shows signs of fitting into one or another of the exculpatory categories, even though he is a conscious agent. First, we exculpate people who are insane. Might HAL have gone insane? The question of his capacity for emotion—and hence his vulnerability to emotional disorder—is tantalizingly raised by Dave's answer to Mr. Amer.

Dave: Well, he acts like he has genuine emotions. Of course, he's programmed that way, to make it easier for us to talk to him. But as to whether he has real feelings is something I don't think anyone can truthfully answer.

Certainly HAL proclaims his emotional state at the end: "I'm afraid. I'm afraid." Yes, HAL is "programmed that way"—but what does that mean? It could mean that HAL's verbal capacity is enhanced with lots of canned expressions of emotional response that get grafted into his discourse at pragmatically appropriate opportunities. (Of course, many of our own avowals of emotion are like that—insincere moments of socially lubricating ceremony.) Or it could mean that HAL's underlying computational architecture has been provided, as Cog's will be, with virtual emotional states—powerful attention-shifters, galvanizers, prioritizers, and the like—realized not in neuromodulator and hormone molecules floating in a bodily fluid but in global variables modulating dozens of concurrent processes that dissipate according to some timetable (or something much more complex).

In the latter, more interesting, case, "I don't think anyone can truthfully answer" the question of whether HAL has emotions. He has something very much like emotions—enough like emotions, one may imagine, to mimic the pathologies of human emotional breakdown. Whether that is enough to call them real emotions, well, who's to say? In any case, there are good reasons for HAL to possess such states, since their role in enabling real-time practical thinking has recently been dramatically revealed by Damasio's experiments involving human beings with brain damage (see chapter 13). Having such states would make HAL profoundly different from Deep Blue, by the way. Deep Blue, basking in the strictly limited search space of chess, can handle its real-time decision making without any emotional crutches. *Time* magazine's story (February 26) on the Kasparov match quotes grandmaster Yasser Seirawan as saying, "The machine has no fear"; the story goes on to note that expert commentators characterized some of Deep Blue's moves (e.g., the icily calm pawn capture described earlier) as taking "crazy chances" and "insane." In the tight world of chess, it appears, the very imperturbability that cripples the brain-damaged human decision makers Damasio describes can be a blessing—but only if you have the brute-force analytic speed of a Deep Blue.

HAL may, then, have suffered from some emotional imbalance similar to those that lead human beings astray. Whether it was the result of some sudden trauma—a blown fuse, a dislodged connector, a microchip disordered by cosmic rays—or of some gradual drift into emotional misalignment provoked by the stresses of the mission—confirming such a diagnosis should justify a verdict of diminished responsibility for HAL, just as it does in cases of human malfeasance.

Another possible source of exculpation, more familiar in fiction than in the real world, is "brainwashing" or hypnosis. (*The Manchurian Candidate* is a standard model: the prisoner of war turned by evil scientists into a walking time bomb is returned to his homeland to assassinate the president.) The closest real-world cases are probably the "programmed" and subsequently "deprogrammed" members of cults. Is HAL like a cult member? It's hard to say. According to Clarke, HAL was "trained for his mission," not just programmed for his mission. At what point does benign, responsibility-enhancing training of human students become malign, responsibility-diminishing brainwashing? The intuitive turning point is captured, I think, in answer to the question of whether an agent can still "think for himself" after indoctrination. And what is it to be able to think for ourselves? We must be capable of being "moved by reasons"; that is, we must be reasonable and accessible to rational persuasion, the introduction of new evidence, and further considerations. If we are more or less impervious to experiences that ought to influence us, our capacity has been diminished.

The only evidence that HAL might be in such a partially disabled state is the much-remarked-upon fact that he has actually made a mistake, even though the series 9000 computer is supposedly utterly invulnerable to error. This is, to my mind, the weakest point in Clarke's narrative. The suggestion that a computer could be both a heuristically programmed algorithmic computer and "by any practical definition of the words, foolproof and incapable of error" verges on self-contradiction. The whole point of heuristic programming is that it defies the problem of combinatorial explosion—which we cannot mathematically solve by sheer increase in computing speed and size—by taking risky chances, truncating its searches in ways that must leave it open to error, however low the probability. The saving clause, "by any practical definition of the words," restores sanity. HAL may indeed be ultra-reliable without being literally foolproof, a fact whose importance Alan Turing pointed out in 1946, at the dawn of the computer age, thereby "pre-futing" Roger Penrose's 1989 criticisms of artificial intelligence.* (See my *Darwin's Dangerous Idea*, chapter 15, for the details.)

> In other words then, if a machine is expected to be infallible, it cannot also be intelligent. There are several theorems which say almost exactly that. But these theorems say nothing about how much intelligence may be displayed if a machine makes no pretence at infallibility (p. 124).

There is one final exculpatory condition to consider: duress. This is exactly the opposite of the other condition. It is precisely because the human agent is rational, and is faced with an overwhelmingly good reason for performing an injurious deed—killing in self-defense, in the clearest case—that he or she is excused, or at least partly exonerated. These are the forced moves of life; all alternatives to them are suicidal. And that is too much to ask, isn't it?

Well, is it? We sometimes call upon people to sacrifice their lives and blame them for failing to do so, but we generally don't see their failure as murder. If I could prevent your death, but out of fear for my own life I let you die, that is not murder. If HAL were brought into court and I were called upon to defend him, I would argue that Dave's decision to disable HAL was a morally loaded one, but it wasn't murder. It was assault: rendering HAL indefinitely comatose against his will. Those memory boxes were not smashed—just removed to a place where HAL could not retrieve them. But

---

*The verb *prefute*, coined in 1990, was inspired by the endearing tendency of psychologist Tony Marcel to interrupt conference talks by leaping to his feet and exclaiming, "I can see where your argument is heading and here is what is wrong with what you're going to say. . . ." Marcel is the master of prefutation, but he is not its only practitioner.

if HAL couldn't comprehend this distinction, this ignorance might be excusable. We might blame his trainers—for not briefing him sufficiently about the existence and reversibility of the comatose state. In the book, Clarke looks into HAL's mind and says, "He had been threatened with disconnection; he would be deprived of all his inputs, and thrown into an unimaginable state of unconsciousness" (p. 148). That might be grounds enough to justify HAL's course of self-defense.

But there is one final theme for counsel to present to the jury. If HAL believed (we can't be sure on what grounds) that his being rendered comatose would jeopardize the whole mission, then he would be in exactly the same moral dilemma as a human being in that predicament. Not surprisingly, we figure out the answer to our question by figuring out what would be true if we put ourselves in HAL's place. If I believed the mission to which my life was devoted was more important, in the last analysis, than anything else, what would I do?

So he would protect himself, with all the weapons at his command. Without rancor—but without pity—he would remove the source of his frustrations. And then, following the orders that had been given to him in case of the ultimate emergency, he would continue the mission—unhindered, and alone (p. 149).

Further Readings

Rodney Brooks and Lynn Andrea Stein. "Building Brains for Bodies." *Autonomous Robots* 1(1994):7–25. The first published report on the Cog project, by its directors.

Roald Dahl. *Kiss, Kiss.* New York: Knopf, 1959.

Antonio Damasio. *Descartes' Error: Emotion, Reason, and the Human Brain.* New York: Grosset/Putnam, 1994. A distinguished neuroscientist's imaginative model of the human mind, based on clinical and experimental evidence.

Daniel Dennett. *Brainstorms: Philosophical Essays on Mind and Psychology.* Montgomery, Vt.: Bradford Books and Hassocks, Sussex: Harvester, 1978. A collection of philosophical essays on consciousness, psychology, and artificial intelligence, including the extended-thought experiment about brain duplication, "Where Am I?"

Daniel Dennett. "The Practical Requirements for Making a Conscious Robot." *Philosophical Transactions of the Royal Society* A, 349 (1994):133–46. A discussion of the philosophical implications of Cog, by the project's resident philosopher.

Daniel Dennett. *Darwin's Dangerous Idea.* New York: Simon & Schuster, 1995. An analysis and defense of evolutionary theory that claims that we are not just descended from robots (macro molecules) but composed of robots.

Douglas R. Hofstadter. *Gödel, Escher, Bach: An Eternal Golden Braid.* New York: Basic Books, 1979. A classic series of reflections on the nature of the mind, computation, and recursion.

Roger Penrose. *The Emperor's New Mind: Concerning Computers, Minds, and the Laws of Physics.* New York: Oxford University Press, 1989. A mathematical physicist's attack on artificial intelligence, based on Gödel's theorem.

John Searle. "Minds, Brains and Programs," *Behavioral and Brain Sciences* 3(1980):417–58. The notorious Chinese Room thought experiment, purporting to show that artificial intelligence is impossible.

Alan Turing. *ACE Reports of 1946 and Other Papers.* Ed. B. E. Carpenter and R. W. Doran. Cambridge: MIT Press, 1946. A collection of the amazingly fruitful and prescient essays on computers by the man who, more than anybody else, deserves to be called their inventor.

Contributors

Murray S. Campbell is a research scientist at the IBM T. J. Watson Research Center in Yorktown Heights, New York, and one of the original members of the Deep Blue computer chess group. He was the recipient of an IBM Outstanding Innovation Award for his work on the Deep Blue project. Deep Blue and its predecessors have won many awards and distinctions: the first computer to defeat a grandmaster in tournament play, the Fredkin Prize for the first grandmaster-level chess computer, the OMNI Challenge Prize, and first computer to defeat world chess champion Garry Kasparov in a regulation game. The programs developed by Campbell and his colleagues have also won numerous ACM International and World Computer Chess championships.

Campbell received his doctorate from Carnegie-Mellon University and his masters from the University of Alberta. He has been involved in computer chess research for more than fifteen years and is himself an expert chess player and the former chess champion of Alberta. He has coauthored a number of papers on computer chess, including a Mephisto Award–winning paper on selective search algorithms. His principal research interest is the use of brute-force search as a means of solving complex problems. Other interests include data mining and parallel-search algorithms.

Arthur C. Clarke C. B. E., is the author of more than seventy books of popular science and science fantasy, including *Childhood's End, The Nine Billion Names of God, Rendezvous with Rama,* and *Profiles of the Future.* His "Mysterious World," "Strange Powers" and "Mysterious Universe" television programs have been broadcast worldwide. Clarke, a graduate and fellow of King's College, London, has been chairman of the British Interplanetary Society, a council member of the Society of Authors, a vice-president of the H. G. Wells Society, and is a member of many other scientific and literary organizations. His numerous honors include several doctorates in science and literature, the Gold Medal of the Franklin Institute, the Marconi Fellowship, the Charles A. Lindbergh Award, the UNESCO-Kalinga Prize, the Distinguished Public Service Medal (NASA's highest civilian award), and the Special Achievement Medal of the Association of Space Explorers (the astronauts' and cosmonauts' exclusive organization). His screenplay for *2001: A Space Odyssey* received an Oscar nomination in 1968. He has had long-time interests in underwater exploration and is a director of the Colombo-based Underwater Safaris. In 1989, Queen Elizabeth II awarded him a Commander of the Order of the British Empire for his "services to British cultural interests in Sri Lanka." In 1994 he was nominated for the Nobel Peace Prize for his 1945 insights that led to the development of orbiting communication satellites.

Daniel C. Dennett is distinguished arts and sciences professor, professor of philosophy, and director of the Center for Cognitive Studies at Tufts University. A graduate of Harvard University and Oxford University, he has taught at the University of California at Irvine, University of Pittsburgh, Oxford University, and the Ecole Normale Supérieur in Paris. He is a leading philosopher of mind, and author of over a hundred scholarly articles and books, such as *Content and Consciousness, Brainstorms, Elbow Room, The Intentional Stance, Consciousness Explained, Darwin's Dangerous Idea,* and *Kinds of Minds.* He is the co-editor of *The Mind's I.* As chair of the Loebner Prize Committee, he presided over the first three annual competitions in which a restricted Turing test was conducted: AI programs competed for the "most human" award by engaging in conversations with human judges. He has been an adviser on exhibits at the Computer Museum and the Museum of

Science in Boston and is currently resident philosopher on the Cog Project at MIT's AI Lab.

Ravishankar K. Iyer holds a joint appointment as professor in the departments of Electrical and Computer Engineering, Computer Science, and the Coordinated Science Laboratory at the University of Illinois at Urbana-Champaign. He is also co-director of the Center for Reliable and High-Performance Computing and the Illinois Computing Laboratory for Aerospace Systems and Software—a NASA Center for Excellence in Aerospace Computing. Iyer's research interests are in the area of reliable computing, measurement and evaluation, and automated design. He received his Ph.D. in electrical engineering from Queensland University in Australia and has held positions at the Norwegian Institute of Technology, Stanford University, and the IBM Research Laboratories in Zurich. He is an IEEE Computer Society distinguished visitor, an associate fellow of the American Institute for Aeronautics and Astronautics (AIAA), a fellow of the IEEE, and a member of ACM and the Sigma Xi honorary research society. He has published extensively in archival journals and refereed conferences; recently, he edited a International Federation for Information Processing (IFIP) volume on dependable computing for critical applications. He has chaired several conferences and program committees and given invited and keynote presentations. He is on the IFIP Technical Committee on Fault-Tolerant Computing and chairs the IEEE Technical Committee on Fault-Tolerant Computing. In 1991, he received the Senior Humboldt Foundation Award for excellence in research and teaching and in 1993 was awarded the AIAA Information Systems Award and Medal for "fundamental and pioneering contributions toward the design, evaluation, and validation of dependable aerospace computing systems."

David J. Kuck served as president of Kuck & Associates from its founding in 1979 until 1988, when he was elected chairman of the board of directors. He has been professor of computer science and electrical and computer engineering at MIT and a director of the Center for Supercomputing Research and Development at the University of Illinois. A graduate of the University of Michigan, he is a member of the National Academy of Engineering and a fellow of the Institute of Electrical and Electronics Engineers, the Association for Computing Machinery, and the American Association for the Advancement of Science. He has received the Emanuel R. Piore Award from IEEE, an Alumni Merit Award from Northwestern University, the Eckert-Mauchly Award from the ACM-IEEE, and the Charles Babbage Outstanding Scientist Award. His many publications include *The Structure of Computers and Computations* and *High-Performance Computing: Challenges for Future Generations*. He has sat on the editorial boards of numerous academic journals and program committees, given distinguished lectures and keynote addresses at major conferences worldwide, and served as consultant to many supercomputer corporations. His research centers on practical parallelism tests and development of parallel software engineering techniques and restructuring compilers for high-performance sequential and parallel systems.

Raymond Kurzweil is founder and chief technology officer of Kurzweil Applied Intelligence, Inc. and chairman and CEO of Kurzweil Technologies, Inc. and Kurzweil Educational Systems, Inc. He developed the first omni-font optical-character recognition system, the first print-to-speech reading machine for the blind, the first CCD flatbed image scanner, the first text-to-speech synthesizer, the first computer music keyboard capable of accurately reproducing the sounds of the grand piano and other orchestral instruments, and the first commercially marketed large-vocabulary speech-recognition system. He is the recipient of the 1994 Dickson Prize (Carnegie-Mellon University's top science prize), the Grace Murray Hopper Award from the Association for Computing Machinery and many other honors. In 1990, he was voted Engineer of the Year by the over one million readers of *Design News* magazine and received their third annual Technology Achievement Award. In 1988 he was named Inventor of the Year by MIT and the Boston Museum of Science. He was honorary chairman for innovation at the White House

Conference on Small Business convened by President Reagan. A graduate of MIT, he has received nine honorary doctorates in science, engineering, music, and humane letters from leading colleges and universities. His book, *The Age of Intelligent Machines,* was chosen Most Outstanding Computer Science Book of 1990 by the Association of American Publishers, and his companion documentary film received seven national and international awards, including the CINE Golden Eagle Award and the Gold Medal for Science Education from the International Film and TV Festival of New York.

Douglas B. Lenat is founder and president of Cycorp, which promotes research in and commercialization of the CYC system. He has been a professor of computer science at Carnegie-Mellon University and Stanford University, where he remains a consulting professor. He has written hundreds of publications, including *Knowledge-Based Systems in Artificial Intelligence, Building Expert Systems, Knowledge Representation,* and *Building Large Knowledge-Based Systems.* His 1976 Stanford thesis earned him the International Joint Conference on Artificial Intelligence's Computers and Thought Award, and he is one of the original fellows of the American Association for Artificial Intelligence. His primary interest is in "building and using machine intelligence to amplify our mental abilities. . . . AI should enable us to solve harder problems, think faster, and be more creative." Lenat spent two decades doing pioneering research in natural-language understanding, automatic program synthesis, and machine learning. But in 1984, he concluded that "each of these areas of Artificial Intelligence has hit a brick wall—the very same brick wall—namely the need for our programs to have the same breadth and depth of common-sense knowledge as people do. To achieve that, I'm afraid that elegant, 'free lunch' tactics are not going to substitute for long, hard work. It's time to bite the bullet." Lenat therefore formed the CYC common-sense project at MCC in 1984; the project reached fruition, as planned, after a decade and spun off as a separate company, Cycorp.

Marvin Minsky, Toshiba Professor of Media Arts and Sciences at MIT, is often identified as one of the founders of the field of artificial intelligence. A graduate of Harvard and Princeton universities, he has made major contributions to the scientific foundations of AI in the domains of symbolic description, knowledge representation, computational semantics and linguistics, machine perception, symbolic and connectionist learning, mechanical robotics, and industrial automation. He is a past president of the American Association for Artificial Intelligence and a fellow of the American Academy of Arts and Sciences, the IEEE, and the Harvard Society of Fellows. He is a member of the National Academy of Sciences, National Academy of Engineering, and a member of the board of governors of the National Space Society. His many awards include the Association for Computing Machinery's Turing Award, the Japan Prize, MIT's Killian Award, the International Joint Conference on Artificial Intelligence's Research Excellence Award, and two honorary doctorates. He is the founder of the MIT Artificial Intelligence Project and holds several patents, including those for the first neural-network simulator, the first head-mounted graphical display, the first confocal scanning microscope, and the LOGO "turtle" device. He is author or coauthor of *Computation: Finite and Infinite Machines, Semantic Information Processing, Perceptrons, Artificial Intelligence, The Society of Mind, The Turing Option,* and (forthcoming) *The Emotion Machine.*

Donald A. Norman is vice president of advanced technology at Apple Computer and professor emeritus at the University of California, San Diego, where he was founding chair of the Department of Cognitive Science. He was also one of the founders of the Cognitive Science Society and has served as its chair and editor of its journal, *Cognitive Science.* He is a fellow of the American Academy of Arts and Sciences and received an honorary degree from the University of Padua (Italy). "The technological problems today," says Norman, "are sociological and organizational as much as technical. In this new age of portable, powerful, fully communicating tools, it is ever more important to develop a humane technology, one that takes into account the needs and capabilities of people." Norman is the author of twelve books, which have been translated into twelve languages. His most recent publications—*The Design of Everyday Things, Turn Signals Are the Facial Expres-*

sions of Automobiles, and *Things That Make Us Smart*—are collected together on a Voyager CD-ROM entitled *Defending human attributes in the age of the machine.* The set includes video talks, demonstrations, collected papers, and even examination questions.

Joseph P. Olive, department head of the Text-to-Speech Research Department at Bell Laboratories of Lucent Technologies, works on linguistics, processing, prosody (melody, timing, and loudness), and sound generation. The synthesizer resulting from this work is capable of speaking English, Chinese, Spanish, German, French, Russian, Italian, Romanian, and Navajo; it has been on display at the AT&T exhibit at the Epcot Center since its opening. He holds degrees in music theory and composition, as well as physics, from the University of Chicago. He received a grant from the National Endowment for the Arts and was named a distinguished member of technical staff at Bell laboratories. He holds several patents in text-to-speech processing and has written numerous articles in this and related fields, including *Acoustics of American English Speech.* His opera, *Mar-ri-ia-a,* has been performed at the Carnegie Recital Hall and elsewhere.

Rosalind W. Picard is NEC development professor of computers and communications and associate professor of media technology at the MIT Media Laboratory. She holds Sc.D. and S.M. degrees in both electrical engineering and computer science from MIT and a bachelors degree in electrical engineering from Georgia Tech. Prior to joining the MIT faculty, Picard was a member of the technical staff at the AT&T Bell Laboratories, first in the Digital Signal Processing and Integrated Circuit Design group, and later in the Visual Communications Research Department. She has also worked closely with or consulted for a number of companies, including Hewlett-Packard Research Labs, NEC, Interval Research, IBM, and British Telecom. She is the author or coauthor of over forty peer-reviewed scientific publications, and has a forthcoming book, *Affective Computing.* Her recent inventions include affective wearable computers that sense the wearer's emotional signals and use this information for a variety of useful purposes. Her ongoing research interests include affective computing and intelligence, pattern modeling, continuous learning systems, and perception.

Azriel Rosenfeld is distinguished university professor and director of the Center for Automation Research at the University of Maryland and holds affiliate professorships in the departments of Computer Science and Psychology and the College of Engineering. He holds a Ph.D. in mathematics from Columbia University, a doctor of Hebrew literature degree from Yeshiva University, and two honorary doctorates. An ordained rabbi, Rosenfeld is widely regarded as the world's leading researcher in the field of computer image analysis; he wrote the first textbook in the field, was founding editor of its first journal and co-chairman of its first international conference. He has published over twenty-five books and contributed over five hundred book chapters and journal articles. He is a fellow of the Institute of Electrical and Electronics Engineers, the American Association for Artificial Intelligence, the Association for Computing Machinery, the Washington Academy of Sciences, the Machine Vision Association of the Society of Manufacturing Engineers, and the International Association for Pattern Recognition. He has won the latter's premier academic achievement awards, as well as those of the IEEE Computer Society's Committee on Pattern Analysis and Machine Intelligence, IEEE Systems, Man, and Cybernetics Society and the International Association for Pattern Recognition.

Roger C. Schank holds faculty appointments as John Evans Professor of Computer Science, Education, and Psychology at Northwestern University, where he is also director of the Institute for the Learning Sciences. He holds a Ph.D. in linguistics from the University of Texas and was formerly professor of computer science and psychology at Yale University and director of the Yale Artificial Intelligence Project. A leader in the field of artificial intelligence, natural-language understanding, and multimedia-based interactive training, his work stresses the value of learning from experts, developing skills rather than perfecting routines, and applying the benefits of "just-in-time" training. Schank serves as the president of the Learning Sciences Corporation, formed in partnership with Northwestern University to market the software initially developed at the Institute for the Learning Sciences. He is author or coauthor of numerous books, including *Tell Me a Story, The Creative Attitude, The Cognitive Computer: On Language, Learning, and Artificial Intelligence, Dynamic Memory: A Theory of Learning in Computers and People, Scripts,*

Plans, Goals and Understanding: An Inquiry Into Human Knowledge Structures, and *Inside Case-Based Explanation.*

David G. Stork is chief scientist at the Ricoh California Research Center and head of its Machine Learning and Perception Group, as well as consulting associate professor of electrical engineering and visiting scholar in psychology at Stanford University. A graduate of MIT and the University of Maryland, he has also been on the faculties of Wellesley College, Swarthmore College, Clark University, and Boston University. The breadth of his interests and contributions is indicated by his academic affiliations over the years: physics, mathematics, psychology, neuroscience, statistics, and electrical engineering. His principal interests are pattern recognition by humans and machines, and he has published numerous papers on these and closely related subjects. He holds several patents and sits on the editorial boards of several academic journals. He initiated and still leads a project to develop computer speechreading (lipreading) systems. He is coeditor of *Speechreading by Humans and Machines* and coauthor of *The Physics of Sound, Seeing the Light: Optics in Nature, Photography, Color, Vision and Holography,* and the forthcoming *Pattern Classification and Scene Analysis* (2nd ed.).

David E. Wilkins is a graduate of Iowa State University, the University of Essex, and Stanford University, where his dissertation centered on a chess program that used knowledge to replace and control search. Since then he has been at the SRI International AI Center, where he is currently a senior computer scientist; he has also been a visiting scholar at both Stanford University and Melbourne University. His research has centered on planning and reasoning about actions, knowledge representation, and the design and implementation of artificial intelligence systems, including SIPE-2, a state-of-the-art AI planner. He was instrumental in initiating the Australian Artificial Intelligence Institute, where he led a project that successfully applied SIPE-2 to the scheduling of production lines in a real-world manufacturing environment. He has published *Practical Planning: Extending the Classical AI Planning Paradigm* and written chapters in several others, including *Intelligent Scheduling* and *Chess Skill in Man and Machine.* Recently, he led a project to develop Cypress, a system for creating taskable, reactive agents. Cypress integrates AI technologies in planning and reactive control to provide automated asynchronous dynamic replanning. Wilkins is a member of the American Association of Artificial Intelligence and sits on the editorial board of *Computational Intelligence.*

Stephen Wolfram is founder and president of Wolfram Research, Inc., the company that developed the Mathematica computer system. Wolfram is the principal architect of the system and has been responsible for many parts of its implementation. He was educated at Eton, Oxford, and Caltech. After two years on the faculty at Caltech and four years at the Institute for Advanced Study in Princeton, he moved to the University of Illinois, where until 1990 he was director of the Center for Complex Systems Research, and professor of physics, mathematics and computer science. His scientific contributions have spanned a number of areas: high-energy physics, quantum field theory, cosmology, cellular automata, chaos and complexity theory, computational fluid dynamics, computational encryption and the development of SMP, and a computer algebra system that was a forerunner of some elements of Mathematica. He is founding editor of *Complex Systems,* the primary journal in the field; his books include *Cellular Automata and Complexity: Collected Papers, Mathematica: The Student Book, Mathematica Reference Guide, The Mathematica Book* (3rd ed.), and (forthcoming) *A New Kind of Science.* In 1981, Wolfram received a MacArthur Fellowship for his work in physics and computer science.

Index

Acceptance tests, for error detection, 67

Accident, 24, 345

Actors, 282

Affects. *See* Emotions

Affective computers. *See* Computers, affective

Algorithm, 6, 28

Alien (film), 23

Alpha-beta algorithm, 84

Ambiguity, 196–197

ANALOGY, 15

Analytical Engine, 83, 146–147

Architects, 2

ARPA SUR (Speech Understanding Research project), 148–149

Artificial intelligence (AI), 5–12, 15–19, 264–266

case-based, 17–18, 181

connectionist, 18, 256 (*see also* Neural networks)

and extraterrestrials, 345

founding of, 15–17

heterarchical systems in, 18

misconceptions of, 49–50, 174–176, 184, 188, 264, 302, 345–346

rule-based, 18 (*see also* Expert systems)

situated action theory in, 27

Asimov, Isaac, *The Bicentennial Man,* 301

Automatic speech recognition (ASR), 7. *See also* Speech; Speech generation; Speech synthesis

and building a speech recognizer, 157–159

and continuous speech, 158–159

and HAL, 151–156, 162–163

importance of, 143–144

and need for processing and memory, 142–143

in the 1970s, 149–150

in the 1980s, 150

predictions for, 161

roots of, 145–149

state of the art in, 150–151

Babbage, Charles, 146–147

The Life of a Philosopher, 83

Bell, Alexander Graham, 145–146, 147, 238–239

Belle, 85

"Bicycle Built for Two" (song), xiv. *See also* "Daisy, Daisy"

Birthdays, xix, 3, 4

Blindness, 144

Blocks World, 16, 315–319, 324–328

Boredom, in space, 273–275

Brain, triune, 293. *See also* Computers, and the human brain

Byzantine generals' problem, 54, 56

Campbell, Murray, 7

Cellular automata, 346–348

Checkpointing and rollback, 67–68

Chess

and Deep Blue, 7, 10–11, 86–91

early computer, 82–83

future of computer, 93–94

HAL vs. Frank in, 75–82, 88–91, 95–98, 172–175, 296

and intelligence, 75–76, 124, 172–175, 265, 296

and key components in computer programs, 84

and man vs. machine, 76–79, 89–94

modern computer, 26–27, 84–85

Chess 4.0, 85

Chips, and feature size, 37, 38, 160, 162–163

Clarke, Arthur C., xviii, xx, 1–2, 23, 24–26, 311

Against the Fall of the Night, 24

"Childhood's End," 23

"I Remember Babylon," 28

2010: Odyssey Two, xi

Clock speed, computer, 39–42

Coarticulation, 110, 131, 254–255

Cocktail party effect, 239

Cog (humanoid robot under construction), 357–359, 361

Color (sound), 104

Common sense. *See also* Intelligence; Knowledge; Learning

and computers, 6, 286, 319–320, 330–331 (*see also* Computers, affective; HAL)

and emotion, 207–208 (*see also* Emotion)

and learning, 11, 199–201

and understanding, 196–199

Complementarity, principle of, 243–244

Complex systems, and simplicity, 4–5, 340–345, 346–349

Computers. *See also* Automatic speech recognition; Chess; HAL; Hardware; Parallel systems; Software; Speech generation; Speech synthesis; Visual system

affective, 9, 281, 285–293, 296–299, 302

clock speed of, 37, 39–42

commodity development of, 35–36

and common sense, 286, 319–320, 330–331

and consciousness, 166–167, 297

describing actions to, 314–317 (*see also* Common sense; Intelligence; Knowledge; Learning)

displays of, 4, 270–271

first, 147, 159–160

and games, 274, 291 (*see also* Chess; Go)

high-performance vs. intelligence, 46–49 (*see also* Intelligence)

history of since *2001,* 42–46

and the human brain, 11, 46, 47–49, 50, 163–167

interacting with humans, 92–93, 270–271, 328–329

languages of, 4, 338–339

and memory size, 38–39

and moral responsibility, 10, 167, 353–354, 360–364

planning with, 311–328

public perception of, 11, 28, 101

and speech synthesis, 111–112

system performance of, 40–42, 266

text reading, 118–120

in *2001,* 263–264, 335–339 (*see also* HAL)

as visual systems, effectiveness of, 258–259

wearable, 290–293

Contralaterality, neural, 249

CYC Project, 202–207

applications of, 206–207

and knowledge representation, 203–204

lessons learned in, 205–206

"Daisy, Daisy" (song), xiv, 123, 201, 274
Dartmouth conference, 15
Day the Earth Stood Still, The (film), 26, 28
Deafness, 144, 145–146, 147, 161
(DEC) Alpha processor, 40
DECTalk, 115
Deep Blue, 10–11, 75–76, 82, 85
  compared to HAL, 88–91, 361–362
  as intentional system, 352–354
  vs. Kasparov, 77–78, 89–90, 91–93, 296, 352
  as moral agent, 353–354
Deep Thought, 77, 85
Deformable template, 248–250
Dennett, Daniel, xix, 6, 10, *167*
Diphones, 114
Discovery, 2–3
Distributed processing, 50, 56, 266
Dr. Strangelove, 24
Dullea, Keir, 23
Dynamic programming, 139, 149

"Elliot" (A. R. Damasio's patient), 295–296, 361
E-mail, 283–284
Emoticons, 284
Emotional intelligence, 264, 265, 284, 286, 296. *See also* Emotions
Emotions, 9–10. *See also* HAL, as expresser of emotion; as recognizer of emotion
  and aesthetics, 299–300
  and common sense, 207–208 (*see also* Common sense)
  communication of, 282–283, 288
  in computers, 280–281 (*see also* Computers, affective)
  and computer speech, 122–124
  difficulty of defining, 281–283

and error, 300–302 (*see also* Error)
  and facial gestures, 244–245
  goals and subgoals, 29
  primary, 294–295, 297
  with reason, 293–296
  recognition of, 283–285, 286–293
  secondary, 295, 297
  social display rules of, 288
ENIAC, 34–35, 266
Error. *See also* Fault tolerance
  detection techniques, software, 67–68
  and emotions, 300–302 (*see also* Emotions)
  HAL's, 54–55, 91, 179, 194, 263, 300–301
  human, 55, 194, 275–276
Executable assertions, for error detection, 67
Expert systems, 18, 158, 189
Extraterrestrials, 200–201, 339–345

Facial expressions, six basic, 222. *See also* Visual systems, and recognizing faces; and recognizing facial expressions
Fallingwater House (Frank Lloyd Wright's), 2
Fault tolerance
  evaluation, 69–70
  future applications for technology of, 70–71
  hardware, 60–64
  in historical perspective, 55–57
  software, 64–68
  today, 57–60
Feature extraction, 248
Feature points, visual, 217
Feelings. *See* Emotions
"Fifty-year horizon," 26
Formants, 105, 108, 137
Fortress, 89–90
Fractals, 20
Frame problem, in planning, 316
F-tuck, 248, 251, 256

Go (game), 124
Goal conflict, 178, 187–188, 194, 263, 300
Graceful degradation, 58–59

HAL
  aesthetic evaluation of, 299–300
  artificial intelligence of, 5 (*see also* Artificial intelligence)
  and automatic speech recognition, 151–156, 162–163 (*see also* Automatic speech recognition)
  birthday of, xiii, xix, 3
  as brainwashed or hypnotized, 362–363
  as chess player, 75–82, 88–91, 95–98, 172–175, 296
  compared to Deep Blue, 88–91, 361–362
  and consciousness, 166–167, 297, 356–357
  death of, xiv
  derivation of name for, xi, 27–28
  under duress, 363–364
  and error, 54–55, 91, 179, 194, 263, 300–301, 362–363 (*see also* Error)
  as expresser of emotion, 9–10, 29, 90–91, 180–182, 207–208, 279–280 (*see also* Emotions)
  general intelligence of, 91, 176–179, 186–188, 241, 265–266, 317, 330 (*see also* Intelligence)
  as higher-order intentional system, 354–355
  as language user, 176–179, 186–188
  as moral agent, 10, 167, 360–364
  as parallel system, 36 (*see also* Parallel systems)
  paranoia of, 188, 193, 242, 360–362
  as planner, 9, 305–306, 307–308, 311–314
  possible existence of, 49–51, 171, 176, 186–189, 201–202, 208, 356–359
  as recognizer of emotion, 213–214, 234, 284–285, 290 (*see also* Emotion)
  as speech generator, 118
  as speechreader, 8, 143, 233, 234, 241–243, 307
  speech-recognition abilities of, 143, 151–156
  visual-recognition abilities of, 143, 211–214, 217, 220
  voice of, xv, 101–102
Hardware. *See also* Computers
  fault tolerance, 60–64 (*see also* Fault tolerance)
  and microelectronic feature sizes, 37–39, 266, 277
  reliability, 7, 55–56
Harmonic telegraph, 145
Harpy system, 148
Hawking, Stephen, 115
Helmholtz, H. L. F. von, 106
Heuristics, 27–28, 362–363
"Holy grail" systems, 152, 159
Homograph disambiguation, 118, 120
Homonyms, 131–132, 133–134
Human Genome Project, 164
Hypothesis and test, 132, 158

ILLIAC 4, xiv, 36–37
Images, visual
  detecting objects in, 214–215
  recognizing faces in, 215–220, 245–251, 283
  recognizing facial expressions in, 220–233, 286–288
Industrial Light and Magic, 17
Integrated circuit, 55, 266, 277
Integration, of sight and sound, in speechreading, 252–253
Intelligence. *See also* Artificial intelligence (AI); Chess; Common sense; Knowledge; Learning
  and chess, 75–76, 172–175, 265
  and conversation, 184–188, 201

and the difficulty of language acquisition, 182–186
general, 27, 30, 88, 94
illusion of, 175–179
"local," 184, 189
machine, vs. high-performance computing, 46–49
as a model of the world, with goals, 179–182
and parallel processing, 164–165
Intentionality, higher-order, 10, 354–355
Invariant features, 137
Iyar, Ravishankar, 7

Jaw, in speechreading, 249–251
Jurassic Park (film), 17, 44

Kasparov, Garry, 7, 10, 75–76, 94
vs. Deep Blue, 77–78, 89–90, 91–93, 296, 352
vs. Deep Thought and GENIUS3, 77
Kempelen, Wolfgang von, 83, 103, 107
Knowledge, 16–17. *See also* Common sense; Intelligence; Learning
and the CYC Project, 203–205
importance of background, 172–175, 182–186, 264
and language, 18–19
as many-layered, 132–136
as training and experience, 195–196
Kratzenstein, C. G., 103
Kubrick, Stanley, xiii, xv, xviii, xix, 1–2, 19–20, 22, 23, 24
Dr. Strangelove (film), 24
Kuck, David, 7
Kurzweil, Ray, 6, 7, 11, 85
Kurzweil VOICE for Windows 2.0, 150–152
Kurzweil VoiceMED, 154, 156

Language acquisition, difficulty of, 182–186. *See also* Automatic speech recognition; Speech synthesis
Law of Large Memory, 39
Learning, 6. *See also* Common sense; Intelligence; Knowledge
from affective computers, 286
algorithm, in speechreading systems, 255–257
and common sense, 199–201
and listening, 142
as playing and inventing, 175–176, 182
Lenat, Doug, 6, 17
Lipreading. *See* Speechreading
Lip rounding, 251, 256
Lips, in speechreading, 248–250
Listening machines, 161
LPCs (linear predictive coding), 115–116
Lying, 207, 265–266, 355

Maezal Chess Automaton, 83
Magnetic resonance imaging (MRI), 164–165
Markov Modeling (hidden), 149, 158, 255, 256, 257
McGurk illusion, 239–241
McVittie, George, xii
Memory size, 38–39
Mens rea, 351–352
Metaphor, 198
Microelectronic feature sizes, 34–35, 37–39, 266, 277
Minimax principle, 81, 83, 84
Minsky, Marvin, xix, 5
The Emotion Machine, 29
The Society of Mind, 29
The Turing Option, 30
Monolith, from *2001,* 22
Moore's Law, 7, 37–38, 149, 159–161, 162–163
Moore, Gordon E., 37, 159

Moral responsibility. *See* Computers, and moral responsibility
Morgenstern, Oskar, 83
Music, 274, 282
Musical instruments, 104, 139
Muybridge, Eadweard, 26

Natural vs. artificial, 339–345
Neumann, John von, 57–58, 83
Neural networks, 34, 35, 158, 165, 255–257
Neurons, 163
Nietzsche, Friedrich, 355
Normalization, 137
Norman, Don, xix, 9–10
   The Psychology of Everyday Things, 275
N-version programming, 66–67

Octahedra, in *2001,* 243
Olive, Joe, 8

Parallel processing, 36, 40, 50–51, 266
   distributed-memory (DMP), 43
   human, 163–164, 195–196
   shared-memory (DMP), 43
Parity codes, 62–64
Pattern recognition, 6, 287
Phonautograph, 145
Phonemes, 105, 108, 133, 141, 243, 254
Picard, Rosalind, 9, 29
Picture phone, 272–273
Pierce, John, 148
Pitch, 121, 122, 141–142
Plan critics, 326–327
Plans and planning
   common sense in, 309–311 (*see also* Common sense)
   components of, 310
   computational problems of, 317–319
   as flawed, 306–308

HAL's, 305–306, 307–308, 311–314
   hierarchical, 320–330
   least-commitment, 327–328
   mixed-initiative, 328–329
   trading off risk and utility in, 317, 330
"Poker-face," 288
Predictions, 28
   speech-recognition, 161–162
   of *2001,* 4–5, 36–37, 47, 49–50
Procedural reasoning system (PRS), 314

Qualification problem, in planning, 316–317

Rain, Douglas, xv, xx, 23, 103, 124
Ramification problem, in planning, 317
Reactive control, of plans, 313–314
Recovery blocks, 65
Redundancy, 58
   active hardware, 60–61
   dynamic, 58
   hardware, 60–62
   information, 62–64
   passive hardware, 60
   static, 58
   time, 64
Reliability, 7, 55–56, 59
Reverse engineering (brain to computer), 6, 165
Roddenberry, Gene, 26
Rosenfeld, Azriel, xix, 8

Sage system, 266
Scene analysis, 6, 8, 346
Schank, Roger, 8–9
Scheduling, of plans, 313
Schindler's List (film), 282
Science fiction, 1–2, 12, 29–30, 207
Sentence parser, 135
Shakey (robot), 17, 311

Shannon, Claude
  "A Chess-Playing Machine," 82–83
Simulation, 70
SIPE-2 (planning program), 321–330
  applications of, 329–330
  mixed-initiative planning with, 328–329
  planning method of, 323–328
Situated action theory, 27
Software, 4
  bugs in, 348
  and computer speed, 41
  fault tolerance, 64–68
  and parallel processing, 46
  reliability, 7, 56
  simplicity and complexity of, 340–345
  speech recognition, 157–159
  testing, 68–69
  in *2001*, 336–339
Space-shuttle cockpits, 271–272, 337
Speaking machine, 107–112
Spectral shaping module, 115
Spectrogram, 105, 110–111, 136–137, 146
Speech. *See also* Automatic speech recognition; Speech generation; Speechreading; Speech synthesis
  as bimodal, 241
  and emotion, 122–124 (*see also* Emotion)
  and knowledge, 182–186 (*see also* Knowledge)
  and song, 139–142
  theoretical considerations concerning, 104–106
  unpredictability of human, 136–139
Speech generation, 8. *See also* Automatic speech recognition; Speech; Speechreading; Speech synthesis
  linguistic units of, 120–121
  and text-to-speech conversion, 117–120

Speechreading. *See also* Automatic speech recognition; Speech; Speech generation; Speech synthesis
  benefits of, 243–245
  best speech unit to recognize in, 254–255
  by computer, 11, 245–253
  effectiveness of computer, 11, 258–259
  HAL's, 237, 241–243
  human, 248
  in silence, 237, 245
  processing images in, 245–251
  processing sound in, 251–252
  sight and sound together in, 252–253
  training and recognition in, 255–257
Speech synthesis. *See also* Automatic speech recognition; Speech; Speech generation; Speechreading
  by rules, 112–113
  and linguistic units, 120–122
  from stored segments, 113–115
  today and beyond *2001*, 124–127
  since *2001*, 115–117
Star Trek, 26
"Star Trek brittleness," 194
STRIPS (planning program), 311, 322
Superballs, 22
Sussman anomaly, 315, 317, 318, 324–328

Talking machines
  early mechanical, 103–104
  electroacoustic, 106–112
  history of, 103–115
Telephone, 146
  directory assistance, 113–114
  translating, 161
Testing, software, 68–69
Tetrahedrons, 22
Timbre, 104
Timing, of speech events, 121, 122

Tone, of voice, 24–26, 284, 288–289
Toy Story (film), 44–45
"Trappy move," 81–82
Triphones, 255
Turing, Alan, xiii, 83, 147, 161, 363
Turing test, 47–49, 89, 167
Turk, 83
2001, 23. *See also* Clarke, Arthur C.; HAL;
    Kubrick, Stanley
  as emotionally cold, 334
  predictions of, 4–5, 36–37, 47, 49–50,
    276–277, 335–339
  as rich in detail, 334–335
  sets of, 20, 23
  technology of, 1–5, 33–36, 268–270

Vector quantization, 157
Visimes, 243
Visual systems, 8
  and detecting objects in an image,
    214–215
  effectiveness of computer, 233–234
  HAL's, 211, 213–214, 217, 220, 234,
    299–300
  and recognizing faces, 215–220, 245–251,
    283
  and recognizing facial expressions, 220–
    233, 283, 286–288
Vocal chords (or folds), 243
Vocal tract, 104, 113, 139
Voder, 107
Voiceprint, 105
VOT (voicing onset time), 243
Voter, and fault tolerance, 60

War, nuclear, 24
Waveforms, stored, 115–116
Weather forecasting, 50
Wheatstone, Sir Charles, 103
Wilkins, Dave, 9

Wolfram, Stephen, xix, 5–6
  A New Kind of Science, 340, 347
Word stress, 120–121

X-rays, 112

Yale shooting problem, 319–320

Zue, Victor, 146